**AN ORIGINAL
HOVE FOTO BOOKS**

COMPLETE MINOLTA
USER'S GUIDE

MINOLTA
DYNAX/MAXXUM
700si

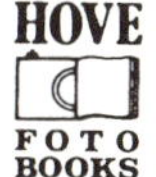

**HOVE
FOTO
BOOKS**

Damian Dinning

MINOLTA DYNAX 700si (International)
MINOLTA MAXXUM 700si (North America)
First English Edition October 1994

Published by Hove Foto Books Limited
Hotel de France, St Saviour's Road
St Helier, Jersey, Channel Islands JE2 7LA
Tel: (01534) 873102   Fax: (01534) 887342

Typeset by Jersey Photographic Museum

Printed by
The Guernsey Press Co Ltd, Commercial Printing Division
Guernsey, Channel Islands

British Library Cataloguing-in-Publication Data
A catalogue record for this book is available from the
British Library

Dinning Damian - Minolta Dynax/Maxxum 700si

ISBN - 1-874031-46-0

Worldwide Distribution:

Newpro (UK) Ltd
Old Sawmills Road
Faringdon, Oxon.
SN7 7DS, England
Tel: (01367) 242411   Fax: (01367) 241124

CONTENTS

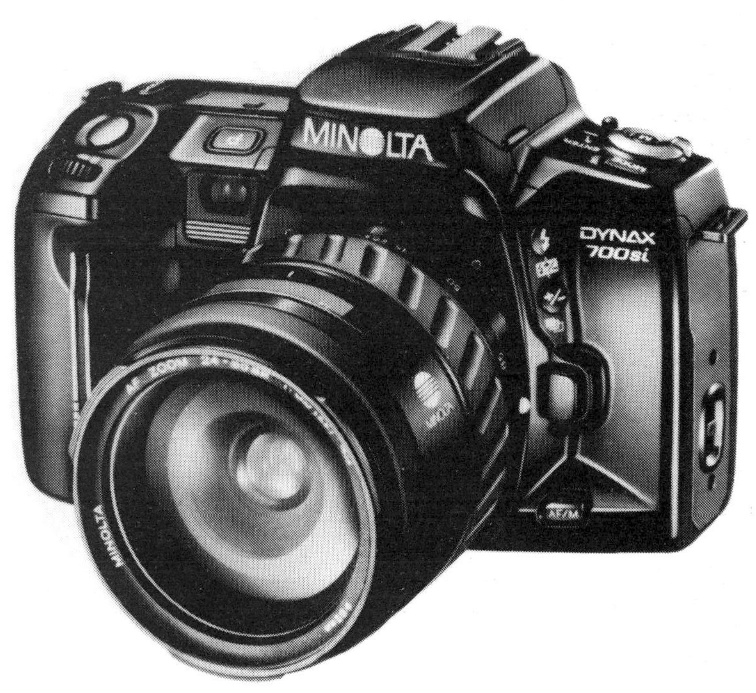

The Minolta Dynax/Maxxum 700si

INTRODUCTION - Damian Dinning

What you are about to read is the result of three years practical experience using Minolta AF SLR's, upon which the 700si has been based, and a great deal of previously unpublished information about Minolta, and in particular the Dynax/Maxxum 700si.

What I have tried to do by writing this book is to drain my memory of all relevant information on the Dynax/Maxxum 700si, to help you, the reader and photographer, into understanding and then being able to get the most out of the camera, by taking better photographs. What I am trying to say is, if the answer is not here, it is simply not available - I hope!

The photograph to me is something incredibly special. What it captures is not always describable. Somehow, in just a split second, a photograph is able to capture a story, record memories of special occasions, holidays, the growing up of our children, and to record our hobbies. A photograph can be something very private or very public.

The fact is that a camera and the photographs that it produces are things that we all take for granted, and yet photographs to all of us are very special for all sorts of reasons. We will always want to take still pictures. A photograph of someone special can be kept in your wallet or the sun-visor of your car. You will never be able to do without it. Anyway enough of the emotional introduction.

I believe that there are two basic groups of photographers. There is the group that believe that photography is an art form and that the process must be done as manually as possible to gain the maximum amount of enjoyment and satisfaction from it. This first group do not always believe in the latest cameras and features such as autofocus, eye-start etc, saying that it takes all the fun out of photography. And there is the group that just want to take good photographs as easily as possible with no fuss whatsoever. About four or five years ago I was a member of the first group - a traditionalist. I then changed to the second group when Minolta launched the 7xi (the camera that the 700si is based on) in 1991.

Some time before the introduction of the 7xi I was one of a few people that knew the specification of the new camera, and, like a number of people, found it difficult to believe that the camera was capable of doing what we were about to tell the world it could do. Due to the secrecy involved before a major product launch we were not even able to go out with the camera and "try it for ourselves". We had to trust them and hope that they had not gone "too far" this time.

With cameras based up until now on conventional computer logic, it was always possible to look at a scene and guess roughly what the camera was likely to do using some technical experience of how the camera was designed to work, this was based on conventional computer logic. But all of a sudden there we were, about to launch a camera that knew what type of picture you were taking, which made use of the very latest Fuzzy Logic (Expert Systems). To say I was worried would be a brilliant understatement!

As soon as the camera was launched I got hold of my sample and went out to take thousands of my own photographs to try and understand what the camera would do and what it would not do. Over three years later, I am still taking pictures which show what the camera will do, but I am finding it extremely difficult to take pictures that show what it cannot do, although it still won't make me a cup of tea.

It is this experience that I am going to give you in the form of this book so that you can take great photographs without having to go through the process of gaining trust and trying to test the camera. My advice to you is to take photographs rather than worrying whether it does what Minolta say it will do. Basically speaking the camera does what this book says it will do.

I must confess that when I started using the 7xi and more recently the 9xi and 700si, when I was taking photographs I would sometimes stop and laugh and think to myself, well how does it know how to do that. This is why I changed to becoming a member of the second group of photographers (the just take good photographs group), because I find it fun just watching the camera do it all for me and then being amazed at the quality of my slides when they arrive though the door.

DEDICATION AND ACKNOWLEDGEMENTS

This book is dedicated to Mutti, for if it were not for her, I would never have been able to write it.

I feel that I must acknowledge the help provided by Alex, and also for the support given to me by John. I must also thank Pat for not leaving John!

The 700si Development Story

It all started in 1981 when just before the introduction of the Minolta X-700, the R & D (research and development) teams were just about to be formed for the next new Minolta SLR.

A meeting between the Marketing and Engineering departments was held to discuss the objectives of the next SLR.

"We can't do that," said the design team chief across the table with finality. "We just can't do it." You marketing people have to understand that any system has its limits. This time, the camera just can't do what you're asking us to make it do." The Head of Product Planning said nothing. Everyone was quiet for a moment.

The engineer reached into his pocket for a pen and started sketching on a scrap of paper. "Unless," he said slowly, speaking more to himself than to anyone else around the table, "unless we could change the ....". The pen started moving furiously. Still nothing was said by the Head of Product Planning.

Many sketches and arguments later, he finally climbed into a cab for the ride home. The engineers still weren't sure, but they had promised to see what could be done about his request.

Four years later, on January 23rd 1985, the World's first effective, body integral, AF SLR was introduced. The Minolta 7000.

A year or two later other manufacturers followed by introducing their own AF SLR's, but it was the 7000 that shaped SLR cameras as we know them today.

At the time, the 7000 was amazing, everyone wanted one. However, professional photographers could not see the benefit, taking the view that they could still focus faster manually. In 1988 Minolta launched the second generation AF SLR. Its faster autofocus speed showed that autofocus was here to stay. Professionals started buying the 7000i to supplement their existing system mainly for use in grab shot situations. In 1991 Minolta then introduced the third generation AF SLR, the Dynax/Maxxum 7xi. Many saw this jump as bigger than the jump between the X-700 and 7000. In 1993 Minolta then once again were the first to introduce the next generation. But this time things were different. Had Minolta gone too far or moved too quickly with the new technology introduced by the 7xi in 1991?

The 700si was a fresh look at AF SLR's. Years of research into what you, the end user, actually wanted from an SLR camera was carried out. The result is the Dynax/Maxxum 700si, a back to basics camera.

THE DYNAX/MAXXUM 700si CONCEPT: THE PHOTOGRAPHER'S TOOL

High Potential Automation

Autofocus

- Wide Focus Area
- Multi-Dimensional Predictive Focus Control

Autoexposure

- Expert Program Selection
- High Speed Sync Flash

Creative Support System

Information

- Metering Index
- Local Focus Area Indicators

Quick Direct Control

- Local focus area selection
- Memory
- All functions illustrated on the body
- Vertical Control Grip (VC-700)

Comfortable Operation

- Large buttons and dials
- Quiet film transport
- Positioning of camera controls
- Vertical Control Grip

The basic concept of the Dynax/Maxxum 700si is to provide the photographer with the highest level of automation possible, but without going over the top just for the sake of automation.

All AF SLR's these days offer extremely sophisticated autofocus and autoexposure systems. But because of the very nature of the way they work and their capabilities we, the photographer, are not fully aware of what the camera has allowed for: e.g. the amount of compensation a camera's metering system has made for a backlit subject if any! If we are not aware of what the camera has already done we may be undoing things or trying to correct for something that the camera may have already done for us.

For this reason there are various systems built into the 700si to allow the photographer to access information if desired, concerning the camera's automatic operations. Once we know what the camera has done we can then either make additional allowances based on this information or simply be happy in the knowledge that the camera has done what we would have done ourselves.

Quite often when I speak to users of the 700si they say to me, "my camera is getting better with age." The reason being, you are becoming accustomed to the way in which it operates. You are subconsciously using the camera in a manner that allows it to perform at its optimum.

As with everything there is of course a learning process, and this is where we come back to the reason for my writing this book: that is, to dramatically shorten the learning period.

GETTING STARTED-
BODY PARTS AND DESIGN

Refer to this first section of the book as a quick reference guide. There is a brief explanation on each of the 700si's controls to allow you to simply flick through this section and get a quick understanding of how to use that particular feature or function. Later in the book we will then concentrate on specific areas by looking at them in greater depth.

Before we go any further I am taking for granted that you have already taken your new 700si out of the box and attached the lens etc, in which case we will not need to waste time by telling you how to do this.

The Top-plate

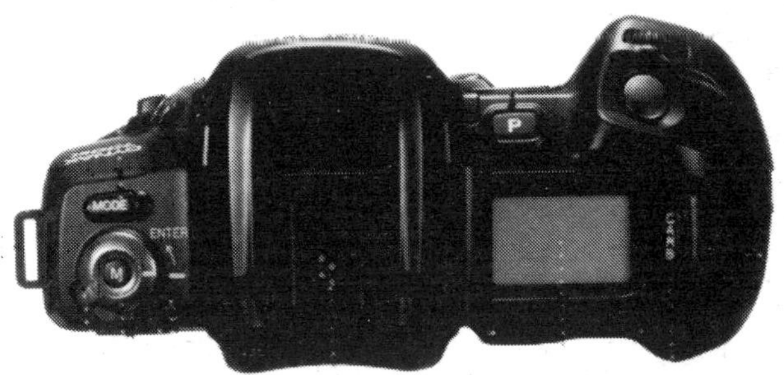

Autolock hotshoe

Slightly off centre is the camera's hotshoe. This is known as the Autolock accessory shoe. It was introduced by Minolta for the first time on the Dynax/Maxxum 7000i in 1988. Since that time Minolta have fitted all their AF SLR's with this type of shoe. Many people, even today, still ask why the design of the standard hotshoe, as still used by all other manufacturers, was changed. Many believe it was done to force them into buying Minolta's own flashguns. This is not true at all. The reasons for changing the design were as follows:

1. Autolocking as soon as the flash is fitted. This allows easier attachment and removal of the flashgun without the need to reach for a pair of pliers to undo the locking ring.

2. More reliable connection of the electrical contacts between flashgun and camera.

3. Precise alignment of the AF-illuminator in the flashgun, in relation to the AF area.

Built-in Flash

Surrounding the hotshoe is the built-in flash unit. This is raised by holding the flash housing at the sides of the pentaprism where there are small grips, and then lifting. When the flash is no longer required, push the flash back down.

The built-in flash has a guide number of 12 (in meters at 100 ISO), and will cover lenses as wide as 24mm focal length.

Ensure that the lens hood is removed when using the built-in flash unit, otherwise flash cut-off may occur at the bottom of the photograph.

Body LCD Data Panel

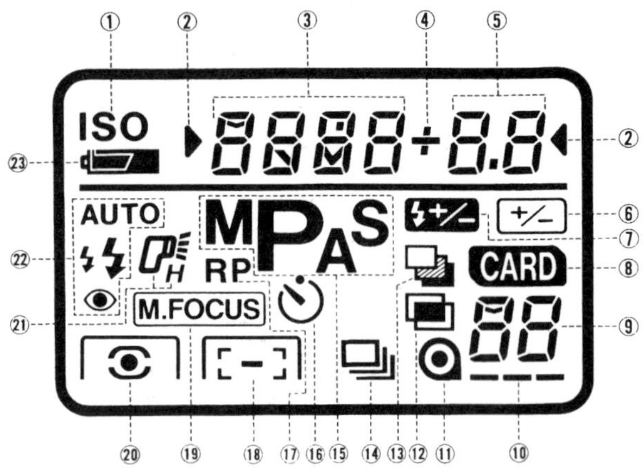

1. Film speed symbol
2. Selectable setting pointers
3. Shutter speed/Film speed/Card name/Local focus-area display/Focal length display(xi lenses only)
4. Compensation indicator
5. Aperture/Exposure compensation/Flash compensation/Card setting display

12

6. Flash compensation reminder
7. Exposure compensation reminder
8. Exposure bracketing indicator
9. Card in use indicator
10. Double exposure indicator
11. Frame counter/Card setting display
12. Film transport signal
13. Film cartridge symbol
14. Drive mode indicator
15. Exposure mode indicator
16. Self-timer indicator
17. Wide/Local focus area indicator
18. Release priority reminder
19. Manual focus indicator
20. Metering mode indicator
21. HSS flash indicator
22. Flash mode indicator
23. Battery condition indicator

To the right of the pentaprism as you look at the top of the camera with the lens pointing away from you is the Body LCD data panel which is used to display all camera operating information which include:

Film speed, shutter speed, aperture, battery level indicator, flash mode, lens focal length (xi lenses only), shutter release priority, exposure mode, metering mode, wide/local focus area indicator, self timer, drive mode, frame counter, double exposure, exposure compensation, flash exposure compensation, manual focus, card type, card in use indicator, high speed sync flash in use.

Although the body data panel is not illuminated (a great shame in my opinion), the use of a bright image design does allow viewing in lower lighting conditions in comparison with previous LCD displays. In low light you may find viewing easier if you look directly down on the display rather than having the camera held at an angle.

Card Button

To the right of the LCD panel is a large button labelled **CARD**. Its use depends upon the card in use, as detailed later on, where applicable. Its main function is to allow a card's function to be switched on or off by simply pressing a single button. This allows a favourite card to be left in the camera, but its function to be called upon only when needed. The **CARD** symbol will appear in the top LCD data panel to alert you when it is in use.

Above the LCD panel is the Program reset button, shutter release and front input dial.

The Panic button

When in a **P**ickle or a **P**anic, hit (preferably press, cameras do not respond positively to violence) the large button marked **P** this will return the camera to point and press mode, resetting all overrides and features to a factory set setting as follows:

Function	Factory Program reset setting
Focus area	Wide focus area
Focus mode	Autofocus
Metering mode	14 Segment Honeycomb-Pattern
Exposure mode	Program
Exposure compensation	+/- 0.0
Flash compensation	+/- 0.0
Built-in flash	Auto on (when raised)*
Accessory flash (when fitted)	Auto on
Film drive mode	Single frame advance
Self timer	Cancelled
Focus/release priority	Focus priority

* **N.B.** Flash mode is reset to the last auto flash mode used. So, if red-eye reduction was the last mode set, then when the P button is pressed the flash mode will return to auto flash mode with red-eye reduction.

The P button can also be re-programmed using the Customized Function Card xi. This I will cover later in the book when we cover this card in detail.

Shutter Release

To the right of the Program-reset button is the shutter release.

The shutter release is a two stage type. Half pressure is used to activate** and lock autofocus/autoexposure. Full pressure releases the shutter. If the shutter release is pressed all the way down in one action without having first pressed the shutter release halfway, the camera will only release the shutter, once autofocusing has been completed (this is known as focus priority).

** When eye-start is switched off.

In manual focus the shutter can be released whether the subject is in focus or not. The 700si can also be set to release priority mode so that when in autofocus mode the shutter can be released even if the camera has not completed autofocusing. This is an advantage when photographing events which are never likely to occur again and it is absolutely vital that an image is recorded on film whether it appears in focus or not. Let me add though that there is absolutely no advantage in this for high speed action photography, it will not increase your success rate of in-focus photographs.

Front Control Dial

The front control dial is mainly used for setting shutter speeds when in program (PS mode), shutter priority or manual exposure modes. It can also be used in aperture priority in preference to the rear dial to select the required aperture. The dial is also used in conjunction with the buttons inside the expansion card door, the two buttons on the front of the camera just above the lens release button and finally the AF button on the back of the 700si, all of which I will be describing later.

Mode Button

Over to the left of the pentaprism is the **MODE** button and the controls for the memory facility.

The mode button is used for selecting one of four exposure modes, Program, Aperture Priority, Shutter Priority and Manual. To select the modes, press and hold the **MODE** button and then turn either of the main control dials, whichever you find most convenient. This way you do not have to remember which dial to turn.

Memory Function

The memory allows the user to store his/her most used features/settings and recall them by pressing a single button. The memory is set by first pressing and holding the small un-labelled button to the right of the memory switch, and then moving the memory switch in the direction of the arrow to the position marked **ENTER. MEmory** will appear in place of the aperture and shutter speed settings on the camera's top LCD data panel. The settings are recalled at any time by simply pressing the button marked **M** in the centre of the Memory switch.

The Front View

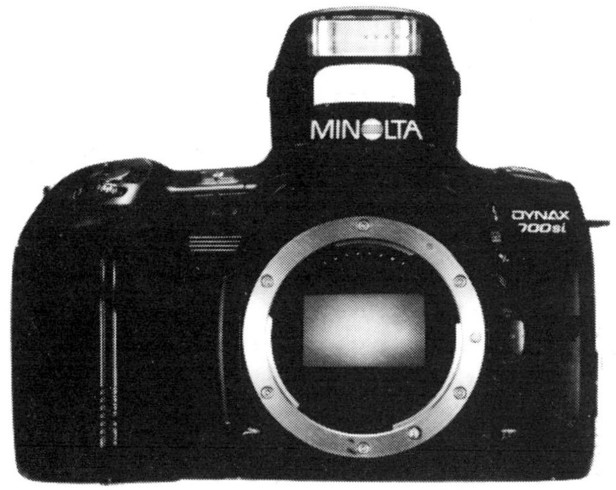

If we now turn the camera so that the lens is pointing directly towards us, we can see on the left hand side, the main handgrip. This has been covered in rubber to increase grip. You will also notice an indentation in the top of the grip for the third finger to rest and to ensure that it does not obscure the AF-illuminator.

Eye-start Grip Switch

Running almost the full length of the grip are two bars. These are the conductive sensors for the eye-start grip switch.

AF-Illuminator

To the right of the grip as we look towards the camera and just down from the P-reset button is the AF-Illuminator. This aids the camera in its autofocusing in low contrast and low lighting conditions. It is also used to provide a warning that the self timer sequence has been activated.

Depth of Field Preview Button

Below this, towards the base of the camera, is the DEPTH-OF-FIELD PREVIEW button. This allows us, when looking through the viewfinder, to see the amount of depth of field (area that will also appear in focus), by stopping the lens down to the selected aperture. Focus and exposure settings are locked when the button is pressed.

N.B. When in autofocus, if focus had not been confirmed with the green in focus signal in the viewfinder, when the button is pressed you will not be able to release the shutter. Therefore please check that the green "In-Focus" light is lit before pressing the depth of field button. With the preview button pressed the shutter can still be released. Please remember that if you had not focused correctly the depth of field viewed in the viewfinder will not be applicable to "your scene".

To the right of the lens are four buttons. Working from the top down. Flash control, exposure compensation, lens release and focus mode switch.

Flash Button

With either the built-in flash raised or a Minolta i/xi/HS series flash fitted to the camera's hot shoe, when in program the flash fires automatically. If the flash control button (labelled with a lightning bolt symbol) is held in whilst releasing the shutter the flash fires regardless of whether the camera thinks that flash is required or not. When in the wireless flash mode, this button is held in whilst taking the picture to select a 2:1 ratio between the built-in flash and the off-camera flash unit(s).

Exposure Compensation Button

The button marked +/- is used to select exposure compensation. By holding the button and turning either of the control dials, the camera's exposure can be biased by +/- 3.0 stops, in half stop increments.

When Honeycomb metering is in use, pressing the exposure compensation button displays in the viewfinder the amount of exposure compensation automatically set by the camera.

If the same button is held in whilst releasing the shutter, a fixed three frame bracketed sequence of -0.5, 0.0, +0.5 stop is activated.

Flash Compensation

Whilst pressing the Flash control and exposure compensation

buttons together, turning either of the input dials selects flash compensation in half stop increments to +/- 3.0 stops.

Lens Release Button

Below these two controls is the lens release button.

Autofocus/Manual Focus Button

Below the lens release is the autofocus/manual focus button labelled **AF/M**. Pressing this selects manual focus. **M.FOCUS** is then shown in the camera's top LCD data panel. Pressing the button again returns the camera to autofocus.

Before we move round to the rear of the camera I would just like to take some time to point out the delicate areas inside the mirror box. With the lens removed you will see the lens mount itself. This is manufactured from oil-impregnated sintered stainless steel. This has self lubricating properties and ensures that the lens is easy to turn in the mount. It also reduces wear and ensures that the lens remains a tight fit, even after thousands of lens changes.

Within the mount itself you will see, by the lens release button, the pin that locks the lens onto the camera. Just down from this you can see the AF drive pin. This moves forward and engages with the AF coupler inside the lens' mount. When the lens release button is pressed in order to remove the lens, this retracts into the camera body to allow the lens to be released.

Just inside the mount itself is a black ring with a small coupler pin near the lens release button. This locates with another pin inside the lens. The distance that this moves by is precisely controlled by the camera depending on the aperture set. Each 5 degree rotation equals one f stop.

At the top of the mount are eight gold electrical pins. They are sprung to ensure a good connection with the contacts on the back of the lens. All Minolta AF lenses have five contacts, except the xi zoom lenses which have eight. Approximately forty pieces of information are exchanged between lens and camera body through these contacts. This information includes, lens focal length or zoom range, current focal length in use, maximum and minimum aperture available, effective aperture on zoom lenses, the type of lens (zoom, macro, wide, tele) and other lens characteristics.

Why was the mount changed?

Whilst we are on the subject of lens mounts, lets spend a little time explaining why the AF series cameras employ a different mount to that of the manual focus Minolta SLR's.

1. The diameter of the mount was enlarged to allow the AF coupler and lens contacts to be included whilst at the same time not hindering lens designs.

2. The larger mount also ensured greater strength for when using large, heavy lenses.

3. The use of the larger diameter also allows for potential future developments.

Inside the mirror box you can see the main mirror and focusing screen. The mirror is not only used to reflect the image up to the viewfinder but it also allows a certain amount of light to pass through which is then reflected off a sub-mirror located just behind. The image is then projected from here into the base of the camera, the location of the AF module.

When you look through the viewfinder you may be able to see small particles of dust or dirt. Although this will not affect the picture, as the mirror swings out of the light path when the picture is taken, it can often be annoying. The safest way of cleaning these surfaces is to use compressed air or a blower brush with the brush removed. **NEVER TOUCH THESE SURFACES WITH ANY OBJECT OR CLEANING INSTRUMENT.** They are very easily marked or scratched. If you cannot blow the dirt away, have a Minolta service facility clean it for you.

The rear view

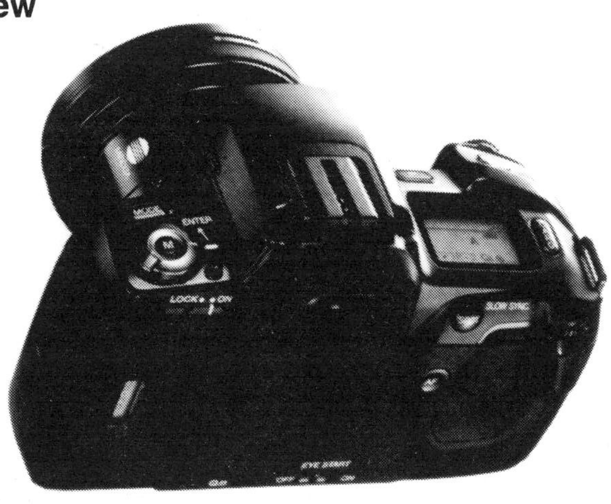

On/Off Switch

Turning to the back of the camera, to the left of the viewfinder eyepiece is the camera's main ON/OFF switch, marked **LOCK** and **ON**. When the switch is moved to the **LOCK** position all camera functions are inoperative and there is no drain on the camera's battery whatsoever. When the camera is not being used for a period of more than approx 10 minutes, slide the main switch to the **OFF** position. When the camera is switched on, an indication as to the battery condition will appear for approximately 5 seconds. This is a four stage indication as follows:

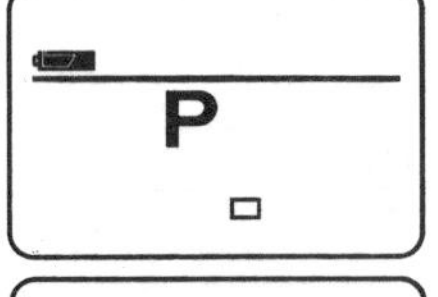

Full battery symbol   Power is sufficient

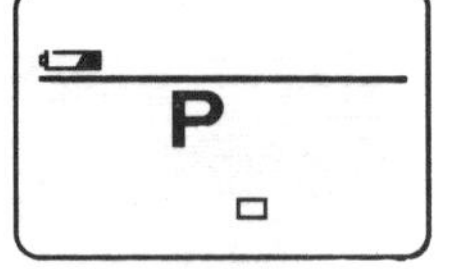

Half battery symbol   Power is sufficient, but getting low. Now is the time to make sure that you have a spare battery to hand.

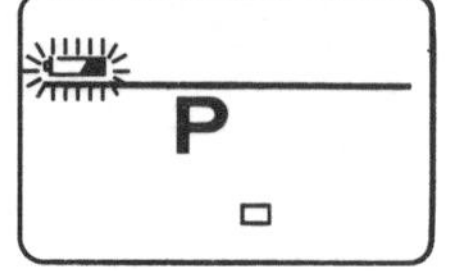

Flashing half battery   If this symbol appears with other symbol operating information on the display, the camera can be operated but power is extremely low, the battery is almost dead.

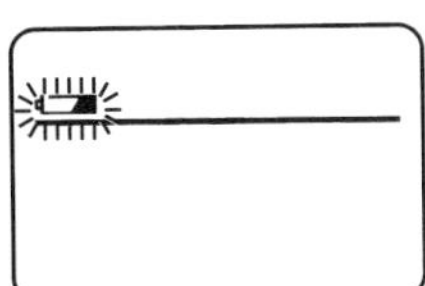

Flashing half battery If this symbol appears with no other symbol operating information or no displays at all, the battery must be replaced. **N.B.** This indicator will appear even if the camera's ON/OFF switch is in the **LOCK** position.

Due to the characteristics of Lithium batteries, sometimes when the camera is switched on after being stored for a period of time, the camera may indicate that the battery is either low or almost exhausted. After some use and switching the camera on and off several times the indicator may show that the battery condition has improved. This is quite normal.

High eye-point viewfinder

The 700si's viewfinder is a high eye-point optical design. This makes it easier for those of you who wear spectacles. It also has an added advantage. Sports photographers sometimes hold the camera away from their eye to increase the effective angle of view through their other eye. This allows you to keep an eye on the action outside of the viewfinder frame. The distance that you can still view the entire frame at is 22.9 mm from the viewfinder protective glass to the eye or 18.9 mm from the eye-cup to the eye.

Viewfinder information

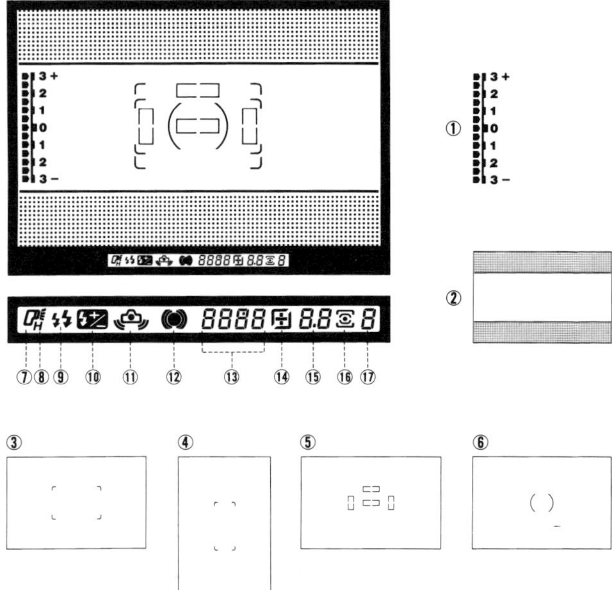

1. Metering Index
2. Panorama Indicator
3. Horizontal Wide-Focus Area
4. Vertical Wide-Focus Area
5. Local Focus Indicators
6. Spot Metering Measuring Area
7. Flash-on Indicator
8. HSS Flash Indicator
9. Flash Signals
10. Flash-compensation Reminder
11. Camera-Shake Warning
12. Focus Signals
13. Shutter Speed/Film-speed/Local Focus Area Indicators/Focal Length(xi lenses only)
14. Compensation/Over/Under Exposure Indicator
15. Aperture/Exposure Compensation/Flash Compensation Display
16. Metering Mode Indicator
17. Remaining Frame Counter

For displaying information in the viewfinder the 700si uses two different types of LCD display. The first is of the conventional type below the image area and illuminated. The second is unique to Minolta, and is called "Advanced Graphic Display Viewfinder". (Who thinks of these terms!) I prefer the term "Head up display".

This is a completely transparent LCD. It is positioned just above the viewfinder screen and is used to superimpose additional information on to the viewfinder screen itself. When information is not being displayed no shadow is evident. Although the amount of information that can be displayed is comprehensive, only the information that is relevant to the current operation or mode selected is shown.

The Head up display LCD is used to show the following information:

Horizontal/Vertical focus area, Local focus area, Spot metering measuring area, Metering index and Panorama indicator.

It is not illuminated but some items are duplicated in the second display for low light operation.

The conventional LCD is used to show the following:

Flash on indicator, HSS flash mode in use, Flash mode, Camera shake warning, Focus status, Shutter speed, Aperture, compensation indicator, metering mode and Remaining frame counter.

This display is permanently illuminated. In bright conditions the brightness of the display is increased. In dark conditions, the display will dim slightly to aid viewing. If the camera is being used in extremely dark conditions, the display may seem too bright and consequently make it difficult for the eye to adjust to the dark conditions and for you to be able to clearly see your subject. In this case, I recommend that you move your eye down slightly in relation to the viewfinder so that you are now unable to see the display. This will make it very much easier for the eye to adjust to the darker conditions.

Eye-Start Eyepiece Sensors

Immediately below the eye-piece are two dark red windows. These are the second set of sensors used for the activation of the eye-start system. They work on a near infra-red principle, one window being an emitter and the other a receiver.

Spot/Slow Sync Button

To the right is the **SPOT/SLOW SYNC** flash button. When the **SPOT** button is pressed the camera indicates the measuring area on the viewfinder screen and takes an exposure reading within this area. The reading is locked. On the left hand side of the screen an indicator also appears which shows the difference between the locked (initial) reading, and the new area which the measuring area covers.

When you use either the built-in flash or a dedicated flash attached to the hotshoe and the **SPOT** button is pressed the function changes to **SLOW SYNC** flash. Here the camera selects a shutter speed based on the background brightness to ensure that this area is also exposed correctly.

The Rear Control Dial

To the right of the Spot button is the rear control dial. Although it duplicates the front dial in some operations, its normal functions are for selecting apertures in program (PA mode), aperture priority and manual exposure modes.

AF Button

On the camera's back cover is a large button labelled **AF**. This is used to indicate on the viewfinder screen the AF sensor selected by the camera for autofocusing, by simply pressing and holding the button, and to lock focus. If the front dial is then turned a new sensor can be manually selected. The camera will then re-focus using the new sensor and then lock focus again.

You will notice that there has been a great deal of thought put into the placement of these last three controls. You will find that when the camera is held in the conventional recommended way with the right elbow tucked in tightly to your body that the thumb can move easily between all three of these controls. A rubber pad has been provided on the back cover to give the thumb somewhere comfortable to rest and aid grip of the camera.

At the base of the camera are the final two exterior controls, on the left is the manual film rewind button and to the right is the Eye-start switch. Both of these are recessed to prevent accidental operation, in particular the rewind button which needs to be pressed with a fingernail or sharp object.

Eye-Start Switch

With the **EYE-START** switch in the **ON** position, AF and AE are activated just by looking through the viewfinder. With the switch in the **OFF** position AE and AF are activated by half pressure on the shutter release.

Film Rewind Button

If you wish to rewind the film before the end, a single press will activate the rewind motor. If the button is pressed a second time or if the button is pressed once the camera has activated rewinding of the film, the camera will change to HI-SPEED rewind if this was not previously selected.

Refer to the section titled "Silent Operation" for further information.

Loading the film

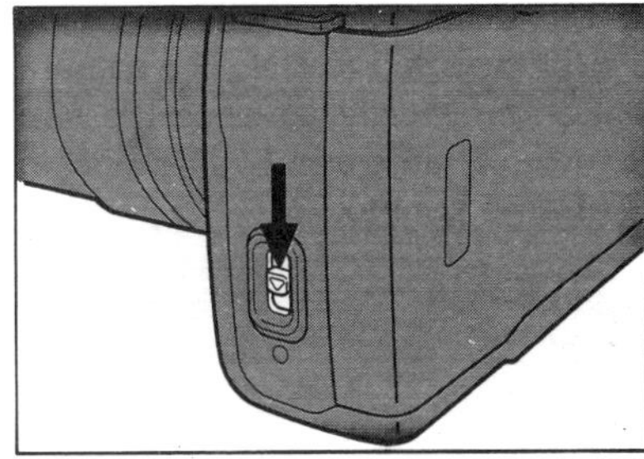

To open the back of the camera slide the back cover switch down. This is located on the left hand side of the camera as we look at it with the lens pointing away from us.

The back cover will spring open. Before we go any further let us just take some time to identify some areas which need to be treated with care.

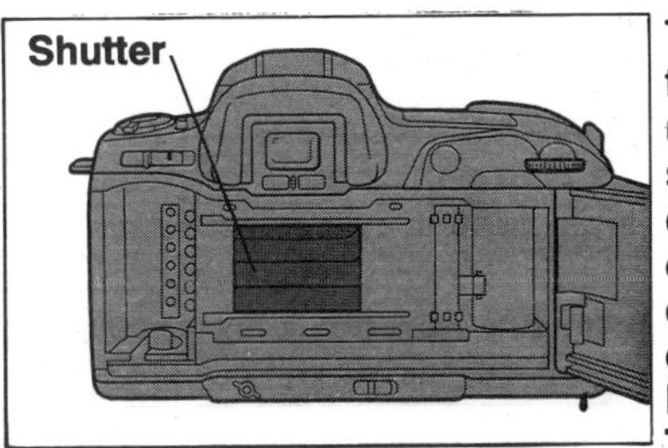

The most delicate area inside the back of the camera is undoubtedly the shutter. The shutter blades, which are clearly exposed in the centre of the camera, are a fraction of a mm thick and hence extremely delicate. **UNDER NO CIRCUMSTANCES SHOULD THESE EVER BE TOUCHED.**

The area around this is the film plane, where the film runs along over the shutter. It is kept flat over the shutter by the pressure plate which is attached to the back cover. You should avoid touching both these areas.

However, if grit, sand or dust falls on these surfaces they could scratch the film. Before loading the film check these areas are clean and blow any dirt away with a blower brush.

DO NOT USE COMPRESSED AIR NEAR THE SHUTTER BLINDS

Inside the film chamber on the left-hand side, you can see 12 silver electrical contacts. These contacts are used to read all of the available DX coding on the film cassette. This information includes not only the film speed and number of exposures but also the films latitude. This third piece of information is used purely by the Fantasy Effect card.

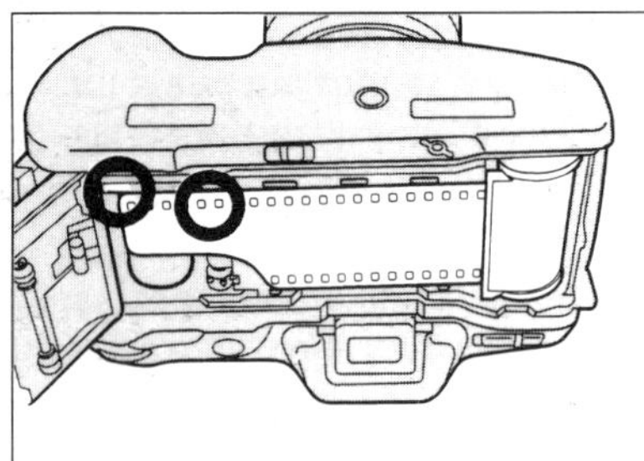

OK, now insert the film into the chamber on the left hand side. You will find inserting it easier by locating the lower end of the film first. Push the film cassette into place until it clicks. Pull the film leader out of the cassette and lay it on the take up drum so that it is level with or slightly forward of the red index mark by the back cover's hinge.

Ensure the film is flat.

Now close the back cover. If the camera was not initially switched on it will advance automatically to number 1 when it is switched on. If the film is loaded correctly number 1 will be indicated in the lower left hand corner of the body LCD data panel.

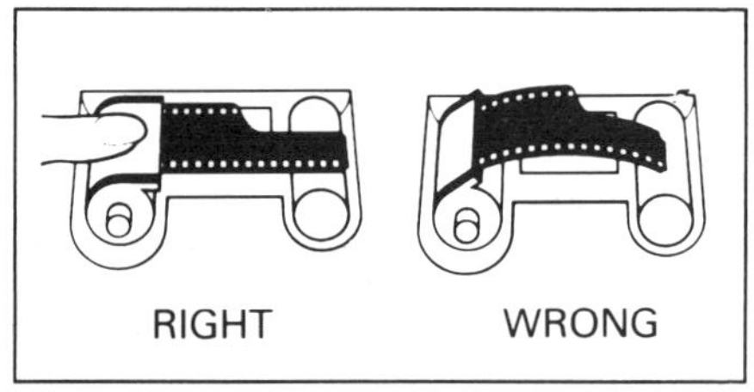

If loading was not successful the frame counter will flash 0. The camera will also fail to function in any way until the film is re-loaded correctly.

For approx 5 seconds after advancing the film to number 1 the LCD panel will also show the set film speed. Incidentally, all camera displays disappear when the camera is switched off, including the frame counter - an annoying oversight in my opinion.

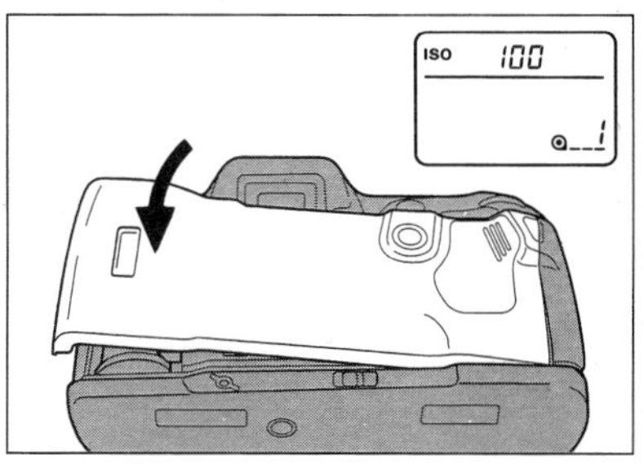

When you reach the end of the film, the camera will re-wind it automatically for you. When rewinding, the LCD panel will only display the frame counter with the number of the last frame taken. Please note that the camera is programmed to rewind the film once the number of frames on the DX coding of the film cassette has been reached. This definitely has its advantages. It overcomes the problem of the processing lab kindly cutting your last picture on the roll in half. It also ensures that the film does not come off its spool at the end of the roll. There is still a mechanism for detecting when the film is physically finished, to prevent the motor breaking the film if the tension in the film is tight (or a film with no DX coding has been loaded).

The disadvantage however, is that if you use one of those films that has 27 exposures for the price of 24 you will not be able to get those last 3 shots, unless you cancel the auto rewind with the Customized Function Card xi.

The "Cupboard"

As we look at the back of the camera, over to the right hand side of the 700si is the Card door. This is opened with your thumb, by pulling open the door at the top left corner where there is an indent in the casing of the back cover/card door. Pull the door open and continue to pull the door open beyond the resistance encountered when the door is at approx 45° (half open) so that the door then stays open at almost 90° to the camera body.

Inside, from the top down are controls for drive mode etc, flash mode, metering mode, film speed override and card adjust functions. With the door open you can see over to the right of the five buttons a slide switch used to eject cards from the door.

Pressing one of these buttons clears the camera's top LCD data panel of all previous irrelevant information and leaves only the features that can be selected/changed. Either front or rear input dials are then used to change a feature or to make an adjustment. Once the change has been made, either pressing the button again or slight pressure on the shutter release confirms the change made. The display will not resume on its own so there are no time restrictions in which you have to make a change as on previous models.

Drive Mode Button (Continuous/Single/Double Exposure/Self Timer)

The top button, in addition to selecting drive mode (single or continuous) is also used to select self-timer operation or double exposure mode. The self-timer delay is fixed at 10 seconds. Focus should be checked before pressing the shutter release all the way down as focus and exposure are fixed as this is done. The AF-illuminator will flash during the 10 second delay confirming that this feature is operative.

Note: When using the self-timer, ensure that you attach the eyepiece cap (normally attached to the camera's strap) to stop any extraneous light entering the viewfinder, as this could affect the exposure reading. To fit the cap, first remove the eyecup, by pushing up on the rubber section with both thumbs. Now slide the cap on to the eyepiece.

Double exposure mode allows you to take two pictures on the same frame without the camera advancing to the next frame.

When the shutter is pressed half way, **M1** appears in place of the frame counter to confirm that the first frame in the sequence has yet to be taken. Once the shutter has been released **M2** remains in place of the frame counter until the final (second) frame in the sequence is taken, the 700si then reverts back to single frame advance. If, after you have taken the first photograph in the sequence you decide not to take another photograph on the same frame but to move onto the next frame, pressing the P-reset button or setting a different drive mode will cancel the sequence and cause the film to be transported to the next frame.

MONEY SAVING TIP - HOW TO DO MULTIPLE EXPOSURES:

To save you buying the card to do standard multiple exposures, do the following operation:

1. Set double exposure in the normal way.

2. Set this in the memory by moving the Memory switch to the **ENTER** position.

3. Take the photograph. (**M2** will appear in lieu of the frame counter)

4. Recall the Memory settings by pressing the **M** (Memory recall) button, **M2** will disappear from the display, but the film will not advance.

5. Repeat steps 3 and 4 until you reach the final photograph in the series.

6. Once you have taken the penultimate photograph, instead of recalling the Memory, press the shutter release all the way down for the final photograph, the film will now advance to the next frame.

Flash mode Button

The second button down in the card door is used to select the following flash modes:

Red-eye reduction, flash without red-eye reduction and wireless/remote flash.

Metering Mode Button

Below the flash mode button is the button for selecting one of the following three metering methods:

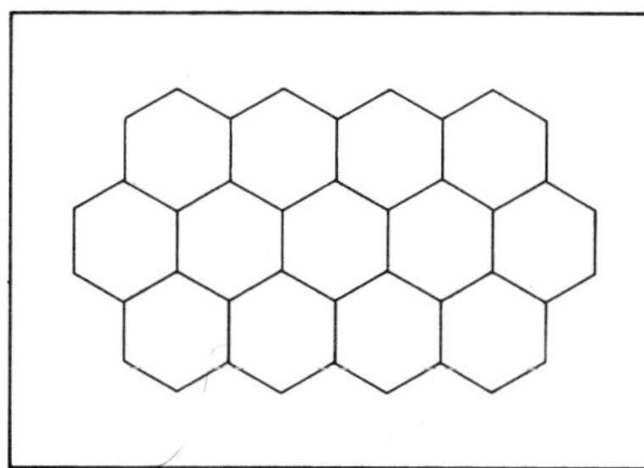

Autofocus Integrated 14 Segment Honeycomb Multi-Pattern Metering System - (You try saying that after a couple of drinks, or before for some people. Who thinks of these feature names?) Throughout the book I shall refer to this simply as, honeycomb metering.

We shall look at honeycomb metering in detail later on.

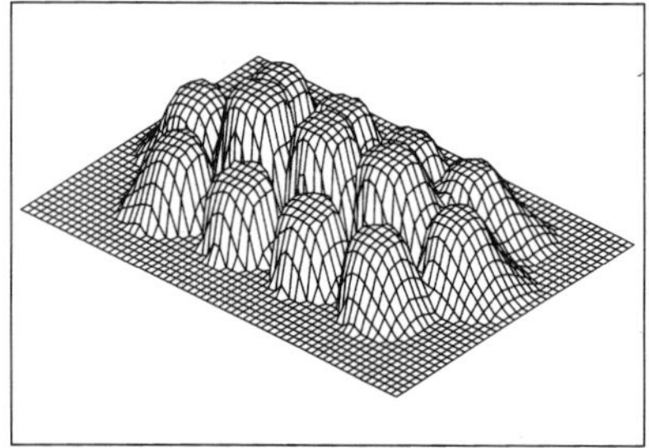

Spot Metering - With this metering mode selected, the camera reads light only from a small area of the scene. This area is approximately 2.7% of the entire frame.

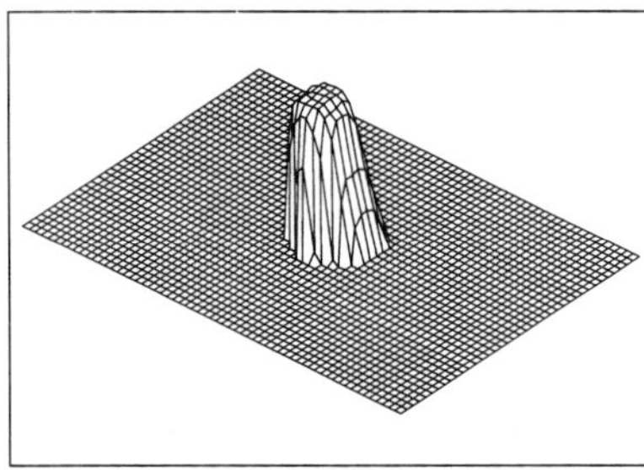

Centre-Weighted Average Metering - Here the camera concentrates 80% of its sensitivity on the three horizontal centre segments and the remaining 20% from the remaining 10 segments. There is no reading from the background surrounding area.

Film Speed Override Button

The film speed is normally set automatically by the camera in the range of 25-5000 ISO/ASA. This is the full range of DX auto film speed settings. If a speed outside of this range is required or you wish to push or pull film by setting a different film speed, simply press the **ISO** button and then turn one of the input dials.

The range available for manual film speed selection is 6-6400 ISO.

IMPORTANT: REFER TO DX OVERRIDE MEMORY UNDER THE SECTION TITLED CUSTOMIZED FUNCTION CARD XI.

Card Adjust Button

The final button labelled **CARD ADJ** is used to adjust settings of certain expansion cards. See relevant section for details of exact operation.

Remote Release Connection

Whilst we still have the card door open, you should just be able to see a small plastic cover with **REMOTE** marked on it. Pull this off with your thumb. Take care not to lose this: its surprising how much such a small piece of plastic can cost to replace. You should now see three gold pins pointing towards you. This is where the electronic remote release RC-1000S/RC-1000L or the Infra-red remote controller IR-1(n) is connected. There is a small storage compartment on the back of the remote release switch casing for this.

The Base

Battery Compartment

The battery compartment is in the main grip. The cover to this is on the base of the camera. The 700si uses a 6 volt 2CR5 lithium battery.

PLEASE READ THE PRECAUTIONS PRINTED ON THE BATTERY.

In the centre of the base plate is a standard threaded tripod bush.
VC-700 Contacts

Over to the right of this as we look at the base with the lens pointing away from us, are two rows of gold electrical contacts. These are used to connect all of the functions of the optional Vertical Control Grip, VC-700, to the camera. To the right of these within the same area, is a blank hole where a location pin on the VC-700 fits.

That gives you a brief run through of the operation of the 700si and should answer most of your initial questions about basic operation, it also means that you should be ready to take photographs.

I suggest that you go and make yourself a cup of coffee and get yourself ready for some serious mind blowing information into how the camera was developed, what it will do and what it won't do (not much).

At times when reading this next section you may sometimes wonder about the relevance of some of the information, bear with me, you'll find it all clicks into place and you will probably thank me for it!

Now settle back , we've got a lot to cover.

EXPERT INTELLIGENCE

An Expert System is one that is literally programmed with the intelligence and experience of an expert in his/her specialist field, in the case of the 700si, a professional photographer. The 700si is able to evaluate the information about the scene and then make a human-like judgement about the scene or subject.

The use of Expert Intelligence, otherwise known as Fuzzy Logic, enables near instantaneous responses to almost any photographic situation. As soon as the 700si is raised to the users eye all of the expert systems come "on line".

Firstly, the AF system must determine the main subject's position within the AF area. This is done by using the distance measured by each AF sensor, the position of each sensor in the frame, the lens focal length and camera orientation.

Once the main subject's position is determined, the AE system uses this information and the output from each of the 14 metering segments to determine the lighting condition of the scene (e.g. backlit, spotlit, slightly spotlit, etc) and to then set the metering pattern accordingly.

The lighting condition, subject position, and brightness detected by each metering segment is then used to adjust the weighting of each segment within the SPC (Silicon Photo Cell). Subject brightness, focal length, widest available aperture, subject distance and subject magnification are used to determine a rough aperture/shutter speed combination.

Expert Program Selection is then used to evaluate a three dimensional description of the subject's motion and balances the shutter speed and aperture settings in order to tailor the exposure to the actual subject or scene characteristics.

So, summing up, the camera first determines the main subject's position. This information is then passed to the exposure system so that it can make a judgement as to the type of subject that you are photographing, and thus select an appropriate metering pattern and aperture/shutter speed combination to give the optimum exposure - simple, really!

Let's now give you some examples of how fuzzy logic is used in the 700si.

Conventional logic operates with answers such as yes and no in

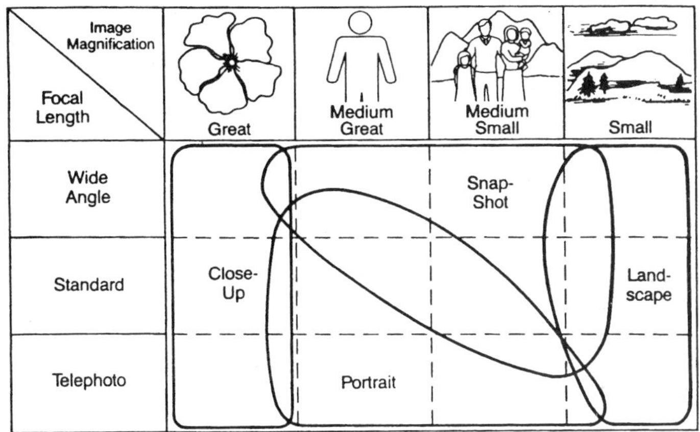

Expert Intelligence with Fuzzy Logic Control

situations which are black or white. Fuzzy Logic, as well as operating in situations which are black and white, also operates in the grey areas in between and is able to answer these situations with responses such as, "slightly" and "if".

Supposing we were to conduct a survey of people's ages, feed them into a conventional computer and to then ask it whether they were classed as young, middle-aged or old. To do this we would need to program it with two thresholds, one between young and middle-aged and the other between middle-aged and old. Let's say for example that these are 40 and 65 (I have tried not to offend) This would then mean that on your 40th birthday you suddenly change from being judged as young to middle-aged. In reality though, this is of course not the case, as we all have our own ideas on how someone is classed in relation to their age.

If we now apply this to a photographic situation, such as determining whether the subject is evenly lit, back-lit or spot-lit, we can see the true benefits of this new fuzzy logic control.

A conventional metering system measures the brightness of the centre of the picture (subject position) and the background area's separately. The difference between these two areas is calculated and then used to determine the lighting condition. If this figure is equal to or greater than 2 EV* (exposure value) then the subject is classed as being spot-lit or backlit, if this difference is only 1.9

[* One EV is the same as one f-stop.]

EV then the camera assumes the scene to be evenly illuminated. But how can such a small change in lighting result in the camera dramatically changing the way in which it sees the scene? A fuzzy logic system however is able to recognise the degree of back lighting in these situations and apply the necessary exposure compensation.

Fuzzy Logic is used to:

1. Determine the main subject's position within the AF area.

2. Select the number of metering segments and the weighting of the segments.

3. Select the aperture/shutter speed combination best suited to the subject.

4. Control the zoom speed of the xi lenses when Image Size Lock and APZ are in use.

AF Sensor Module

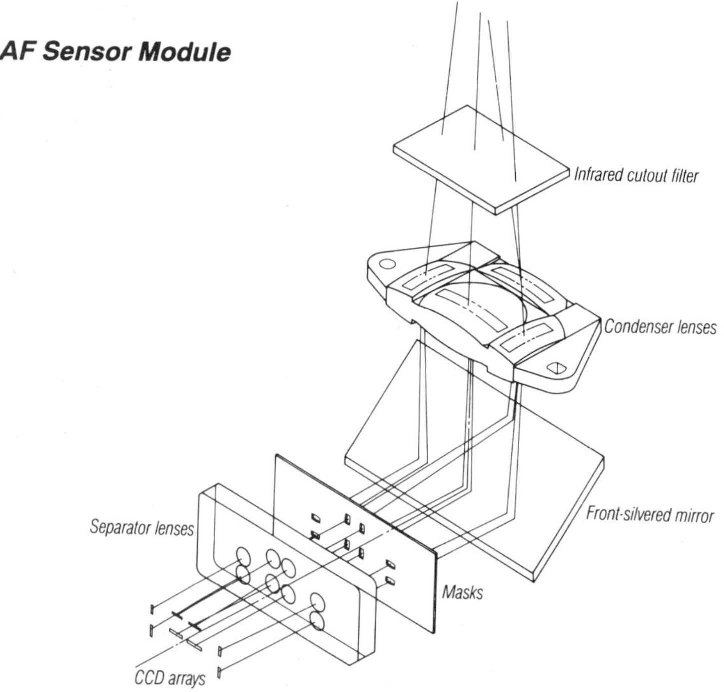

THE 700si's AUTOFOCUS SYSTEM

We are now going to look at how autofocus works, why the 700si focuses on the items that it does, what its capabilities are and how to control it to get the best out of it in the unlikely event of it getting stuck, or how we can help it out.

We all seem to take it for granted that everyone understands how autofocus works these days, but unless you remember clearly the introduction of the Minolta 7000 in 1985, it's unlikely that you understand or even know how the camera does its job in the way that it does, partly or even fully. The better your understanding of how the AF system works the easier you will find it to control and to overcome potential problems.

First the basics

The autofocus system's main components are the AF module, autofocus drive motor, AF CPU (Autofocus Central Processing Unit), and a ROM IC (Read Only Memory Integrated Circuit).

Light that passes through the lens enters the camera body and is reflected up to the pentaprism in the viewfinder where you see the image. The main mirror is a semi-silvered type so that whilst most of the light is reflected up to the viewfinder, a high percentage passes through the main mirror. This light is then reflected by a small sub mirror, located directly behind the main mirror, into the AF module, the most important element of the system.

Once the image enters the AF module it passes through an infra-red cut off filter through a condenser lens and splitter lenses which split the image into two duplicate images. The two images are now projected on to a pair of Charge Coupled Device's (CCD) which are in line. This device is used to convert an optical signal into an electrical signal that can be decoded by the AF CPU.

The CCD is split up into a number of areas which are known as elements or Pixels. The brightness is measured in each area, producing a signal or wave form.

The distance between the two images varies depending upon the focus condition. This distance is compared to a reference signal in the AF CPU. If the distance is greater than that of the reference signal then the lens is focused behind the subject, if the distance is smaller than the reference signal then the lens is focused in front of the subject. This is how the AF CPU knows which direction the lens must be moved.

The lens position and focal length are then supplied to the AF CPU from the ROM IC in the lens. By using this data the AF CPU is able to calculate how far the lens must be moved. The camera's micro-motor is then activated. Once the motor has shifted the lens by the required amount it is then instantly stopped and the subject is now in focus.

Easy!?

Potential problems with autofocus

I have explained how the system works but let us now look at some situations that can fool autofocus systems and why this occurs.

Low contrast

The most common situation where autofocus is unable to work is low or zero contrast. I will explain why. Supposing we paint the left hand side of a wall black and the right hand side white. With the camera's AF area positioned centrally on the area where the two halves meet, a waveform with a strong peak will be generated by the signal from the CCD. If you draw a straight horizontal line, this will represent the signal for the black area. If you now draw a straight vertical line up from the right hand side of the first line and then another straight horizontal line from the end of the vertical line to the right, this is what the output from the CCD will look like as a waveform. Remember that there will be two duplicate images of this on the CCD. One image on the left hand side and the other on the right hand side. This will give the AF computer two reference points to work from. The distance between them on the CCD is compared with a reference distance in the AF computer's memory etc.

If we were to point the AF area at a subject that had even brightness across it, lets say a plain white wall (zero contrast subject), the waveform will be a single straight horizontal line. Because there is no contrast, there are no reference points and so it makes no difference what the camera does to the lens setting, the waveform will always look the same, so the camera will not know whether the subject is in focus or out of focus.

Other situations in which the AF system may not be able to focus correctly are: when alternating identical light and dark lines completely fill the AF area, on very bright subjects and when two or more subjects overlap in the AF area.

Before we go any further, I must stress that the first and especially the second of these three situations are extremely rare occurrences. I will explain why the system may not work in these situations.

Light and dark lines

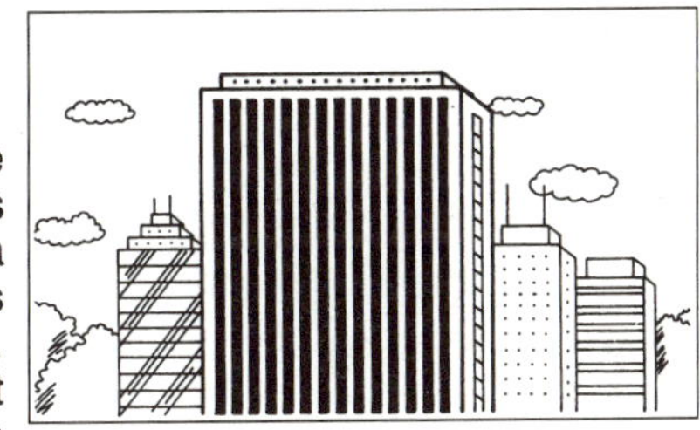

Firstly lets look at the alternating light and dark lines example. Imagine we paint a wall with identical thickness black and white vertical lines. Plenty of contrast, yes, but here is where the problem lies. When the two duplicate images are projected onto the CCD, there are no apparent reference points. The waveform will feature many identical steps, but the AF computer does not know which peaks on the left hand side image to match up with the peaks for the right hand side image. It's a similar situation to the zero contrast example, no reference points, no autofocus.

Very bright subjects

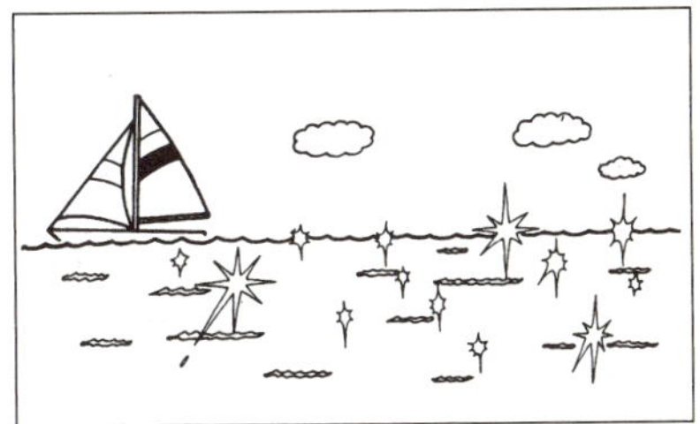

Refer to sub-section titled **EV minus 1 low light AF performance** (see page 53).

More than one subject in the AF area

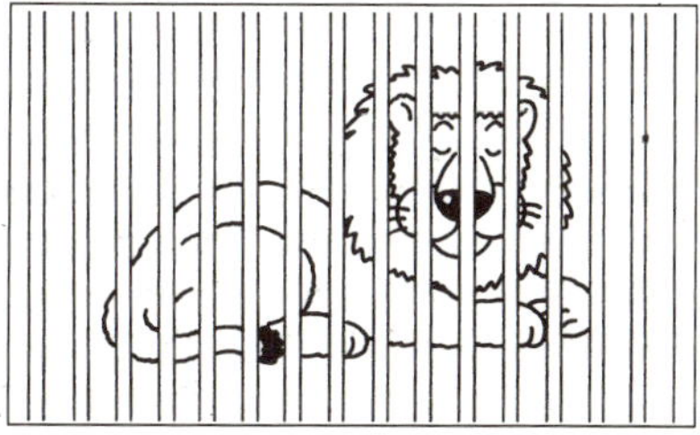

The third situation is a classic problem for AF cameras. Essentially the CCD is giving conflicting signals. The camera does not know which reference point to use for its calculations. Put another way it hasn't a clue as to which subject you want to focus on. The AF system used by the 700si is unique amongst all other AF systems in the way in which it decides what to focus on and what not to focus on. We shall cover later in this section how and why the 700si decides to focus on what it does. But occasionally it may have difficulty in certain situations when there are two or more subjects within the AF area. For when this does happen we will look at what to do so we can still make use of the AF system.

All of the first generation AF SLR's and the majority of them today only use one AF sensor. With the exception of one or two Canon and Nikon AF SLR's, this sensor only works on vertical contrast. So, in our original situation where we had a half black, half white wall, if we were to turn the camera through 90° the waveform would be one straight horizontal line, because the brightness in each area of the CCD is the same. Basically, the contrast is in the wrong plane.

Now you have an understanding of how autofocus in general works you will be able to start to adjust the way you use the camera to get the most out of the AF system.

Alternative Systems

Motor in the body versus motor in the lens

The very first AF cameras all featured a motor in the lens design. The Minolta 7000 was the world's first body integral AF SLR. Not only were the AF sensors and AF computer in the body, but also the motor for driving the lens.

Since Canon introduced the EOS range which use motors in the lens, there has always been a big argument as to whose system is best.

There are in fact advantages and disadvantages to both systems.

Motor in the lens disadvantages

The disadvantages for this system mainly relate to the cost. It is obviously more expensive to incorporate a motor into every lens. If there is an improvement in AF speed due to an improvement in the body integral system all lenses become faster. However, with the motor in the lens system, you would need to buy a whole new range of lenses, and I can tell you now, I for one would not be rushing out with my cheque book!

Motor in the body disadvantages

The motor in the lens is very quiet, it also starts and stops sooner apparently.

Ah....... Well.....

The motor in the body is not up to the job of focusing large telephoto lenses.

STOP! .... Not Minolta lenses.

Let me explain. It's all due to rear focusing, internal focusing, double floating etc. lens designs, newly developed low viscosity lubricants, low friction gearing and specially selected gearing ratios. Clear? I thought so.

During the time Minolta spent developing the original 7000 system they paid particular attention to the lenses. Rather than utilising conventional lens designs, Minolta radically changed the design of all the lenses to ensure fast focusing. This was mainly achieved by reducing the mass of the focusing optics and the movement of the optics to focus the image.

Inevitably a wideangle lens will be faster in focusing than a large telephoto lens, but even the 300 f/2.8 and 600 f/4 APO lenses are incredibly fast. In fact I have personally used these lenses with no problems at all on 200 mph F1 cars.

The system used by the 700si is fundamentally the same as that used by the 7000 in 1985 and in fact all other AF SLR's today, and is known as "Phase detection" or "Passive".

What makes the 700si different then?

Its choice of main subject to be focused on and the amazing speed by which it can focus on still, as well as very high speed, subjects. Let's first look at the main points of the 700si's AF system, which are:

- **Ultra Wide AF Area**
- **Fuzzy Logic control for subject position**
- **Multi-Dimensional Predictive Focus Control
  (Omni-Directional Predictive Focus Control, in some markets)**
- **Automatic Focus Mode Selection**
- **High Sensitivity AF Sensors**

Previously we looked at problems that an autofocus system may come across and why. The above five features employed by the 700si are designed to reduce and in some cases even eliminate potential problems occurring.

Ultra-wide AF area

The 700si uses the largest AF area of any AF SLR available on the market today. The benefit of a large AF area is that it makes it very much easier to focus on the following subjects:

- Off-centre subjects.
- Erratically moving subjects.
- Low contrast subjects.
- Fast moving subjects.

The 700si's AF area is made up of four AF sensors. Two are vertical (left and right sensors), whilst the remaining two are horizontal (centre and top sensors).

The centre and top sensors are used for vertical contrast, whilst the left and right sensors are used for horizontal contrast. Each sensor is sensitive enough to focus on diagonals.

The centre sensor is the largest of all the four sensors. It is approximately 25 % larger than the top sensor and approximately 67 % larger than the left and right sensors.

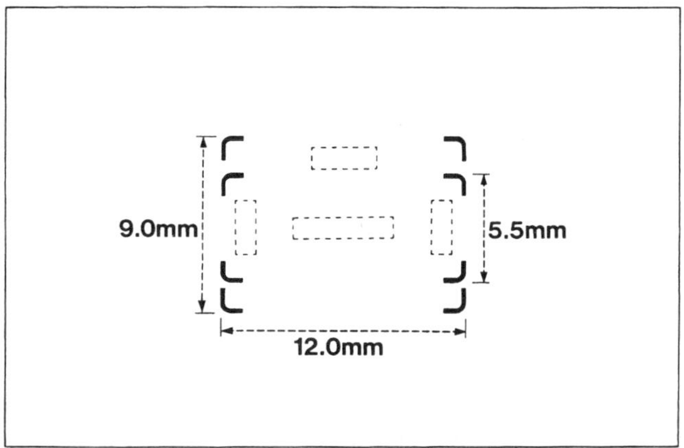

Position of AF sensors and focus areas within viewfinder frame:
Vertical-mode AF area : 9x12mm
Horizontal-mode AF area : 5.5x12mm

The total size of the AF area is 9 x 12 mm, three times the size of the Minolta Dynax/Maxxum 7000i. It is approximately five times the size of other AF SLR's available today.

The AF area is indicated on the focusing screen by four small brackets. As long as your main subject is positioned within this area the camera should be able to focus on it.

Rule of Thirds

The AF area markings are at the intersection points of the "Rule of Thirds" guideline for composition. If you divide your picture up into thirds, both horizontally and vertically you will find that there are four intersection points. This is where the AF area markings are.

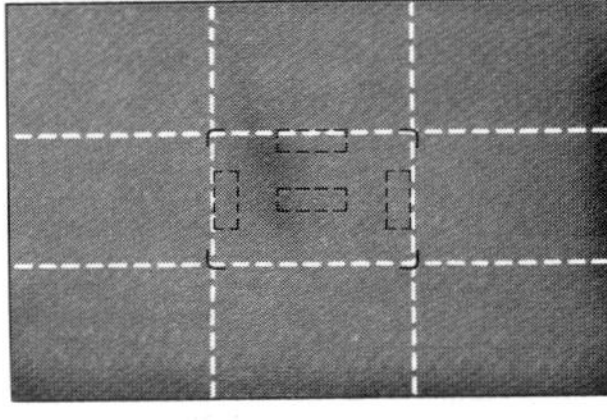

The Rule of Thirds states that if your main subject is placed at one of those points a more balanced composition will result. For example: for portraits where the subject is looking to the left, place their head at the top right intersection point. They should now be looking towards the open part of the picture which creates interest. For landscapes, rather than positioning the horizon in the centre, position it across two of the intersection points, this creates a better balance. If you were photographing a scene where there was no horizon but just grass and a small house in the distance, position the house at one of the four intersection points. It works very well, try it.

So basically, what I am trying to say is that it is highly unlikely that your main subject will be positioned outside of the AF area.

Fuzzy logic control for subject position

The 700si makes use of fuzzy logic to determine which of the four AF sensors detects the main subject. The first AF SLR's, and in fact most of today's models, use only one AF sensor. The introduction of the Minolta Dynax/Maxxum 7000i in 1988 saw the first application of a multi sensor system. The benefits of this system have already been explained in the section, "Ultra-wide AF area", and clearly shows the benefits over a single sensor system. However, there are complications. The problem is, which one sensor to use for focusing? Conventional AF SLR's always try and focus on the nearest object within the AF area, accepting that there is sufficient contrast on the subject for accurate focusing. However, your actual subject may not always be the closest object in the frame.

Due to this, Minolta developed a new and unique system to help combat this problem and of course at the same time increase the success rate of correctly focused photographs. As previously explained in the section titled "Expert Intelligence", it is not always necessary to store every conceivable situation into the camera's memory so that it is able to recognise the actual current situation in question.

Although the 700si uses a far more advanced system for subject detection than other AF SLR's, because it makes use of fuzzy logic it is reliant on fewer rules for the selection of which sensor to use for focusing on the main subject. This makes the 700si's focusing faster as well as more accurate and reliable.

This is how it works:

First, information from all four focusing sensors and the lens CPU are transformed into 6 different types of subject distance data. This, together with the camera's orientation, (vertical/horizontal) are input to the Fuzzy Inference module. There are now 7 pieces of information. These are inferred with 7 inference rules that the module is based on. Using these rules a certainty grade of the subjects within the following four areas are evaluated. From this a choice is then made to select just one sensor. It is this sensor that is used to focus the lens.

The four areas that are evaluated are:

1.   Spot area in centre sensor
2.   Centre sensor
3.   Top centre sensor
4.   Sensor which detects nearest object

Basically, the sensor chosen is the one that has the highest probability of being positioned on the subject.

Let's now go a bit further and hopefully it should all piece together. Essentially the system will choose a sensor based on the type of photograph or more specifically the type of subject.

For Close-ups the 700si will place emphasis on the centre sensor. However, for high magnification subjects the 700si may use just a small section of the centre sensor. As an example, this avoids problems where the AF system doesn't know whether to focus on the petals of the flower in the foreground or the centre of the flower in the background. The use of a small section allows the 700si to focus through and "into" the flower.

Automatic Focus Area Selection

For Portraits the 700si will place emphasis on the top centre sensor which covers the subject's eyes. However what happens when you hold the camera vertically? Inside the camera's main handgrip are a couple of ball bearings. You can probably hear them if you shake the camera close to your ear. They are used to inform the camera as to its orientation.

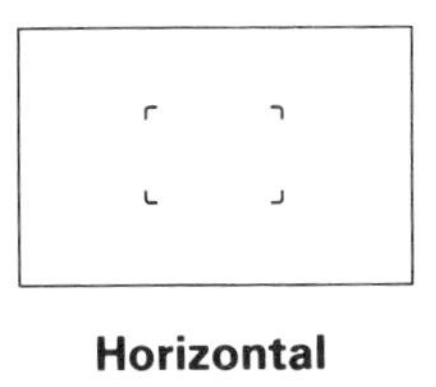

Horizontal

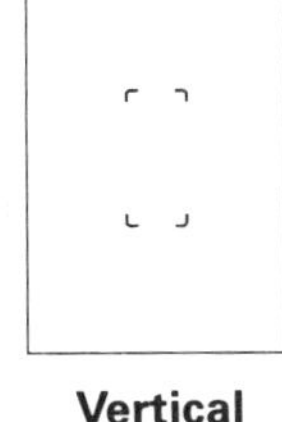

Vertical

So, for vertically framed portraits with the handgrip at the top the 700si's AF system will emphasize the use of what was originally the right hand sensor. If the camera is held with the grip at the bottom, then the system will place emphasis on what was originally the left hand sensor.

Incidentally, this orientation information is also used by the exposure system, so that the metering system knows the position of the sky.

For landscapes the 700si places emphasis on whichever sensor detects the nearest object. This helps to increase the depth of field, which is ideal for this type of photograph

Finally, for sports the camera will use whichever sensor detects a moving subject. If this subject changes its relative position in the frame, maybe because it is moving erratically, then the AF system will detect this and immediately switch to a new sensor which covers the same subject.

Due to this type of situation, I personally have found that the 700si has an uncanny ability to follow the action even when obstructions are passed, whilst panning for example.

Another example is when shooting through trees or undergrowth at animals or scenery. Here the system ignores very close subjects and continues to focus on the subject or scene.

You are probably now thinking to yourself one of two things. Either that's very clever or, like me, how basic!

But remember what I said in the Expert Intelligence section. When analyzing anything in life we don't think about every individual situation, we ask ourselves a few questions and then come up with a suitable response for that situation.

High Speed Autofocus - The fastest!

When the Minolta 7000 was launched in 1985 the speed and accuracy of autofocus was incredible for that time period, but it was clear that there was room for improvement. There was no doubting that the 7000 was an incredibly successful camera, perhaps the most successful of all time. It's hard to imagine there ever being an epoch breaking camera like the 7000 again, but there were many professional and good amateur photographers who took the opinion that autofocus would never replace manual focus. In 1988 Minolta showed, with the introduction of the 7000i, that autofocus was here to stay. Many professionals bought 7000i's as a supplement to their existing equipment for those applications where there was little time to capture an image, such as for fashion shows. Let me give you some idea as to the improvement in focusing speed made with the 7000i over the original 7000. The 7000 when fitted with an original 35-70 lens would focus from infinity to 1m in 0.45 seconds. The 7000i when fitted with the same lens would take 0.25 seconds. However, since the introduction of the 7000i the original AF lenses have been gradually upgraded to "Dynax/Maxxum Spec". This term basically means that the lens is faster focusing than its predecessor. For example when the 7000i is fitted with the original 35-105mm lens the time for the lens to be shifted from infinity to 1.5m is 0.30 seconds. When the 7000i is fitted with the new version the time drops considerably to 0.14 seconds, a 100% improvement, just by changing the lens. When you look at these times you can start to imagine why a number of people took the view that it would be unlikely that autofocus speeds would be dramatically improved upon in the near future.

Think again. The introduction of the next generation, the Dynax/Maxxum 7xi in 1991, saw autofocus times halved yet again.

The figures quoted so far relate to the time it takes for the lens to be rotated. But a major part of the total time needed for focusing is used for calculating subject distance etc. We also have to bear in mind the maximum speed of the subject that is able to be tracked. Let us now look at some data for this.

Assume we are tracking a car that is moving directly towards us and which is filling the frame. The lens in use is 300mm focal length. The 7000 would be able to keep the car in focus at all times as long as the subject does not exceed 10 mph, the 7000i would manage up to 70 mph whilst the 700si will be able to keep the subject in focus at up to 200 mph! This example is for a high magnification subject. If the car filled only 2/3 of the frame then the maximum speeds would be, 20 mph (7000),120 mph (7000i) and in excess of 250 mph (700si).

Let us look at another example.

Let's say for example that we are going to photograph an Olympic athlete running the 100m event. With a 7000i we would be able to photograph the subject with a 300mm lens from 18m away. With the 700si we can photograph the same subject as close as 9m, which in turn allows us to capture our subject with very high magnifications.

So, summing up, the time it takes for the 700si to focus on your subject is approximately half that of the 7000i, which allows us to capture subjects moving three times the speed.

In independent tests the AF system that the 700si employs continues to out perform all others in focusing speed.

How is it done?

Improvements in three key areas allow this to be possible.

1. An improved microcomputer with higher data processing speed. The 700si makes use of a 16 bit CPU which operates at a clock speed of 20 MHz. The 7000i used an 8 bit CPU running at 10.5 MHz. This allows processing of up to almost 8 times the amount of information and at almost five times the speed.

2. New algorithms for processing position data for high speed subjects. Once the subject has been detected, its movement characteristics then determine the way in which the 700si will

handle the data from the four AF sensors. Essentially the 700si tailors its operation precisely to the subject.

3. High response lens drive motor. The new motor operates at a higher RPM than the 7000i's (which incidentally was in excess of 6000 RPM). In addition the new motor reaches its maximum speed and stops sooner.

Multi-Dimensional Predictive Focus Control (Omni-Directional Predictive Focus Control, in some markets)

The Minolta Dynax/Maxxum 7000i was the first camera to feature Predictive focus control, now a standard feature on almost all AF SLR's. The first AF SLR's calculated the subject position prior to the mirror moving up and the aperture closing to the selected setting. Therefore during the time that the mirror etc would move the subject would also move, but to an out of focus position. Predictive focus control was designed to overcome this problem. With predictive focus the camera calculates not only the subject position, but also the subject's speed, either towards or away from the camera. Because the camera now knows the subject speed it is able to predict where the subject will be at the time the shutter opens.

To reduce the time delay even further, the system makes use of the time when the mirror is moving up. Most AF SLR's set the predicted focus setting before the mirror moves up, but on the 7000i, the lens continues to move right up until the shutter blades of the first curtain start to move.

Now we have looked at the basics behind previous systems we can now look at the system used in the 700si.

Most AF systems with predictive control give a very high success rate on subjects up to their maximum possible tracking speed (120 mph for the 7000i). Because the 700si's system is capable of tracking subjects at much higher speeds, the focusing accuracy has to be much higher. Let me give you an example to show how critical focusing is on a high speed subject.

Subject	Formula 1 car
Speed	200 mph
Lens	300 mm f/2.8
Subject Distance	25m
Shutter Speed	1/500

Believe it or not, just whilst the shutter is open the subject will move approximately 20cm. When you bear in mind that at f/2.8 for that subject distance there is only approximately 40cm of depth of field either side of the point of focus I am sure you can realise how accurate the autofocus system has to be.

Predictive focus systems only take into account subjects moving in the same direction and at a constant speed. If we were following a high speed moving subject that was changing both speed and direction there will be a number of shots taken that will be out of focus. To combat this the 700si features what is known as Multi-Dimensional Predictive Focus Control.

This new system is unique to Minolta and allows the AF system to take into account complex subject movements.

This is how it works.

If you were to track a subject performing a U-turn and then plot its path on a graph of image velocity at the film plane against time you can see that there is a characteristic waveform. In the 700si system for every type of subject movement there is a unique waveform which is referred to as an algorithm.

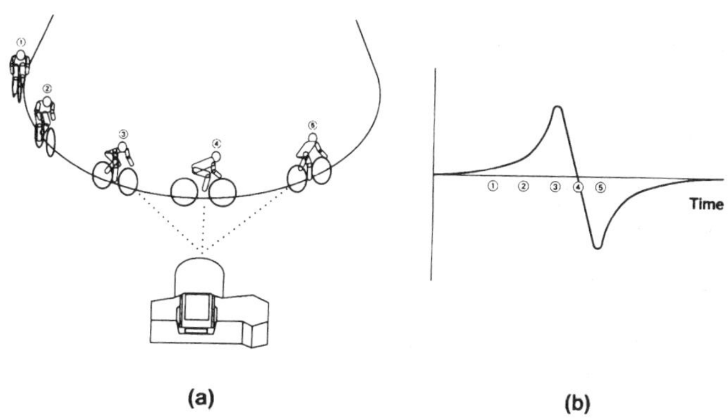

(a)   (b)

This improvement has been made possible by the camera taking hundreds of readings every second. This gives the AF computer more information and allows it to take into account small changes in subject speed and types of movement and therefore is more accurate. Previous systems would be able to take just two consecutive readings and be able to calculate the subject speed towards or away from the camera only.

Two readings are not enough to calculate whether the subject is accelerating or decelerating. The system must take three or four to be able to calculate this. To calculate complex movements even more readings must be taken. The drawback is of course, this takes longer, so this is why a much faster computer was used in the 700si. The 700si has the ability to take almost 8 times the amount of information into account over previous systems within the time it took those systems to take just two readings.

Once the camera has detected a moving subject it will start to form a 3 dimensional image of it. Once this has been done it will control the autofocus based on the algorithm that most closely matches that of the actual subject. If we refer to the diagram on page 47 again, what becomes hard to believe is that between points 1 and 3 the 700si would have already decided what the subject's movements will be!

Now I know exactly what you are thinking, what if the subject's movement characteristics change? The answer to this is simple, it will immediately switch to the new algorithm that corresponds to the new movement, because it is continuously updating the algorithm by calculating the subject's movements in real time.

How is the subject's speed calculated?

Remember when the AF system is calculating the adjustment for autofocus, it generates two images on the CCD (focus sensor). The distance between these two images is compared with

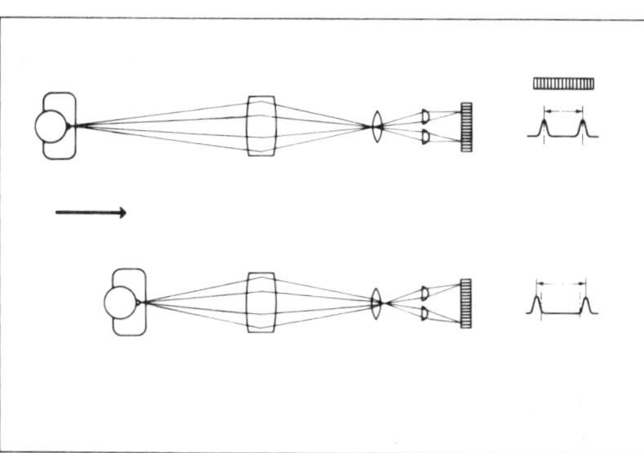

reference signals and the camera knows how much and in which direction to move the lens. Great.

The camera takes two consecutive readings. By comparing these two readings the 700si knows how fast the subject is moving.

D1 is the initial distance between two points on the CCD.
D2 is the second readings distance.
Vz is the velocity along the z axis (towards/away from the camera)
T is the time measured for the two readings.

Therefore:
$$Vz = (D2-D1)/T$$

For a subject moving parallel to the film plane the speed is calculated as follows:

This time the two reference points used for focusing move across the CCD. The deviation from their original position is x.

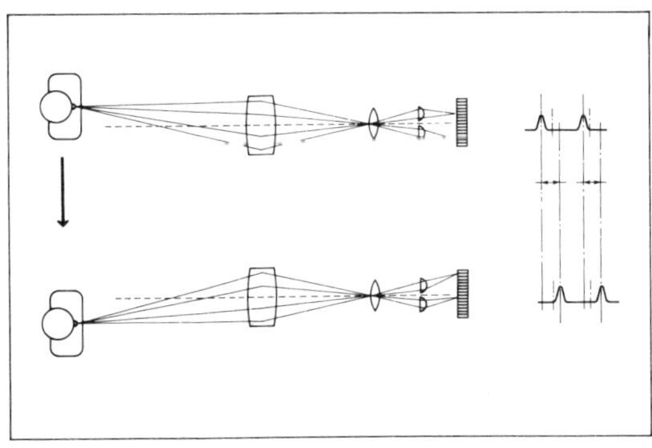

Vx is the velocity in the x axis, from left to right.

Vy is the velocity in the y axis, from top to bottom.

Therefore:
$$Vx = x/T$$
and
$$Vy = x/T$$

However, because the AF system can only measure the subject's movements when the mirror is down, it is unable to take into account any sudden changes that the subject may make after the mirror has started to move up. I must add though that this is **extremely** unlikely and any change that may occur in most cases will be within the depth of field available.

Below is a table showing the types of movements that the 700si can follow.

1. Subject approaching
2. Approaching and rapidly decelerating
3. Approaching from a standstill
4. Receding
5. Receding and rapidly decelerating
6. Receding from a standstill
7. Traversing the scene - **Refer to the Panning card for tips**

8. U-turn away from the camera
9. U-turn towards the camera

Just to reiterate, other AF systems can only function accurately for subjects 1 and 4.

Automatic Focus Mode Selection

Minolta Dynax/Maxxum's are the only AF SLR's that feature automatic focus mode selection in all modes of operation. When you press half way down on the shutter release the camera selects which AF mode best suits the subject based on its speed at the film plane.

The 700si has all three AF modes.

    1.   Single AF (also known as one-shot AF)
    2.   Continuous AF (also known as servo AF)
    3.   Multi-Dimensional Predictive Focus Control

This is done simply by continually taking subject distance readings for 3/10 of a second. If within that time the subject speed at the film plane does not exceed the standard value, focus will be locked. If it is greater than the standard value, continuous AF is selected. Speed at the film plane is different to actual subject speed. Image magnification is relative to speed at the film plane. Here's an example. Imagine you are tracking a high speed subject moving at over 200 mph approaching from over a mile away. The lens will more than likely be focused on infinity. The subject could move over half a mile and yet the lens will probably still be on the infinity setting. In this situation the camera will infer the subject as either stationary or slow moving.

Now imagine you are photographing an Olympic runner approaching the camera from only 20m away. In one second the subject will move 10m, and obviously to take into account the change in subject distance the lens will have to move at very high speed to be able to keep the subject in focus. In this example the camera will judge the subject as a very high speed subject, although its actual speed is very much less than in the previous example.

So, summing up. If the subject is inferred as being stationary, focus will be locked with half pressure on the shutter release. If the subject is inferred as being a high speed subject, continuous AF is selected and the focus cannot be locked with half pressure.

Sometimes the camera may not select continuous AF for a moving subject but it will make use of predictive focus control so that any movement is taken into account, and hence the subject will not be out of focus.

However, what a large number of users tend to do in this situation is to press half way on the shutter release and hold it there for a brief time. This then causes the focus to be locked and therefore predictive focus is then effectively switched off. To overcome this potential problem, use the camera in the following way:

First press half way down to activate the AF system and then release the shutter release. This gets the initial focus setting close to the one that will be used for the photograph. Therefore the camera has less of an adjustment to make when the picture is taken. When you see the subject in the frame at the position that you would like to take it press all of the way down on the shutter release in one smooth action without pausing or hesitating. This will ensure that predictive focus works regardless of autofocus mode (continuous/single).

An even easier method is to rely purely on the eye-start system. Here the camera adjusts focus continuously without having to press halfway. In this case only ever press all the way down on the shutter release when you wish to take the picture. Remember pressing halfway even with eye-start on, will lock focus if the subject is inferred as being stationary.

Summing up

Stationary subjects — Focus locked with half pressure

Slow moving subjects — Predictive Focus - focusing carried out whilst mirror swings up.

Fast moving subjects — Continuous and Predictive AF selected. Most of the focus adjustment made prior to the mirror swinging up. Focusing continues until the shutter opens.

Very fast subjects — Continuous and Predictive AF selected. In addition, just prior to mirror swinging up, subject's movements double checked. Most of the focus adjustment is made prior to the mirror swinging up. Focusing continues until the shutter opens.

Extra Information

When the shutter release is pressed part way and the camera selects continuous AF rather than locking focus, the AF system will remain in continuous AF until the shutter is released, even if a moving subject comes to a halt. If this occurs and you wish to focus lock once the subject has stopped, release the shutter release and then press part way again.

If you prefer to be able to select continuous AF, perhaps because you prefer not to use the eye-start system then there are several ways in which this can be done.

1. Using a Customized Function xi card you can reprogram the focus lock button on certain Dynax/Maxxum lenses (see focus lock for list), so that pressing this button activates continuous AF as long as the button is held in.

2. Insert Sports/Sports 2 card. One of these card's functions is to keep continuous AF on permanently. Refer to Sports/Sports 2 card in expansion card section for further information.

3. The third way is a little tricky. Point the camera at the ground in the distance and then, not too slowly, point the camera down so you end up with the camera pointing at the ground in front of you. The tricky bit is pressing the shutter release part way just as you start to point the camera down. This is the best way of fooling the AF system into thinking that you are following a high speed subject. If it has worked you will get the continuous AF signal in the viewfinder rather than the focus locked signal. Now you have activated continuous AF, do not lift your finger off the shutter release, otherwise you will have to start again! With practice it gets a lot easier, take my word for it.

Incidentally, don't worry, exposure will not be locked.

The standard value referred to at the beginning of this sub-section is set at the development stage of the autofocus system. It is set in a way to give the most reliable selection of focus mode for the given situation. The value has been set so that continuous and predictive focus are used only if the subject's speed is so great that if the shutter release was pressed in one action predictive focus would not be able to capture the subject "on its own". In this case continuous and predictive AF are used to ensure that the subject can be focused upon.

Refer to the section titled "Eye-start" for further information.

Refer to "Taking Control" for more information on focus lock.

High sensitivity AF sensors

The 700si makes use of high density AF sensors. A high density sensor is broken into even smaller elements or pixels than previous systems. This makes focusing even more accurate, especially in low light and low contrast situations. In addition, due to alterations in the algorithms used for low light and low contrast situations, focusing speed and accuracy has been further improved over previous models.

The centre sensor comprises 276 pixels, the top sensor 226 and the left and right 167 each. This gives a total of 836 pixels, the highest number of pixels in any AF SLR.

It is the use of these new sensors that make the multi-dimensional predictive focus system possible, because the system is able to detect small changes in subject distance and speed within a short space of time.

EV (exposure value) minus 1 low light AF performance

Due to the use of high density CCD's, the 700si's AF sensitivity range is minus 1 EV to 19 EV (100 ISO). In exposure terms that is equivalent to 30" at f/4 to 1/8000 at f/8 (100 ISO).

What does this mean?

The sensitivity range is quoted so that we are able to recognise the limits of the AF system in bright and dark conditions. EV 0 is roughly equivalent to the illumination given by a single candle. EV minus 1 is currently the lowest lighting level that any AF SLR will focus down to. If the lighting is darker than this the AF system will not function at all. The same will hold true if the conditions are too bright.

Why?

Remember the way the CCD works. It essentially measures the brightness in each of its areas. If the scene is too dark, there will not be sufficient light to generate a waveform for focusing calculations. The waveform will be a straight line. This is the same for situations that are too bright

So, what can we do?

If the conditions are too dark, not a lot. But you may find that if there are slightly brighter areas present in the scene, locking focus on a similar distant object that has more illumination may allow you to stay in autofocus.

We have more options available at the other end of the scale. We could either try focusing on a similar distance subject and then locking focus. There is a better solution though. By using a polarizing or neutral density filter we can effectively increase the range to EV 21, equivalent to 1/8000 at f/16 with the filter fitted. This will reduce the illumination falling on the CCD and allow the camera to still autofocus.

Incidentally the AF system, according to independent tests focuses twice as fast at EV 10 and above than it does at EV 3 and below. You can draw you own conclusions from this.

Three frames per second AF linked continuous motordrive

Due to the speed of the overall autofocus system the 700si is able to shoot continuously at three frames per second when following moving subjects, even if the subject is moving at almost 200 mph. This is hard to comprehend when you bear in mind that in between frames the mirror is down and stabilised only for a fraction of a second. Yet that is enough time for the autofocus system to check and make any major adjustments before the mirror swings up again for the next frame to be taken. In fact the system is capable of functioning at 5 frames per second! For the 700si however, it was decided that a more compact and lightweight body along with a quieter motor drive was more important. In fact at this time, apart from the Dynax/Maxxum 7xi and 9xi which shoot at 4 and 4.5 FPS respectively, there are no other AF cameras that can shoot at over 3 FPS, **WITH FOCUS PRIORITY**, on every frame.

Tip (but be prepared to use some film!)

Let me explain something to you. I have not yet found a subject that moves so fast that the AF system cannot focus on it. I am not a professional photographer, I just enjoy taking action pictures. But it has to be said that I seem to achieve an uncannily high success rate for these types of subjects. The main reason for this is the use of the motordrive.

Occasionally (very rare occurrence) when shooting very fast moving subjects the camera may make a blunder, and get an out of focus picture; lets face it, nothing's perfect!

When photographing extremely high speed subjects my advice is, use some film. If you select continuous drive, rather than shooting one picture at a time, shoot a small sequence, not only does this give you a higher chance of capturing the subject with the composition you are seeking but it also almost guarantees, even if the first shot in the sequence is out of focus, that all the following shots will be in focus.

Why is this?

Basically, the camera could possibly, because of a number of factors, select the wrong AF mode for the first shot. But after the first shot has been taken the camera will engage continuous and predictive AF, regardless of its initial calculations and the subject's movements, it will also refocus for every following frame. This I guarantee (almost) will increase your success rate.

AF Illuminator

Built in to the camera's body between the main hand grip and the pentaprism is the AF-illuminator. This allows the 700si to focus in total darkness and zero contrast. The range is 0.7 - 7m depending on the ambient light level.

The AF-illuminator is in fact a patterned beam of near infra-red light. The infra-red light illuminates the subject so that the camera can see and the pattern generated allows the camera to focus on zero contrast subjects. This is its only purpose, it does not actually measure subject distance.

Because the beam is near infra-red it is not always possible for the human eye to see the beam projected on to the subject. If you turn all the lights off in the room at night and point the camera at a plain white surface, you should be able to see a red pattern projected briefly on to the surface.

Between EV 9 and EV 3.5 it is activated automatically when there is insufficient contrast to allow the camera to focus using any of its four sensors. Below EV 3.5 it always functions to ensure accurate focusing.

The AF-illuminator will not function if the focal length is greater than 300mm or if you are using either the 300mm f/2.8 or the 3x-1x Macro Zoom. You may find that when using focal lengths close to 300mm that the camera has difficulty in focusing on low contrast subjects. This is due to parallax caused by the illuminator being positioned off the lens axis, which of course is unavoidable.

Remember to ensure that the lens hood is removed as this may obstruct the path of the illuminator with certain lenses. Also ensure that you hold the camera with all of your fingers on the rubber section of the hand grip, otherwise once again the beam may be obstructed.

There are a few potential drawbacks though. Whenever the AF-illuminator is activated, predictive and continuous AF no longer function. This is purely because the AF-illuminator cannot fire continuously to allow the camera to take the number of continuous readings that are needed to allow the camera to focus accurately.

To overcome this potential problem, when photographing moving subjects, the AF-illuminator will not function if the subject is out of range. In this case the camera will continue to try and focus purely with the available light.

When the lighting levels drop to a level that causes the AF-illuminator to function continuously, the biggest problem will be the subject moving considerably during the exposure and causing a blurred effect. In this case the focus should still be accurate enough.

To ensure the highest accuracy and success rate, remember to press the shutter release all the way down in one smooth action. Because continuous and predictive AF are no longer functioning, if you press half way down on the shutter release focus will be locked. As the subject continues to move it will be out of focus.

Another drawback to bear in mind is that the beam from the built-in AF-illuminator only provides coverage of the centre sensor. The AF-illuminator built-in to Minolta flash units is a three beam illuminator which covers, in addition to the centre sensor, the left and right sensors. There is also some overlap into the top sensor. The LED's that provide the beam are also more powerful and thus allow an increased range of up to 9m.

However, the flashgun's illuminator will function most efficiently when using lenses whose focal length is between 28 and 105mm.

In some situations you may not wish to use flash photography. In this case switch the flash off, but keep it on the camera. Although the flash has been switched off the AF-illuminator will still function in low lighting conditions. In bright conditions where there is low contrast the camera's illuminator will function instead.

If the camera's AF illuminator functions the camera will only be able to use the centre sensor. This will in turn mean that the camera only uses 7 of its total of 14 metering segments, as it is not able to access information from the other focusing sensors. This would therefore be another advantage in attaching a Minolta flash unit to overcome this potential problem.

This does not mean that you will get bad photographs. I am simply saying that you will not be getting the camera's maximum potential performance. I have simply just taken the time to explain how you can increase the camera's performance in certain cases.

Extra information: Should you, for any reason, wish to be able to disable the AF-illuminator, insert the Sports/Sports 2 card.

The 700si's built-in illuminator will not function if you select the left, right or top sensor. In this case attach a Minolta accessory flash.

TAKING CONTROL

So far we have only looked at the automated side of focusing with the 700si. But we need to know what to do to be able to take control when the camera may not do what you want it to do.

The most accepted form of overcoming any problems with autofocus is to immediately switch to manual focus. However, in my opinion, there are easier ways in which to get the camera to focus on the point that we would like. Incidentally, if previously there were any problems that you have been experiencing in terms of the camera not focusing on your actual subject you may find that by having a better understanding of the overall system gained in the previous sections you may have overcome these already.

The AF button

The most useful feature on the 700si to aid the "taking control" process is the large **AF** button on the back cover.

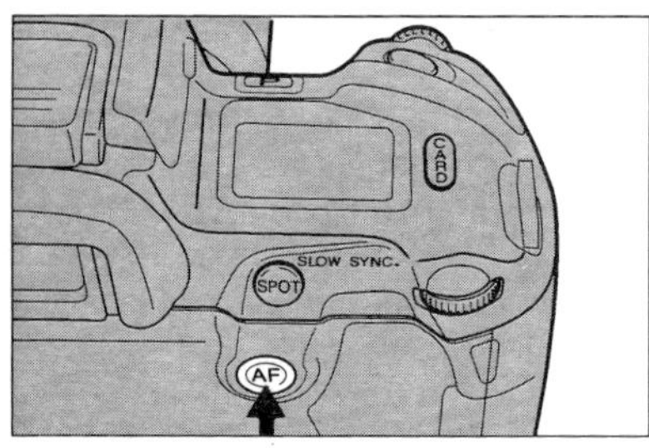

Looking through the viewfinder, if you press and hold the **AF** button the camera will lock focus and then indicate on the focusing screen within the AF area which one of the four AF sensors has been used to focus the lens. Remember, although the camera compares the distance measured by each sensor there can only be one focus point that provides the sharpest focus. So, for further control, depth of field can be utilised to increase or decrease the range that also appears in focus.

You may find sometimes that by pressing the **AF** button twice within the same scene that the camera displays a different area each time. The reason for this is that the selection of the sensors is based on a number of factors which include distance, brightness, and most of all contrast. The camera may waver between two sensors if they are both detecting similar levels of contrast.

Continue to keep the **AF** button pressed. Now turn the front dial. As you turn the dial you will be able to change from the camera's selected sensor to any of the other three sensors and back to the original. As you select each sensor you will see that the camera immediately refocuses using that sensor so that you may be able to see the effect on depth of field and the appearance of the rest of the scene depending on the composition. Once you release the AF button the camera will only focus using that sensor. The local AF area will remain indicated on the screen, so that you know where to position your subject.

To return to wide focus area, press the **AF** button again and turn the dial one click in either direction.

Extra Information: Selecting an individual sensor switches the Multi-Dimensional Predictive system to normal Predictive focus.

It also causes the exposure meter to only read the brightness in the seven segments that surround that sensor. In some situations this could be a benefit by forcing the exposure meter to only read within a controlled area, a bit like a very large spot metering area.

Generally though it inhibits the maximum potential of the overall system. Having said that though, if the camera had focused on the wrong part of the scene it is likely that it would be concentrating its metering on the wrong part of the scene also, which could possibly lead to an incorrect exposure.

If you find that you frequently select an individual AF area, you may prefer to re-program the focus lock button which is on some manual zoom and prime lenses. These are listed under the "focus lock" section. Pressing the button with it programmed for this function causes the AF system to switch from wide area AF to the centre AF area. When the button is released the area changes back to wide.

To re-program this facility refer to the section "Customized Function xi card".

The **AF** button can also be used to activate the AF system without having to press the shutter release. However, remember focus will be locked once the subject is in focus.

Focus lock

I personally find the easiest way of getting the camera to focus on my subject is to use the focus lock facility. The simplest way of locking focus has already been mentioned a number of times, that is to press half way down on the shutter release. However, if the camera senses any movement on a high magnification subject, which could be caused either by the subject moving slightly or you moving very slightly yourself, continuous AF may be selected and focus cannot be locked with this method. In this case the use of the **AF** button on the back cover may be preferable. Because of the function of this button, as already mentioned, you will see confirmation of the area that the camera is focusing on in the viewfinder. This also gives you an idea as to what part of the scene the camera is concentrating its exposure reading on.

Other methods for locking focus are pressing the depth of field button or using the button on the lens barrel of certain manual zoom and prime lenses. The lenses that currently feature this facility are as follows:

        28-70 f/2.8 Dynax/Maxxum/G
        70-210 f/4.5-5.6 Dynax/Maxxum
        70-210 f/3.5-4.5 Dynax/Maxxum
        80-200 f/2.8 APO Dynax/Maxxum/G
        100-300 f/4.5-5.6 Dynax/Maxxum
        100-300 f/4.5-5.6 APO Dynax/Maxxum
        50 f/2.8 Macro Dynax/Maxxum
        100 f/2.8 Macro Dynax/Maxxum
        85 f/1.4 Dynax/Maxxum/G
        200 f/2.8 Dynax/Maxxum/G
        300 f/2.8 Dynax/Maxxum/G
        600 f/4 Dynax/Maxxum/G
        500 f/8 Mirror Dynax/Maxxum

Pressing the focus lock button on these lenses not only locks focus but can be used to instantly engage shutter release priority rather than the standard focus priority.

Although an extremely rare occurrence, there is sometimes an occasion when the camera indicates that it cannot guarantee that the subject is in focus, although in the viewfinder it may appear to you to be in focus. If this occurs, hold the button on the lens barrel in and then press all the way down on the shutter release. This will allow the shutter to fire whether the subject is in focus or not.

Precaution

Especially if you are using the 700si with "Eye-Start" switched off, be sure to check that the green "in focus" indicator appears before pressing the button on the lens to lock focus, otherwise you could take the picture but the camera may not have finished focusing (eye-start on) or started focusing (eye-start off).

Finally, you can also lock focus when using an xi series lens by pulling the zoom ring directly back towards the camera body. You should ensure that you wait for the image to appear in focus before pulling the ring back, because the AF system is temporarily deactivated as soon as the ring is pulled back. Take care not to turn the ring as this will then engage powered manual focus.

The final way of getting the camera to focus on the part of the scene that you are interested in is simply to move the camera slightly to change the composition. This may then cause the camera to refocus on the desired area. You can then of course lock focus and return to your original composition if required.

What appears to be a problem subject for a large number of photographers is aircraft. This is due, in many cases, to the lack of contrast on the subject, and not, as many people think, the speed of the subject. I would doubt that you could ever get close enough to a high speed plane where the AF system could not keep up with it.

The best advice I have for taking photographs of single aircraft is to ensure that they fill the entire AF area. If they are much smaller than this, the chances are that they are so small that it will be difficult for the sensors to get a strong enough waveform that can then be used for focus calculations. Without wishing to offend, if the aircraft is that small in the frame you are probably wasting your time and film taking it in the first place, as the final photograph may not look that good.

As speed of the aircraft is not really an issue you may find manually selecting an individual sensor improves the AF operation for this particular type of subject. As to which one to use, this will be down to which you find works best. Remember, the left and right sensors detect horizontal contrast and the top and centre sensors detect vertical contrast. Also bear in mind that the top sensor is smaller than the centre sensor and this may make things easier or more difficult, depending on the actual situation.

The final way of overcoming any problems the AF system may be experiencing is to select manual focus. This is done by pressing the button marked **AF/M**, which is positioned just down from the lens release button. **M.FOCUS** will then be indicated on the body LCD data panel. All you need do now is to turn the focusing ring on the lens until the image appears sharp. To return to autofocus press the **AF/M** button again or press the Program reset button on the top plate. Remember, pressing the P button will also reset all other camera functions.

When you switch the camera on, autofocus is automatically set. The lens will then be reset to a standby setting suitable for that focal length and type of lens. This setting was determined in development as a good initial starting point for photography with that lens, with the aim of reducing the time it takes to capture the first shot on film.

A green "in focus" dot will only be shown when the AF sensor that the 700si's AF system would normally choose detects an in focus image. However, if the reason for manual focusing is because the camera is unable to focus at all, no signal will be shown.

The shutter can be released even if the subject is out of focus.

With an xi series lens fitted, manual focusing is possible simply by pulling the zoom ring back towards the camera body and then rotating the ring to the left or right depending upon the direction required. If prior to pulling the ring back you had not selected manual focus with the **AF/M** button and you then release the zoom ring the camera will re-focus.

Viewfinder Focus Signals

In the viewfinder, to the left of the shutter speed indication, are the focus signals. These confirm the state and mode of focusing.

With either the blinking green dot or brackets shown, focusing cannot be confirmed.

With the green dot and brackets shown, focus is confirmed and continuous AF is in use.

With the green dot only, focus is confirmed and locked.

No indication is shown whilst the 700si is focusing.

Shutter Release Priority

The 700si is set to focus priority as standard. This ensures that the shutter is released only if the camera is able to focus on the subject and once the camera has finished autofocusing. I strongly recommend that you leave the camera in this mode.

However, you may wish to ensure that you get at least something on film whether it is sharp or not. In this case you can select release priority. This is done by pressing together the ISO and drive buttons in the card door. **AFP** will now appear in the body LCD data panel. Turn either dials one click to change to **RP** (Release Priority). Press the shutter release lightly. The normal display will now reappear with the addition of a small **RP** icon located by the exposure mode. To return to focus priority, repeat the operation, or press the Panic **P** button.

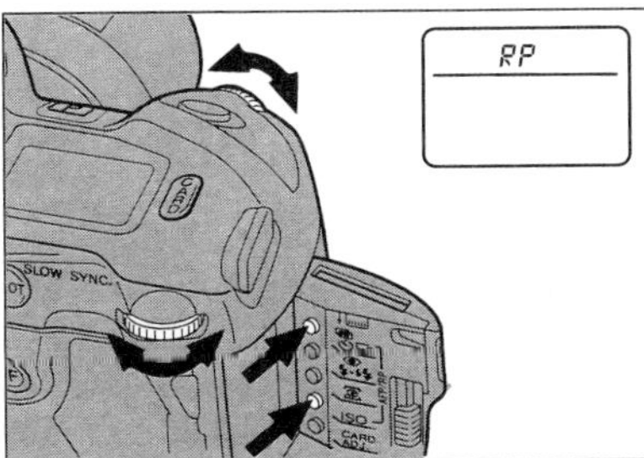

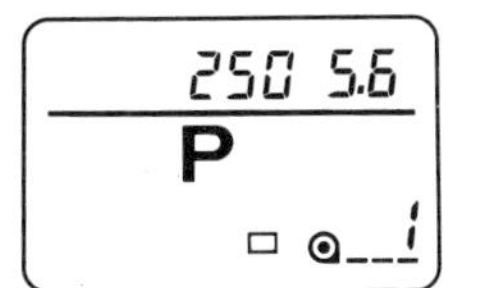

Using the Memory facility you could store **RP** and then recall it simply with the press of a single button at will.

EYE-START

The focusing speed of most Modern autofocus SLR's is extremely fast these days and most of these SLR's can focus more accurately and much faster than even the most seasoned professional photographer.

Probably the biggest delay in taking pictures is not the time that the lens is being controlled, but the time taken for the photographer to decide to take the picture and to then press the shutter release part way to activate the autofocus system. By reducing this delay to an absolute minimum, or even eliminating it completely, the photographer can take photographs when they wish to and not have to wait a fraction of a second while the AF system comes "on line".

Enter "Eye-start". The basic concept behind Eye-start is that just by looking through the viewfinder the AF and AE systems come on line, instantly.

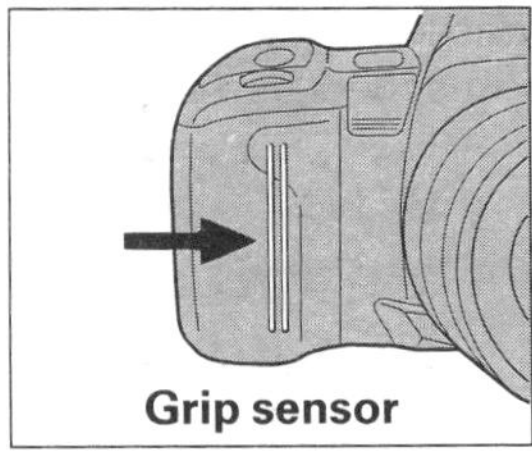

Grip sensor

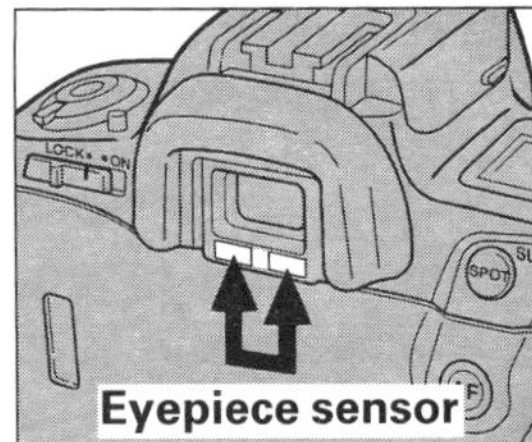

Eyepiece sensor

When you grip the camera you bridge the gap b e t w e e n conductive bars positioned on the main hand grip. This makes a circuit which in turn activates a near infra-red emitter/receiver sensor positioned just below the eyepiece. A low power near infra-red beam is emitted from just below the eye-piece. When an object is positioned close to the viewfinder (within 3 - 5cm) the near infra-red beam is reflected back to the eye-piece, to the receiver. With both sensors activated the 700si recognises that you are looking through the viewfinder and holding the camera. The eye-start system now activates both the metering and autofocusing systems.

There are two main advantages of using the Eye-start system.

The first of these is that the time delay that has always been associated with AF SLR's has been eliminated.

To prove this to yourself, look through the viewfinder, position the AF area on your subject and then press the shutter release part way. The question is, were you able to press the shutter release part way before the camera had activated the AF sequence using the eye-start system? The chances are that the subject was already in focus before you even thought about where your subject was positioned in the viewfinder!

The second advantage is that the camera is able to gather more information about the subject or scene before you decide to take the picture. This gives the camera the ability to gauge more accurately the type of subject or scene and predict the likely movements of the subject, or in fact the way in which the camera is being used! (No, I'm not joking.) For example, if the photographer looks through the viewfinder and then zooms backwards and forwards and moves the camera around the surrounding scene or constantly tries different ways of composing the scene or subject, the camera will select a slower autofocus speed and increase its reaction time, purely because with this type of operation it is not necessary to drive the lens at its fastest speed. If however, the photographer looks through the viewfinder and is always tracking or following the same subject (for example a racing car) then the lens will be driven at a much faster speed as well as the reaction time being reduced, to ensure that when you do wish to take the photograph that it will be able to focus and release the shutter in the smallest amount of time.

There are other benefits to the camera controlling the AF speed based on the subject. Firstly, selecting slower AF control speeds reduces the noise generated by the camera moving the focusing lens. The second benefit, although only a minor one, is the increased battery life. Controlling the focusing lens at a slower speed and increasing the camera's reaction time reduces the load on the battery.

In some situations you may find eye-start annoying. Personally I leave it on, mainly because it makes using some of the features a little easier by not having to keep pressing half way on the shutter release to bring up the viewfinder information. If however you find the eye-start system distracting then simply slide the eye-start switch to the off position. Now the camera will only focus when your finger is pressed half way on the shutter release.

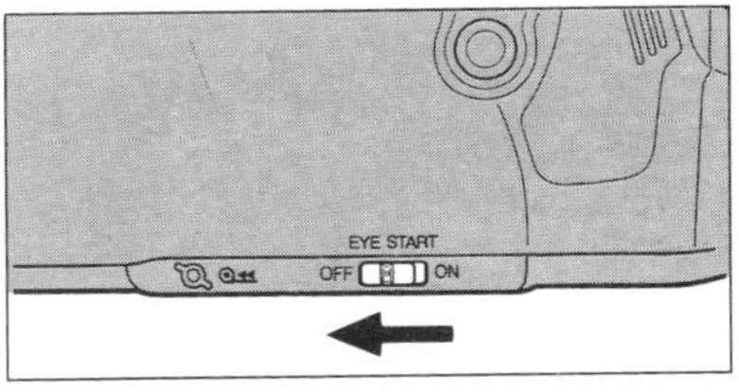

Potential problems with eye-start

The main problem with the eye-start system is centred around the grip switch.

Because it is a conductive sensor if you suffer from dry skin or you are taking pictures in cold conditions where your skin is likely to dry out, or maybe if you are wearing gloves, the sensor will no longer function and eye-start will not operate. In this case the most reliable way of overcoming this problem is to switch the grip sensor off. This is done using the Customized Function Card xi. With the sensor disabled eye-start will function just by bringing the eye up to the viewfinder. However, when carrying the camera on the shoulder strap you may find that the eye piece sensor is activated by being close to your body. If you find this a problem either switch off eye-start or the camera completely when carrying it.

Spectacles should not affect the operation of the eye-piece sensor.

It is also convenient to have the grip sensor switched off when using the camera on a tripod. This allows you to simply look through the viewfinder without having to touch the camera and yet both focusing and metering systems will be activated.

If you do not own a Customized Function Card xi then simply pressing part way down on the shutter release will activate both focusing and metering systems, effectively bypassing the eye-start system altogether.

There may be the odd occasion when due to the operation of the eye-start system you may find that the camera seems unsure as to what to focus on. It may even hunt for focus back and forth. If this occurs you will probably find that when you press part way or all the way down on the shutter release that it focuses on your subject without any problems. The reason for this is that by pressing the shutter release you are in a way telling the camera to sort itself out and make a firm decision. It then switches to its fastest AF drive speed and will then lock on to the subject.

Tip: My advice to you is, use the eye-start system. However, any experience that you have built up when dealing with fast moving subjects when using either autofocus or manual focus will have to be thrown out of the window. You may have already come to this conclusion earlier in the book. This is undoubtedly the case when using eye-start.

When photographing moving subjects, **DO NOT** pre-focus on an area and wait for the subject to enter this area and then press down on the shutter release.

With eye-start, as soon as you see the subject in the distance position it in the frame and then continue to keep it in the frame until you take the picture.

Although I accept that this may not always be possible, I personally find that this gives a much higher success rate.

Is autofocus performance affected by extreme temperatures?

The straight answer to this would be yes. With extreme temperature the distance between lens mount and film plane changes, which will affect focus and of course the sharpness of the image on film.

However, due to the installation of thermistors in the AF system circuitry, the affect that varying temperatures would have is taken into account by the AF CPU. So the answer is in fact no.

METERING AND EXPOSURE

The metering system of the 700si is probably the most understated element of its specification and one that so far has not been given it's due.

The main areas of interest that we shall be covering in this section are as follows:

- **AF Integrated 14 Segment Honeycomb Metering**
- **Spot Metering**
- **Expert Program**
- **Metering Index**
- **How the 700si's metering system was developed**

A group of engineers within the R&D department studied thousands of portrait, landscape, closeup and snapshot photographs in order to determine the factors which contribute to a good image and how the camera could play a more active role in the image making process. Based on the report from this team Expert Program Selection was developed.

RAPID, a high speed digital image processing system was used to store and analyze each photograph. Such information as the distribution of subject brightness was examined in every photograph. This system was also used to simulate Expert Program Selection.

The use of a re-writable micro-computer which was attached to a circuit board outside the camera allowed a morning team to check the operating system each day. A day team would then conduct test shooting sessions with the newly tuned software on board. A night team would then evaluate the results and adjust the software. This allowed the software to be adjusted twice a day. This procedure was also used for developing the AF system.

AF Integrated 14 Segment Honeycomb Metering

This has to be the most widely used exposure control mode on the 700si. As can be seen in the illustration, the camera employs a metering system which is made up of 13 honeycomb shaped

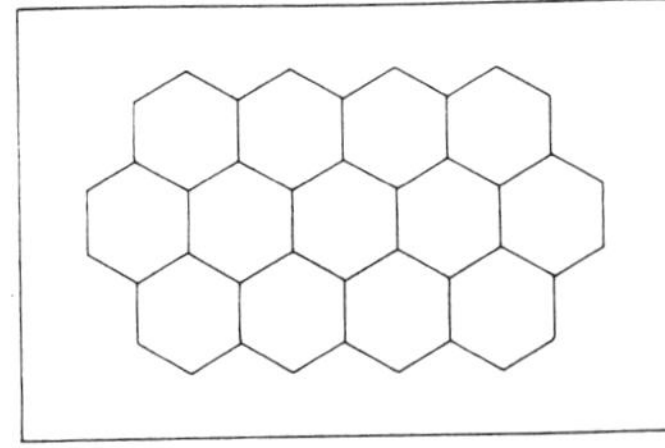

segments which cover the majority of the picture area, the background surrounding area is the 14th segment.

As in the Autofocus system, Fuzzy Logic is used extensively in a number of ways, amongst which are:

1. The determination of the type of lighting in the scene.
2. The selection of and the weighting of the 14 segments.

Why use honeycomb shaped metering segments?

The use of honeycomb shaped segments maintains exposure continuity within the picture area as the composition is changed or if the subject moves.

With conventional metering patterns, as the subject position changes or if the composition is changed, the exposure reading also changes. This is because when the subject is say, to the left of the frame, a particular pattern is chosen which covers the subject, as the subject moves, the change in metering pattern results in either more or less of the background also entering the metering area which will then of course affect the exposure reading, especially if the subject is either spotlit or backlit.

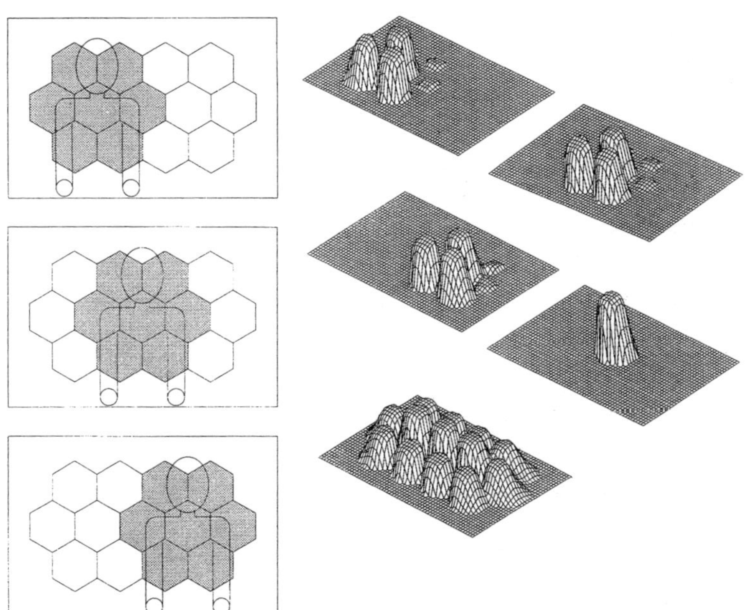

Putting honeycomb metering into an extremely basic form, the 700si, once it has recognised the type of scene, starts using a metering pattern comprised of a certain number of segments with a particular weighting. It then fine tunes this pattern to come up with the best possible exposure for the way in which the scene has been composed. So that's the basic form; let's now look at it in more depth.

The first task is for the main subject's position to be determined and this of course is where the AF integration comes into the equation. The subject's position is fed into the AE system. The exposure system then decides on an appropriate metering pattern based on the subject's position in the frame, distance of the subject from the camera, image magnification and the camera's orientation.

Measuring the illumination in all of these segments, the exposure system then concentrates on fine tuning the metering pattern. Firstly, Fuzzy Logic processing is used to assess the type of lighting situation, whether it be backlit, spotlit or an averagely lit scene or subject. This is achieved by the camera measuring the brightness in all of the metering segments. If the subject is recognised as being either backlit or spotlit, it then compares the segments which cover the main subject with those of the background or foreground, Fuzzy Logic Processing is then applied again to determine the degree of back lighting or spotlighting.

Conventional cameras that operate on conventional logic measure the brightness levels for both the subject and background areas. The difference between these two values is then used to judge the type of lighting. For example if the subject's brightness is 2 EV or greater than the background then the camera classes the subject as spotlit. If the difference is actually measured at being only +/- 1.9EV then the camera classifies the lighting as average illumination. How can such a small change in conditions affect the judgement of the scene so adversely?

EV difference between background and subject

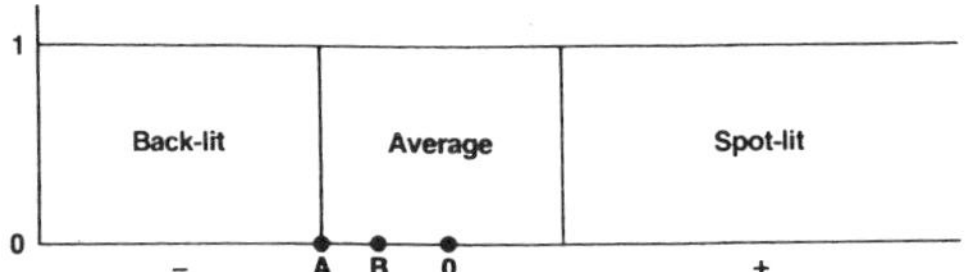

Conventional Computer Logic - A = 2EV; B = 1.9EV

When Fuzzy Logic is applied to the same situation the camera's exposure control computer is able to calculate the degree of back lighting or spotlighting and then make the necessary adjustment to the exposure settings to give exactly the right balance between foreground and background areas.

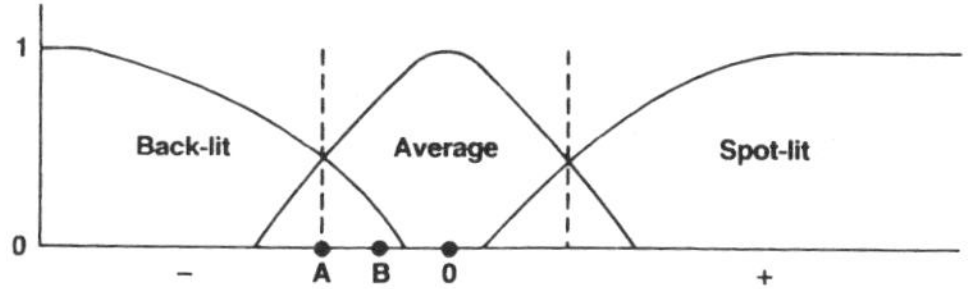

Fuzzy Logic - A = 2EV; B = 1.9EV

Fuzzy Logic is also used in the weighting of the segments, and it is this which gives the metering system the correct balance between foreground and background areas. For example, unlike other cameras the 700si will, in the weighting of the segments, emphasise the metering segments which cover the main subject and then, depending on the degree of subject illumination or the back lighting, the 700si will adjust the exposure settings so that the remaining segments also have some affect but to a much lesser degree. In some cases, depending upon the subject's actual position, the 700si may choose to use only one honeycomb segment. Basically speaking, the 700si has the ability to take a spot exposure reading practically anywhere in the scene. In some other cases the 700si may choose to use say 5 segments, that cover the main subject for 80% of the exposure reading, then another 5 segments for 15%, and then 3 segments for the remaining 5%.

Here are some example metering patterns that the 700si may use for certain situations.

If the subject is judged to fall on or near the portrait area and the background brightness is evaluated as being close to that of the subject, a centre-weighted pattern is selected.

If, however, the subject is judged to be backlit, the camera

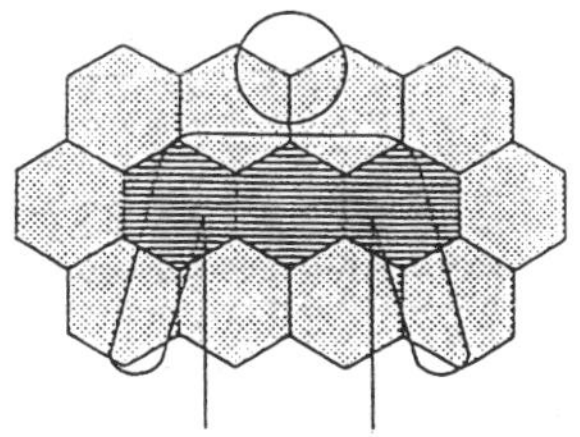

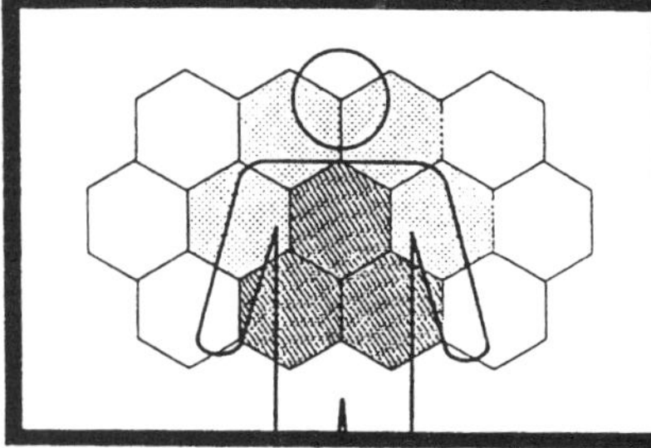

will concentrate its exposure reading within the seven segments that surround the AF sensor judged to detect the main subject's position. It then evaluates the brightness within each segment to determine the most likely position of the subject. The weighting of the segments are then adjusted further to favour the smaller area. As the degree of back-lighting increases, the weighting of the segments becomes more and more spot orientated. If the camera is set to Program and a Minolta i/xi/HS series flash is fitted the flash will fire automatically to provide fill-in, to balance the background exposure with the subject.

When taking portraits, if the camera is held vertically, the 700si will use a centre-weighted metering pattern, but because the 700si knows the position of the sky and land in the scene it is able to adjust the weighting of the segments to ensure that ultimately the subject is properly exposed, and, depending on the lighting condition, may also balance the exposure so that the background is not too dark or too light. If the subject is judged to be backlit then, as in the previous example, the segments used and the weighting will change accordingly.

For close-ups the 700si will read the light in all of the metering segments and adjust the weighting of those segments that detect very light and dark areas that would normally adversely affect the exposure reading.

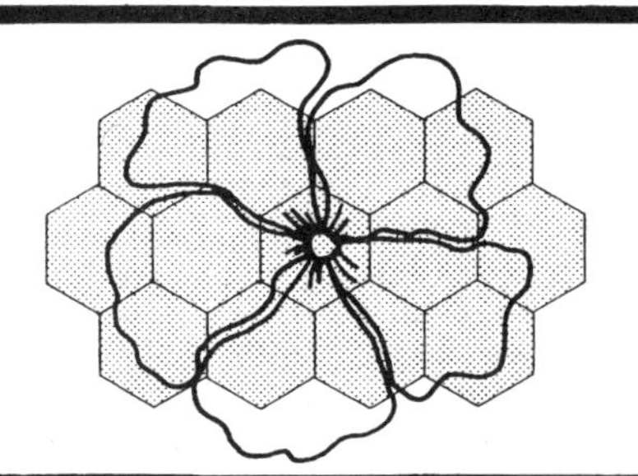

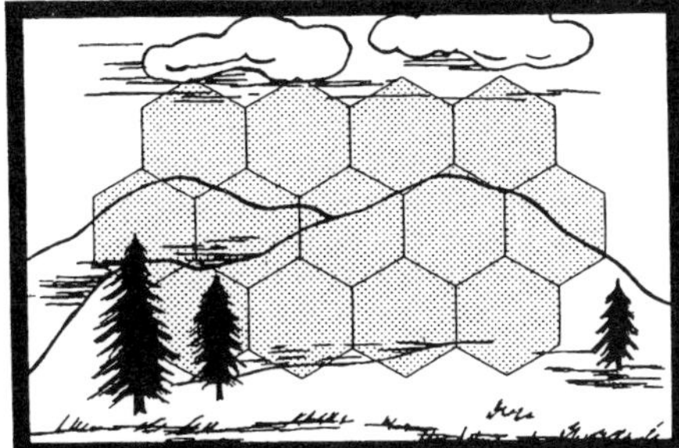

All of the metering segments are also employed when taking landscapes. However, should there be a small, extremely bright area, such as the sun, the segment that covers that area will be switched off. For example, when taking sunsets or scenic photographs where there is direct sunlight, taking any account of the sun will dramatically affect the overall exposure reading. If, for example, a centre-weighted metering system was used to expose an evening sunset, the exposure from this system could be up to 6-7 stops different depending upon the time of day and the position of the sun in the frame.

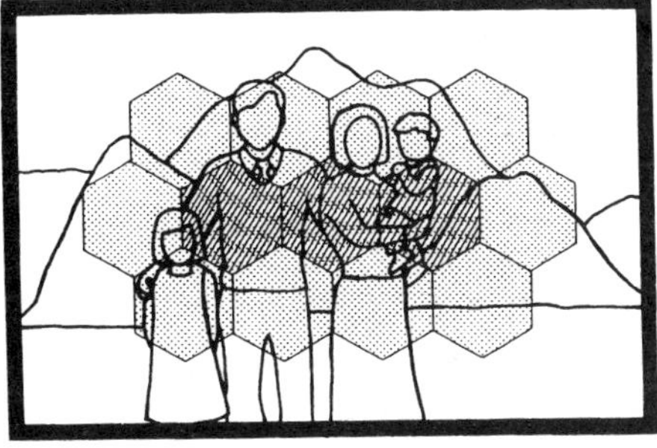

Snapshots are within the transitional zone. If all the segments read nearly the same brightness, an average reading of all areas is used. If the metering of all areas indicates that the areas around the subject are brighter, a more centre-weighted pattern is selected. As the degree of back lighting increases the camera may use the seven segments that surround the focusing sensor that detects the main subject's position.

Sports photographs can normally be handled easily by centre-weighted metering. But as there are no rules for taking sports photographs the metering system will be tailored to the actual environment that the camera is being used in, for example the subject's distance, size, position, and of course the type of lighting will all be taken into account for the final exposure.

When shooting scenes or subjects that are spotlit, and which have very high contrast, the metering system may favour reading for the brighter areas as this will produce a dramatic silhouette effect. Reading for the darker areas would only wash out the brighter areas.

What has to be realised is that the above are just initial metering patterns which are then adjusted and fine tuned to the actual situation in question. All other metering systems rely on the camera being programmed to recognise every conceivable situation. The camera's metering system will then analyze the scene or situation in question and then try to match this with a pre-programmed example. If, however, that particular situation does not precisely match one of its examples the camera will be incapable of giving a good result. Many manufacturers talk about the number of situations that they have been programmed to recognise or the number of algorithms that are available. If we assume that there are an infinite number of photographic situations, being programmed for 84,000 of them equates to a very small percentage. For every day use that's fine, but not everyone takes every day type pictures.

The 700si, however, will first determine the type of scene and then choose settings based on its programmed experience. It is this that gives the 700si the flexibility to react to almost any scene, and give, at least, a good exposure. Most of the time, however, it will come up with settings that even the most experienced photographer would have difficulty in improving upon.

If this all sounds too hard to believe then when you next use a 700si in your normal line of photography, and when you think that the camera's settings could be improved upon, take two photographs, one taken with the camera's settings and one taken with your settings. Then **you** can decide who is best. It's already beaten me too often!

Centre-Weighted Average Metering

If honeycomb metering is so good why use centre-weighted?

Many experienced and professional photographers have built up their experience with cameras that employ centre-weighted metering systems. It is easy to predict when the metering system will give an erroneous reading and to then apply the necessary degree of exposure compensation to the situation in hand.

As good as modern metering systems are, it is almost impossible to apply a degree of exposure compensation as the camera's metering system may have already taken into account the difficult lighting. Hence why centre-weighted average metering is available.

The camera takes 80% of its exposure reading within the three centre honeycomb segments and the remaining 20% from the surrounding 10 segments.

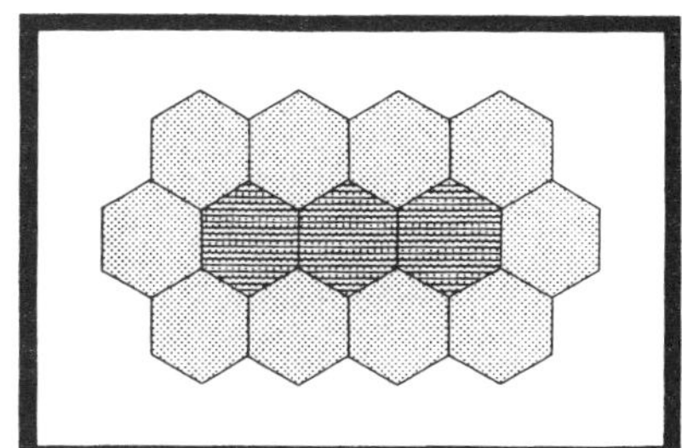

Spot Metering

Spot metering only measures the light within the central honeycomb metering segment. This is approximately 2.7% of the viewfinder area. When spot metering is in use this is represented by a 5.5mm diameter circular area in the centre of the frame.

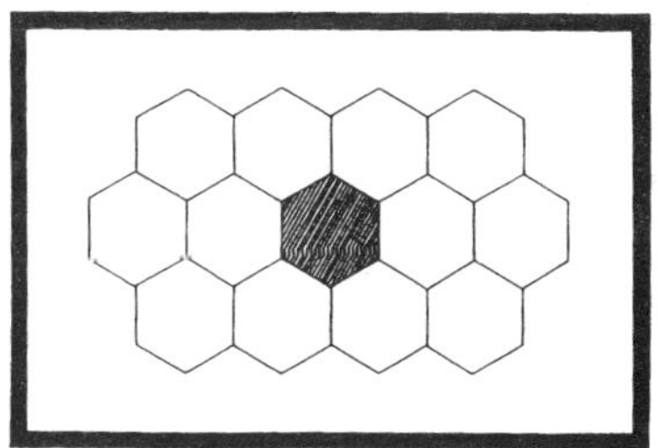

Reasons for using Spot metering:

1. To base the exposure on a small single area.

2. To take several small individual areas within the scene using the Multi-Spot Memory card.

3. To bias the exposure for highlights/shadows, using the Highlight/Shadow card.

4. The subject's lighting level is different to that within the focus area.

Spot metering can be engaged permanently or only when it is needed. The easiest way of using spot metering is to use the SPOT button on the back cover, to the right of the eyepiece. As soon as you press the button the metering area appears on the viewfinder screen and an exposure reading within that area is locked. So in practice place your subject or the area which you wish to read the exposure in the centre of the screen and then press and hold the **SPOT** button, then fire the shutter.

The added benefit of using spot metering in this way is that it allows you to flick backwards and forwards between two metering modes.

To select spot metering permanently, press the metering mode button inside the card door (third down). The display will clear, leaving only the metering mode icon. Turn either of the control dials to select spot metering, which is indicated as a single dot. Press the shutter release part way to enter the selection. The metering area will now be shown on the viewfinder screen. The camera will now always take its exposure reading from this area. To take an exposure reading of a particular part of the scene which is off-centre, press and hold the **SPOT** button to lock the exposure reading and then release the shutter.

How to select the three metering modes

Inside the card door, the third button down, is the metering mode button. Press this and then release it. The body LCD data panel will clear leaving only the metering mode icon. Each click of either the rear or front input dials selects a new metering mode.

Metering range and what it means

The metering range in Honeycomb and Centre-weighted metering is EV 0 to EV 20. In Spot metering the range is EV 3 to EV 20.

If the scene or subject brightness is outside this range, the metering mode indicator in the viewfinder will blink to warn of this.

As with the autofocus sensors the metering sensors have a range in which they operate. Outside this range, the exposure reading will be inaccurate and "over" or "under" exposure may occur. Whilst there is nothing you can do at the lower end of the range, apart from recomposing so that a brighter part of the scene either fills or enters the frame, there is more you can do at the brighter end of the range. Using either a neutral density or polarizer filter will reduce the amount of light entering the camera and will have the affect of extending the upper sensitivity range to the equivalent of EV 22.

Expert Program Selection

Early program cameras, had just one program line. The program line is a series of aperture/shutter speed combinations that are selected by the camera based on the illumination or scene brightness (EV).

In the early 80's there was an advance in Program mode cameras. Here the user had a choice of three program lines (wide, standard and tele). By changing from one program to another the combination of aperture and shutter speed changed. For example when using wide angle lenses the camera would be biased towards smaller apertures for greater depth of field. When using the telephoto program setting the camera would be biased towards faster shutter speeds to help reduce camera shake and subject blur.

When the Minolta 7000 was launched in 1985, and because each and every AF lens contained and still contains a ROM IC which sends information such as the focal length in use, the available aperture range, etc, etc, to the camera, the 7000 was able to automatically select program wide, standard or telephoto. This is the same system used today by most manufacturers.

The launch of the Minolta 7000i in 1988 took this one step further. Instead of just three program lines the camera had a choice of up to 12 program lines within each zoom lens. This improved the accuracy of this system.

The basic concept of the above methods of aperture and shutter speed selection was relying on an assumption as to the type of photograph that you may tackle with a certain type of lens. For example, when using wide angle lenses the most likely types of photographs taken such as landscapes require smaller apertures for greater depth of field, and for telephoto lenses it is likely that faster shutter speeds will be required to freeze the action for fast moving subjects and to overcome camera shake that always becomes a problem with this type of photography. So as long as the lighting conditions are reasonable and the photographer is using the right type of lens for the subject being photographed the aperture/shutter speed selection should be fairly good.

But, we do not always use the theoretically correct lens for our subject, which may be due to the composition required or the fact that the user may simply not own that focal length lens.

This is where Expert Program comes in.

By gathering various pieces of information about the scene or subject the 700si can establish the "type" of scene or subject and then select an aperture/shutter speed combination tailored to the actual picture being taken and not a similar pre-programmed example. The 700si deals with every situation individually.

As already stated, today's conventional AF SLR's select apertures and shutter speeds based purely on the lens' focal length and the scene illumination. The 700si however, takes into account not only the above but also the subject distance, image magnification, subject speed and the type of movement. Once this information has been analyzed the 700si will select an appropriate aperture/shutter speed combination, within the program area for that type of lens. This gives the 700si the ability to select small apertures for greater depth of field, when taking landscapes or close-ups, whether the lens in use is telephoto or wide angle.

It is the use of Fuzzy logic processing that makes this all possible. With conventional logic, every situation must be catered for, but this is simply not possible. There must be an area of overlap between two or three situations where a suitable combination would be appropriate to either situation. For example, when you are photographing the family in front of a building or scenery. This type of scene could be classed as either a portrait or a landscape. In fact the 700si would classify this particular situation as a snap-shot and therefore control the depth of field so that both the subject and background appear in focus.

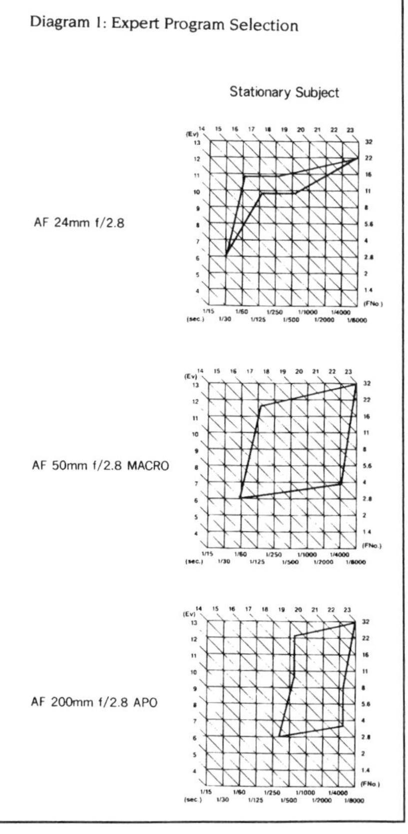

Summing up, when photographing landscapes the 700si will select small apertures to increase depth of field, regardless of the lens focal length.

For Close-ups, the 700si will select smaller apertures to compensate for the loss of depth of field experienced as the image magnification increases.

Note: The 700si always assumes that it is being hand held. Therefore, if the light level is low, the camera will be limited in the apertures that it can select, due to its being programmed not to use a shutter speed that could cause camera shake.

When taking portraits the 700si will control the depth of field based on the subject's distance and the lens focal length in use, otherwise referred to as the image magnification. Ultimately its aim is to ensure that the entire subject is in focus, whilst blurring the background as much as possible.

When the 700si detects a moving subject, it will determine its speed, type of motion and magnification. From this information the 700si will select an appropriate shutter speed to freeze the action.

Creative Program Control

Although the selection of aperture and shutter speeds whilst in program is automatic, there may well be a situation where the photographer decides to use his/her own expertise for that situation. For example, if the photographer would prefer to create a special effect by decreasing the shutter speed or increasing the depth of field even further, this is possible, at the turn of a dial.

Rotating the front dial changes the shutter speeds in 1/2 stop increments and causes the 700si to enter **Ps** mode. The apertures will be adjusted automatically by the camera to maintain correct exposure. Rotating the rear dial changes the apertures in 1/2 stop increments and puts the 700si into **PA** mode. Here the shutter speeds are adjusted for correct exposure.

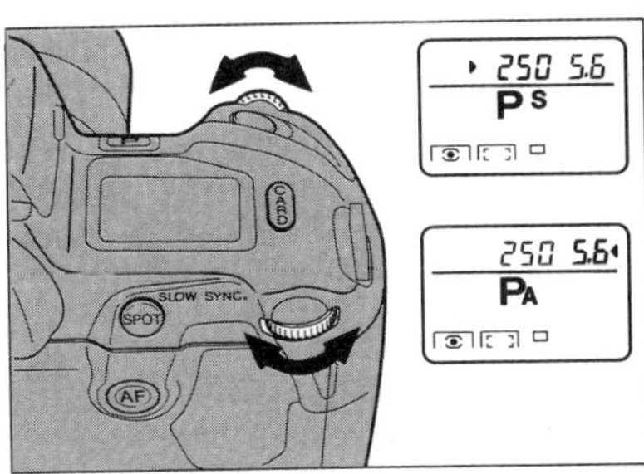

Many AF SLR's today feature some form of program shift. This is where the program line has been shifted by adjustments made by the user. The problem with this system is that as the lighting changes, both values change.

With the 700si the aperture or shutter speed has been set (depending upon which dial was turned) by the user just as in aperture or shutter priority.

So summing up Creative Program Control is an immediate way of accessing aperture or shutter priority without having to first change the exposure mode.

Extra Information

Pᴀ/Pꜱ modes cannot be selected with flash photography. Similarly, the built in flash or accessory flash will not fire if Pᴀ/Pꜱ mode are in use.

In Pᴀ mode if the shutter speed blinks turn the rear dial until it stops blinking, otherwise over/under exposure may result. Similarly, if the aperture blinks in Pꜱ mode, turn the front dial until the blinking stops.

To return to normal Program (P mode), press either the **MODE** or flash button.

Creative Exposure Control

The Creative Program Control facility is designed to offer a quick temporary override of the camera's normal settings. However, for those photographers that like to choose a shutter speed or aperture and then stick to it, there is of course the aperture or shutter priority exposure modes.

To change the exposure modes:

Press and hold the **MODE** button which is just in front of the Memory dial. Then turn either of the dials until the required mode has been selected. A letter will appear in the body data panel to indicate which mode is set.

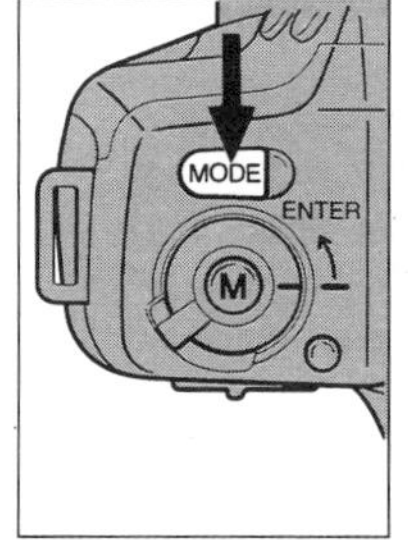

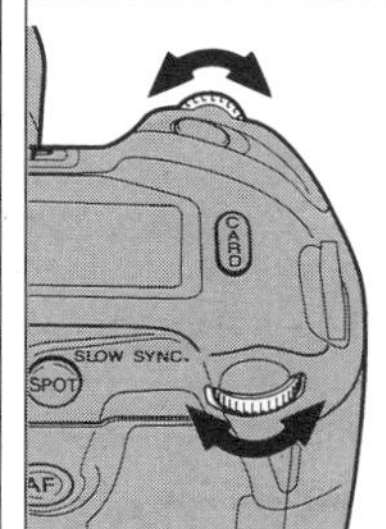

P	**Program**
A	**Aperture Priority**
S	**Shutter Priority**
M	**Manual**

A pointer will also appear to indicate the user-controlled setting/s.

Program is the most widely used exposure mode on cameras these days. And when you have a camera such as the 700si which selects the exposure based on the subject or scene, why use the other modes?

For a number of reasons, not everyone wishes to have the camera taking control of every function available. For many, setting manually, as much as possible, is part of the enjoyment in photography.

Aperture Priority

We may use aperture priority when we want to control the background appearance. Do we want a sharp or blurred background? Well, that depends on who is behind the camera and what is being photographed.

What is depth of field?

Depth of field is the area in front of and behind the subject that also appears to be in focus. This should not be confused with depth of focus. This is the area in front of and behind the film plane where the subject will still appear sharp. This distance is incredibly small.

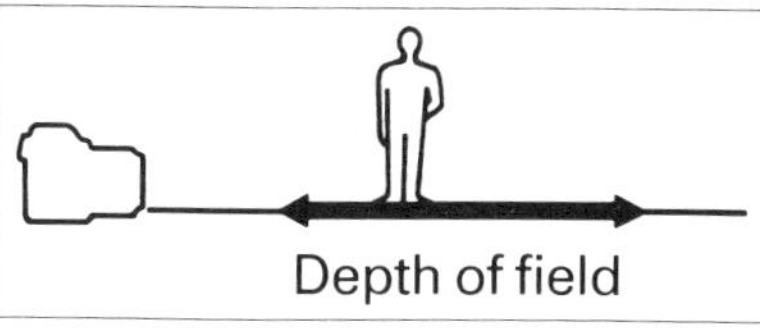

How is it controlled?

The size of the aperture, lens focal length and subject distance are the three main factors for controlling/affecting the amount of depth of field. The total depth of field is normally expressed as being 1/3 in front and 2/3 behind the subject. This is true in most cases, but quite often it is equal.

Summing up: Using smaller apertures (larger f. numbers), the shorter the focal length and the greater the subject distance, the larger the depth of field. This is a pretty good guide. However, there are a few exceptions. E.g. Using a 35-70 f/4 zoom to photograph our subject we find that for the subject to fill the frame we are 10m away with the lens set to 70mm. The aperture used is f/4 due to light restrictions. To increase depth of field we zoom to 35mm but have to move to 5m away from the subject so that they are still filling the frame.

At 70mm, the depth of field is 4m behind the subject and 2.24m in front.

At 35mm, the depth of field is 5.3m behind the subject (1.3m more than at 70mm), but only 1.69m in front of the subject (0.55m less).

Bear that in mind!

Depth of Field Preview

That leads me on nicely to mention the depth of field preview facility. The feature that 95% of users ask for (mainly because the magazines tell them they have to have it), of which 90% do not know what it does, apart from make the viewfinder dark, 5% who just do not use it and 5% that do make use of it.

I hope that this does not give the impression that I do not use the depth of field preview facility. Far from it, I am one of the 5% group that does make use of it. I use it for almost every aspect of my photography, including portraits, landscapes, close-ups, motor sport. I can almost hear you saying, why motor sport?

I find getting the right balance of shutter speed/depth of field one of the most difficult aspects of motor sport photography. Focusing I have no problem with, as I rely purely on the AF system.

With this type of subject it is important to:

1. Select a shutter speed that provides sufficient sharpness on the body of the car but is slow enough to show motion in the wheels.

2. Ensure that the level of depth of field must be sufficient to ensure that the entire car is in focus, but to also ensure that the background is as blurred as possible.

This combination is not always possible, as the use of slow

shutter speeds results in too much depth of field. In this case the selection of the right film speed based on the day's conditions is essential.

So, how do we use it?

Focus on your subject, then press and hold the depth of field preview button. You will find this easier to press if you use one of the fingers on your left hand rather than your right hand. The 700si's preview facility is an electro-mechanical type; i.e. an electrical switch that controls a mechanical mechanism, in

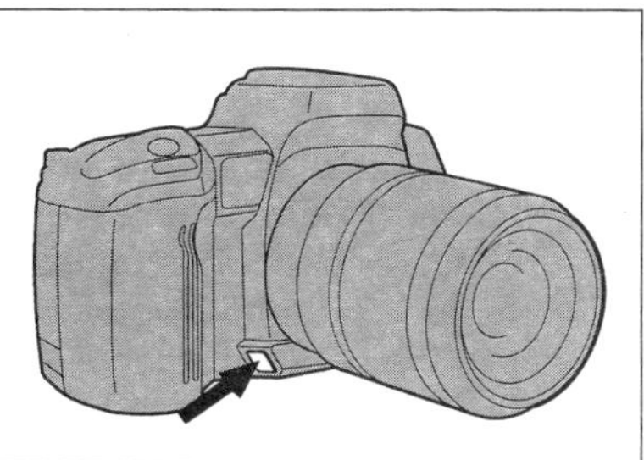

this case the aperture control ring. Due to this design the aperture can be stopped down to that manually set or the automatically calculated setting in all four exposure modes.

With the button pressed the aperture closes to the set/calculated setting. The viewfinder may now become very dark, this is due to less light entering the camera body through the lens. This will not however affect the photograph, as the shutter speed set/calculated will compensate for the reduction in light.

With the aperture closed down you should now see the "range" that will appear in focus on the final photograph using that aperture setting. This will be most noticeable on subjects that are positioned just in front and behind the subject that were originally out of focus. With the lens stopped down (as long as the aperture set is small enough) these areas should now also appear in focus.

Extra-Information: The shutter release can still be released with the preview button pressed in (only if the "In focus" signal was given prior to pressing the button).

Focus and exposure are locked when the button is pressed, therefore release the button to set a different aperture if required and then press again to check.

Shutter Priority

Shutter priority is most normally associated with sports

photography applications, when a fast shutter speed is needed, for example, to freeze the action.

I tend to use shutter priority when panning subjects. I select my favourite shutter speed, stick to it, and then let the camera set the aperture for me.

However, when I need the fastest possible shutter speed, maybe because the available light is dropping and I am following fast action, I tend to use aperture priority. This allows me to open the aperture fully and get as much of the available light into the camera, and hence give the fastest possible shutter speed. This of course will reduce the depth of field.

Manual

Finally, we have manual. Here both shutter speed and aperture are set by you. Why? Because you want to create a special effect or maybe you want to lock the shutter open for a night time shot of the stars. Another example would be when using an exposure meter. Manual is the only mode you can use to key in the metered settings from the hand held meter.

In aperture priority and manual exposure modes, the apertures can be changed in half stop increments.

In shutter priority and manual the shutter speeds can also be selected in half stop increments from a range of speeds from 30" -1/8000. In manual we can also select **BULB** exposure. This allows us to lock the shutter open to photograph subjects like the stars and fireworks. It is best used with either the RC-1000S or RC-1000L remote releases, mainly for convenience rather than for overcoming the possible problem of camera shake. Of course it would be essential to have the camera already mounted on a tripod.

In Program and aperture priority, shutter speeds are stepless, although in the viewfinder and body data panels the camera will display the shutter speed in 1/2 stop increments.

If the shutter speed in Program or aperture priority is too slow a camera shake warning symbol will appear to the left of the shutter speed in the viewfinder. If this appears use flash, mount the camera on a tripod or select a larger aperture (aperture priority). The exposure will still be correct if you do not do this, but camera shake may result. With practice you may find that by holding your breath and tucking your arms tight into your body that you can hold the camera steady at speeds much slower than is recommended.

The warning is activated when the shutter speed roughly equals 1/focal length in use. (E.g. With a 50mm lens in use, shutter speeds slower than 1/60 second will cause the indicator to blink. With a 500mm lens, shutter speeds slower than 1/500 second will cause the indicator to blink).

When in manual exposure mode an indicator will appear on the left hand side of the screen to display the amount of over/under exposure in comparison to the camera's recommended exposure. A plus or minus also appears in the LCD panel at the bottom of the viewfinder to indicate whether your settings will give under/over exposure. When the pointer is at zero or there is no plus or minus symbol, the exposure set is the same as that calculated by the camera.

Metering Index

I would say that this is my favourite and most frequently used feature of the 700si's entire specification.

Its primary function is to allow you to be able to understand the settings automatically selected by the camera. Knowing what the camera has done allows you to make further adjustments if needed based on your own experience.

The information displayed varies depending on the metering mode and exposure mode in use. Let us start by looking at its use with honeycomb metering.

With honeycomb metering in use and either program, aperture priority or shutter priority selected, the metering index is displayed when the exposure compensation button is pressed.

The indicator will appear on the left hand edge of the focusing screen.

The pointer on the scale indicates the degree of exposure compensation automatically set by the camera. Put another way, it is the difference between the exposure measured using honeycomb metering and centre-weighted metering. The pointer represents the reading for honeycomb metering, whilst the 0 represents centre-weighted.

The idea is that with a good knowledge of centre-weighted metering, which is relatively easy to predict the failings of, you can compare with honeycomb metering to establish whether the camera has already taken into account the type of lighting situation etc.

Here's an example.

You are photographing a friend, sitting indoors in front of a window. Quite often conventional metering systems either concentrate on the bright light coming in through the window, resulting in the subject being extremely underexposed, or they average the two areas which then results in the subject being underexposed and the window area overexposed.

On the other hand, the camera may well get the exposure correct, by emphasising the dark area where the subject is positioned.

The problem here of course is, that we do not know what the exact result is likely to be. And this is where the metering index is invaluable. When you press the exposure compensation button you will be able to see instantly what the camera has done.

We know that centre-weighted will be an average of the two areas. So we are looking for plus exposure compensation on the index. Experience tells us to increase the exposure in this case over the reading given by centre-weighted, by, let's say, 2 stops. Before we do this though, check to see where the pointer is on the scale. If it is positioned at +2 the camera has done precisely what we would have done manually. So, in this case no further compensation is needed.

Exposure compensation

If however the pointer was only at, say, +1, then we would need to add an extra +1 stop compensation. This is easily done: whilst still holding the compensation button in, turn the front dial until the pointer moves up to the +2 position. Now take the picture.

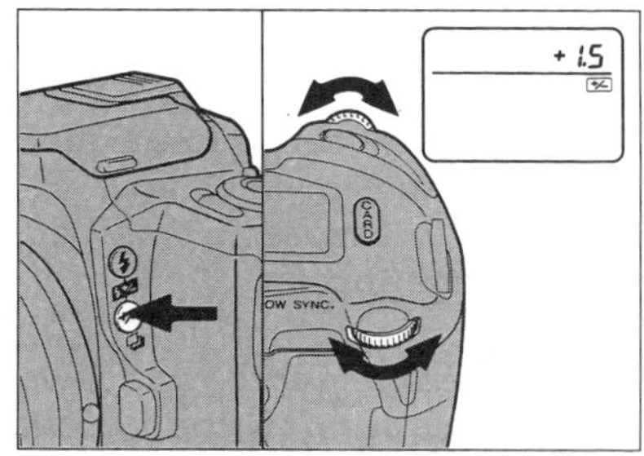

Remember though that you have now set +1 stop compensation. A reminder will be shown in both the viewfinder and body LCD panels. To cancel, press the button again and then turn the dial until 0.0 is shown in the LCD panel at the bottom of the screen and on the camera's top LCD panel. Pressing the P-reset button will also cancel the compensation set.

The range of the exposure compensation is +/- 3 stops in half stop increments. Remember that this factor can be set in the memory and recalled instantly when needed.

Exposure Bracketing

The 700si has built-in exposure bracketing. This allows a fixed three frame sequence to be quickly taken. The sequence is, -0.5, 0.0, +0.5. The exposure increments are fixed. If you would like to shoot wider than this then you will need to use either the Bracketing Card 2 or the Exposure Bracketing Card.

However, because the bracketing sequence is around the metered value, including any exposure compensation set, you could for example set an exposure compensation value of +0.5, and bracket around this which will give you the equivalent of 0.0, +0.5, +1.0.

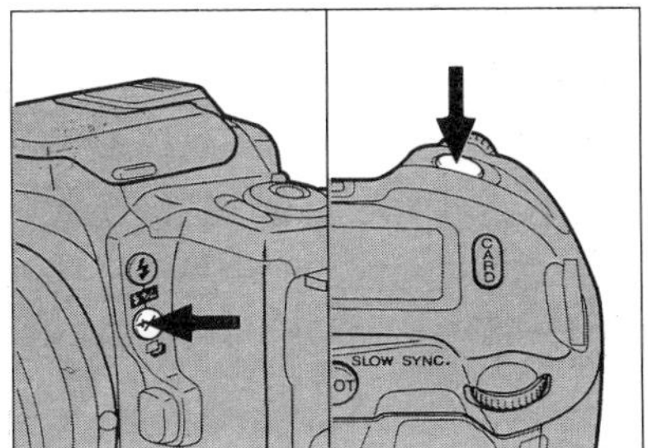

To use the bracketing function press and hold the exposure compensation button whilst releasing the shutter. The 700si will automatically be set to continuous drive mode.

Ensure that you do **NOT** release the shutter until the entire sequence has finished, otherwise the bracketing sequence will be cancelled. The 700si will stop automatically after the three frames have been exposed.

Looking through the viewfinder with the exposure compensation button pressed and the shutter release pressed part way, you will see three pointers on the metering index. Each pointer represents one of the frames in the bracketing sequence. After each frame in the sequence is taken the relevant pointer will disappear. Although, in my opinion, this is not necessary, it is a nice touch. You get the feeling that they have thought of everything!

This, combined with the metering index, has got to be one of the most thought about and easiest to use creative features Minolta have ever introduced.

To gain the best from this feature, you should operate it in this way:

Looking through the viewfinder you first wish to check the amount of exposure compensation automatically set by the camera. For this you press and hold the exposure compensation button in. The metering index will appear on the left hand side of the screen. The pointer position is the amount of compensation set. To modify this amount, whilst still holding the button in, turn the front dial (you can use the rear dial as well, but I think you will agree that the front dial is far more comfortable). This will move the pointer up or down. At the same time you will see at the bottom right corner of the viewfinder the amount of exposure compensation set by you. Remember the pointer position includes the compensation set by the 700si.

Once you have done this, you may wish to add some insurance. For this, continue to keep the compensation button pressed whilst releasing the shutter for the three frame bracketing sequence.

All that from one Button.... Brilliant!

Tip: When using the Metering Index I strongly recommend that you have eye-start switched on, it makes it very much easier to use this feature. Otherwise, with eye-start off, you will need to press the shutter release button part way and then release to get a pointer on the scale. However, if you recompose the scene you will need to press part way down on the shutter release and then release again to get a new reading for that scene.

Exposure is not locked. When you press the shutter release all the way to take a picture and the compensation button is still pressed you will get a bracketing sequence around the settings measured at the time of the picture being taken.

The Metering Index is not only useful for checking the amount of compensation that has been automatically set, but it can also be used to build up an understanding of how the metering system works. Although admittedly that could take some time. If this is your intention, remember the use of the AF button to see which sensor has been used. This will give you an idea of where the camera is concentrating its meter reading on.

When in Manual exposure mode the index remains on permanently to indicate the difference between the exposure calculated by the camera, using whichever metering mode is selected, and the exposure you have set.

If centre-weighted or spot metering is set the indicator only displays the amount of exposure compensation set when the compensation button is pressed

However, if you use the spot metering button (it makes no difference which metering mode was previously set), the indicator will appear on the screen at the same time as the spot metering measuring area appears. When the spot button is first pressed the brightness within the measuring area is assessed and a pointer initially appears by 0 on the index. As the camera is moved the camera will continue to measure the brightness within the spot area and display the difference between the two readings by moving the pointer up or down the scale. (E.g. If the pointer is positioned by +2, that indicates to us that the area spot metering is currently covering is 2 stops brighter than that of our original area.)

Extra information: The pointer position also takes into account any exposure compensation set manually.

If the pointer flashes at +/- 3 the reading is beyond 3 stops.

Even in manual focus, because the camera is still monitoring information from the AF sensors, honeycomb metering is still operative. On the 7xi, the 700si's predecessor, when you switched to manual focus the metering system would be automatically set to centre-weighted metering.

However, the 700si continues to monitor the AF sensor that it would use if it were autofocusing, although you may have focused on a separate part of the scene.

When using the metering index to check the amount of exposure compensation set by the 700si you may find in some situations that the display is difficult to read. In this case, with the compensation button still pressed, move the camera so that the indicator is on a brighter background. **DO NOT PRESS THE**

SHUTTER RELEASE BUTTON AGAIN, otherwise a new reading will be taken.

How can we best use this information?

Look at the scene you are about to photograph and judge what you think to be the highlight (brightest) and shadow (darkest) areas that are relative to the composition of the overall scene, NOT simply any two discriminate points of maximum contrast.

Once you have done this position one of the areas in the centre of the frame and then press and hold the spot button. Now, whilst still holding the spot button in, move the spot area over to the second part of the scene. The pointer will then show what is known as the brightness range of the scene.

Generally speaking slide films have a contrast latitude of approx 5 stops whilst most print films have a latitude of 7 stops.

This means that if we were photographing with slide film and the brightness range was just within the 5 stop range available, then the darkest area would be exposed as a shadow (black) area and the brightest area would be exposed as a highlight (white) area.

If the brightness range was higher than the film range (latitude), then the highlights would be washed out and the shadows would be blocked out, basically there would be no visible detail in these areas. A compromise would have to be met, i.e. biasing the exposure towards one end of the range.

We could also use this facility to compare the brightness between the main subject and other areas of the same scene. For example, first measure the brightness of your main subject, by pressing and holding the spot button in. Now position the spot metering area on other parts of the scene which are of interest to your composition.

The areas which show very little brightness difference will be exposed exactly the same as our original area or as your eye sees those areas when looking through the viewfinder.

The final example for using this facility would be for determining the contrast range, which is similar to the brightness range check, but expressed as a ratio rather than an exposure difference. Operation is the same as for the brightness difference check.

So, firstly take two readings of the highlights and shadows that are essential to the composition, and look at the difference between them. By referring to the table below you will then be able to calculate the subject contrast.

Difference in metered exposure	Subject contrast	
1	2:1	
2	4:1	
3	8:1	
4	16:1	
5	32:1	
6	64:1	Beyond slide film latitude
7	128:1	
8	256:1	Beyond print film latitude

Now there is a problem when the subject contrast is greater than 8:1. That is, the metering index only displays to +/- 3 stops in half stop increments.

This is how we overcome it:

Firstly, we must determine a mid-tone area (an area that reflects approx 18% of the light falling on the subject, back to the camera) within the scene. (See grey card below).

Take a spot meter reading of this area and keep the SPOT button pressed. Move the measuring area indication on to the highlight and shadow areas. Make a mental note of the deviation from zero for each area. Ideally, if the areas are black and white, they should each be between 2 and 2 1/2 stops from zero. This will be within the latitude for slide film and will ensure that they are exposed as highlights and shadow areas. If the deviation from zero is equal, this further proves that our original mid-tone area is correct. It is this area that should be used for correct exposure.

See Multi-Spot Memory and Highlight/Shadow cards for more information on this subject.

Grey Card

If you photograph a white subject in front of a white background, it will be 2.3 stops underexposed and will appear grey rather than white.

If you photograph a black subject in front of a black background it will be overexposed by 2.7 stops and so it will once again come out grey.

If you photograph a grey scene, it will come out grey.

Why?

A white surface (high reflectance) reflects approx 85-90% of the light falling onto it towards the camera.

A black surface (low reflectance) reflects approx 2.5-3%.

A grey surface reflects approx 18%. Hence the term 18% grey card. And it is this reflectance factor that all camera exposure meters are calibrated to. Put another way, the camera's exposure meter assumes that all subjects and scenes reflect 18% of the light towards the camera. Hence, when the subject reflects more or less light to the camera, you get over or underexposure.

To compensate for this type of situation you simply increase the exposure by 2-2 1/2 stops for a highlight scene and decrease the exposure by the same amount for a shadow scene. There is a problem with this though. If the scene is mainly black but there are also white areas in the scene, underexposing by 2 stops may be too much. The best alternative would be to spot meter for the black area and then set exposure compensation for this reading. An even easier alternative would be to use the Highlight/Shadow card. For more information on this refer to the card section.

If the scene is half black (shadow) and half white (highlight) a straightforward average of the two areas will give the correct exposure. For this you should be able to rely on the camera's honeycomb system. However, to ensure you get the correct result you could select centre-weighted metering or use the multi-spot memory card and take one reading of each area.

Extra Information: Although not as easy as the above ways of utilising the metering index we can also use the indicator to display the difference between spot metering and honeycomb or the difference between spot and centre-weighted.

This is how it's done:

Difference between Spot and Honeycomb metering

This allows us to check exactly what compensation the camera has made for spot-lit subjects.

1. Set camera to Honeycomb metering
2. Press and hold **+/-** button
3. Press and hold **spot** button
4. Release **+/-** button

Pointer position = Honeycomb metering.

Therefore if the pointer is at +2, the exposure measured by honeycomb metering is 2 stops brighter than the exposure measured by spot metering. If you continue to keep the SPOT button pressed whilst releasing the shutter, the exposure will be set based on honeycomb meter reading.

Difference between Centre-weighted and Spot metering

1. Set camera to centre-weighted metering
2. Press and hold **+/-** button
3. Press and hold **spot** button
4. Release **+/-** button

Pointer position = Spot metering.

Therefore, if the pointer is at +2, then the exposure measured using spot metering is 2 stops brighter than the reading measured using centre-weighted metering.

If you continue to hold the +/- button in whilst releasing the shutter, the exposure will be set according to the reading obtained using centre-weighted metering.

Exposure Lock

The 700si does not feature a dedicated exposure lock facility. However, it is possible to lock the exposure in other ways.

1. Pressing part way on the shutter release locks exposure and focus for a stationary subject.

2. Pressing the AF, depth of field or focus lock (on some manual zoom and prime lenses) button will lock exposure and focus for both stationary and moving subjects.

ADVANCED GRAPHIC DISPLAY VIEWFINDER

Almost all modern SLR cameras feature an LCD (Liquid Crystal Display). This is normally positioned at the bottom of the viewfinder, just below the photograph area.

Top of the range SLR cameras today feature an entire plethora of information in the viewfinder. This information has included exposure mode, aperture, shutter speed, exposure compensation, flash ready indicator, metering mode, focus status etc, but up until the introduction of the Dynax/Maxxum 7xi in 1991 no camera had been designed in such a way as to allow the photographer to control the major camera functions whilst looking through the viewfinder.

One of the main reasons why built in motor drives on modern SLR's have become so popular is not just because it makes it easier to capture fast moving subject sequences, but because the photographer does not have to remove his/her eye from the viewfinder to advance the film in between frames.

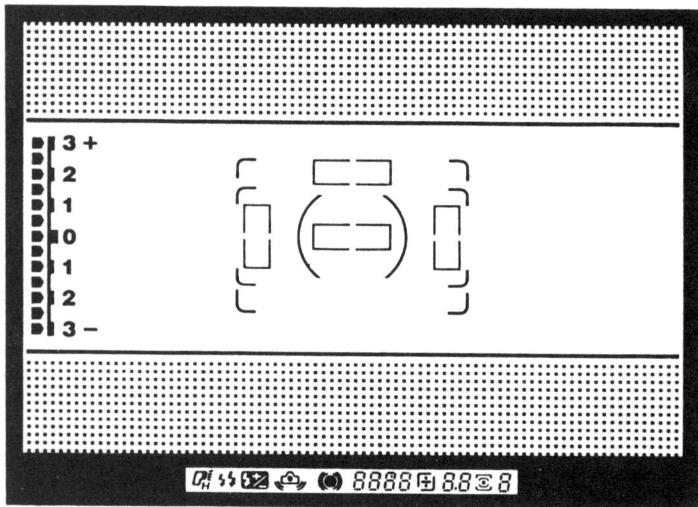

The Advanced Graphic Display viewfinder, as featured on the Dynax/Maxxum 700si, is the result of the very latest LCD technology. Conventionally, LCD panels have been of a non-transparent design.

The use of this new type of display makes it possible to increase the amount of information that is relayed back to the photographer through the viewfinder. You would be forgiven for thinking that having all of this extra information in the viewfinder will mean added complications and confusing operation. However, this could not be further from reality. Only the information that is relevant at that specific moment in time to the way in which the camera is being used or controlled is displayed, ensuring that operation is never complicated, if anything, it is easier than on previous cameras.

In very low lighting situations it may become difficult to read the viewfinder overlays. For this reason some of the information is duplicated in the conventional LCD readout below the picture area so that settings can still be adjusted whilst looking through the viewfinder.

To compensate for the loss of light (approx 6-7%) through the transparent LCD panel installed just above the focusing screen, the main mirror has been given a new special coating which reflects more light up to the viewfinder, this results in an image brightness approximately the same as that of the Dynax/Maxxum 8000i.

Panorama Indicator

To select the Panorama indicator, press and hold in both the **AF** and **CARD** buttons whilst switching the 700si on. To cancel, repeat the procedure.

Selecting this manually allows you to compose for the panoramic format but have the pictures printed to the correct proportions at a later date without having to install the panorama adaptor.

When this is selected the camera will change the AF area to that for vertical framing. Therefore the top sensor is switched off and the camera will only use the left, right and centre sensors for focusing. However the top sensor can still be selected manually with the **AF** button.

The program area is also modified slightly to favour even smaller apertures for greater depth of field control.

Focal length display

With an xi lens fitted to the camera, you can view the current focal length set in both the viewfinder and body data panels. When you pull the ring back, the focal length in use will be shown where the shutter speed is normally indicated. The display will revert back to the shutter speed after a few seconds.

Frame counter

When you load a film, the 700si reads the number of frames the cassette holds off the DX coding. When you reach the last nine frames a countdown indicator will appear to the right of the metering mode indicator in the viewfinder. This is very handy for when you are shooting motor drive sequences. It is not intended to replace the frame counter, more to act as a reminder that film reserves are getting low.

Other information

The viewfinder will also show information such as flash on, flash mode, HSS flash operational, flash compensation reminder, exposure compensation reminder, focus status, aperture, shutter speed, film speed, metering mode, local focus area indicator and camera shake warning.

MEMORY

The Dynax/Maxxum 700si features very few new features, but takes the best features from the best features from the best cameras. One of the few new features is the Memory facility.

There are several benefits, the main one is the ability to store your favourite combination of settings, 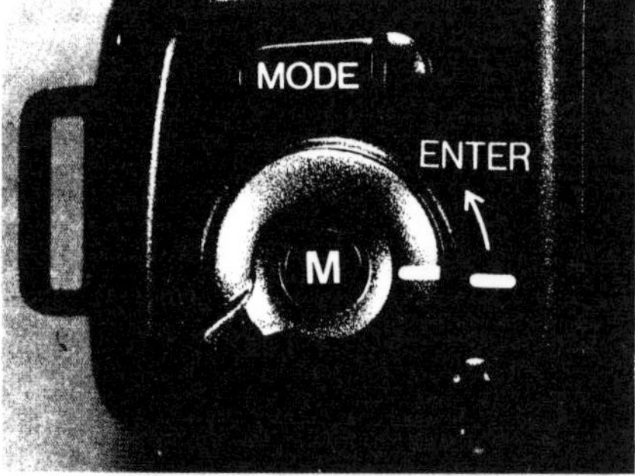 features and functions, and recall them quickly and easily with a single press of a button.

This then allows you to switch between the camera's default settings (program reset button) and your settings stored in the Memory.

To program the memory after the camera settings are made,

press and hold the Memory switch release, whilst turning the Memory switch to **ENTER**. **MEmory** will then be shown on the body data panel to confirm the settings have been stored.

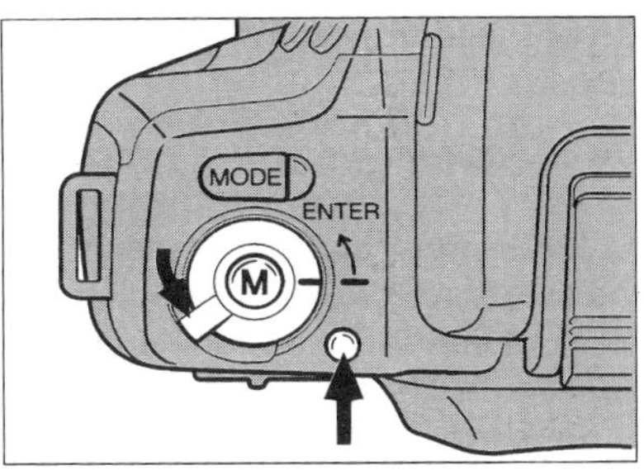

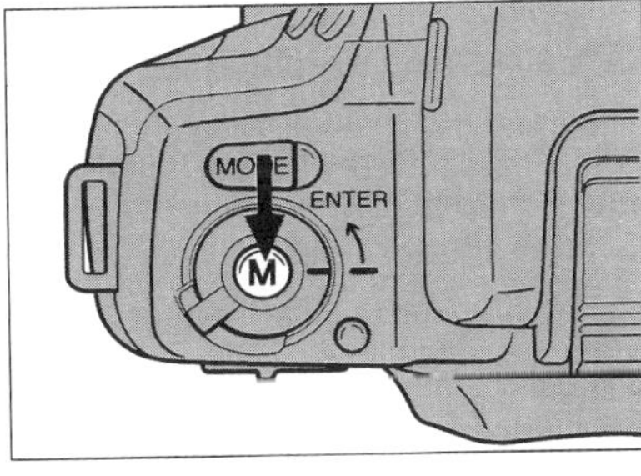

The settings can then be recalled at anytime by simply pressing the recall button (**M**) in the centre of the Memory switch.

Functions	**Settings that can be stored in Memory:**
Exposure Mode	P/A/S/M
Aperture Setting (in A/M modes only)	f/1.0-f/64 depending on lens
Shutter Speed (in S/M modes only)	1/8000-30" and bulb
Drive Mode	single, continuous, double exposure or self timer
Flash Mode	red-eye reduction on, red-eye reduction off or remote off camera flash
Exposure Compensation	+/- 3.0 stops in 1/2 EV steps
Flash Compensation	+/- 3.0 stops in 1/2 EV steps
Metering Mode	honeycomb, spot or centre-weighted
AF Area	wide or any of the four local sensors
AFP/RP	focus or release priority

Settings that cannot be stored in the Memory:

Flash On/Off

Eye-start On/Off

Depth of Field Preview

Temporary Spot with Spot Button

Manual Fill-Flash On

AE Bracketing

P_A/P_S modes

Card Details

Card On/Off

Panorama/Standard Format Frame

AF/MF

ISO Settings

In addition to using the Memory to recall our favourite settings we can use it to select one commonly used feature. For example, rather than pressing two buttons and then turning a dial to select release priority, this feature can be stored in the memory and recalled at any time.

Here's another example. You normally use the camera in program most of the time, but you tend to use continuous drive frequently. This could be stored in the Memory on its own, and recalled at will. To do this, press the program reset button. Now set continuous drive. Store this in the Memory.

Pressing the program reset button will restore to single drive, pressing the **M** button will instantly set continuous drive. It is not necessary to clear the Memory, as you are still able to adjust the settings after having recalled the Memory.

Only one combination of settings can be stored at any one time. However, it is possible to reprogram the program reset button, by using the Customized Function Card xi, in a similar fashion.

If you would like to modify one or two of the settings in the Memory, the easiest method of doing this is to first recall the Memory. At this stage cancel or add to the recalled settings. Now store this new combination in the Memory. This is very much easier than cancelling everything and starting afresh.

SILENT OPERATION

Well not exactly silent operation, but certainly reduced noise level in comparison with previous Minolta AF SLR's. Various measures have been taken to reduce the overall noise level generated by the 700si.

Particular attention was paid to the film transport. Firstly, using a floating motor which is then mounted on two polymer shock absorbers to help prevent vibration and noise from being transmitted to the 700si's body. Secondly, the motor's speed is computer controlled to maintain a constant speed which also helps in reducing noise and vibration.

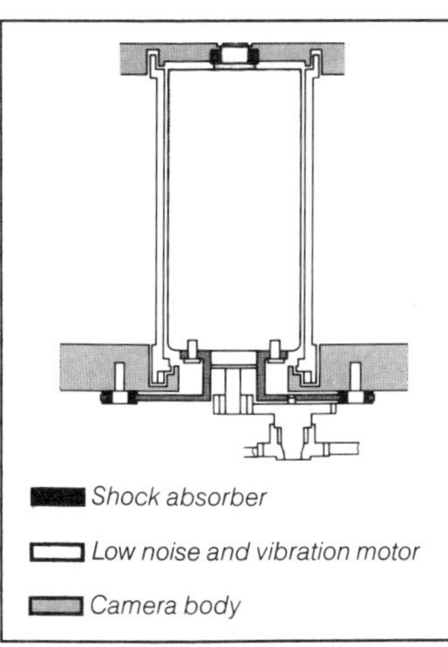

Shock absorber

Low noise and vibration motor

Camera body

The transport gears have been manufactured from soft material which reduces friction and gear clash, therefore improving speed and further decreasing operating noise. Additional shock absorbers are placed at the impact points of gear trains which are also moved by spring loaded switches.

As a result of the above measures, film load, film rewind, shutter release, mechanical charge and autofocus are all much quieter than the 700si's predecessors, especially film rewind which is approximately 60% quieter.

To help significantly reduce noise and vibration when loading and rewinding film, the 700si is set to Silent Load/Rewind mode as standard. In this mode the motor is slowed down considerably. However, this mode of operation may not be desirable in action situations, when the film needs to be rewound and a new one loaded as quick as possible. In this case you can select High Speed Load/Rewind. To do this press and hold the drive mode button whilst switching the camera on. The

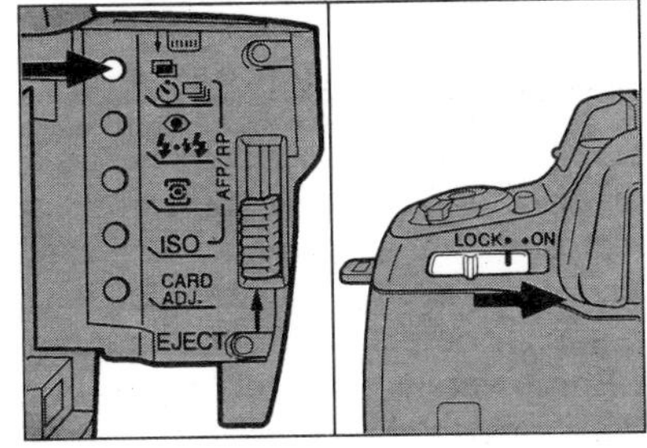

body LCD panel will display **ON** to confirm this mode has been selected. Performing the same operation again will switch this mode off and **OFF** will be displayed in the LCD panel to confirm this.

With Silent Load/Rewind selected, once film rewinding has started, pressing the film rewind button will cause the film to rewind at high speed for that roll only.

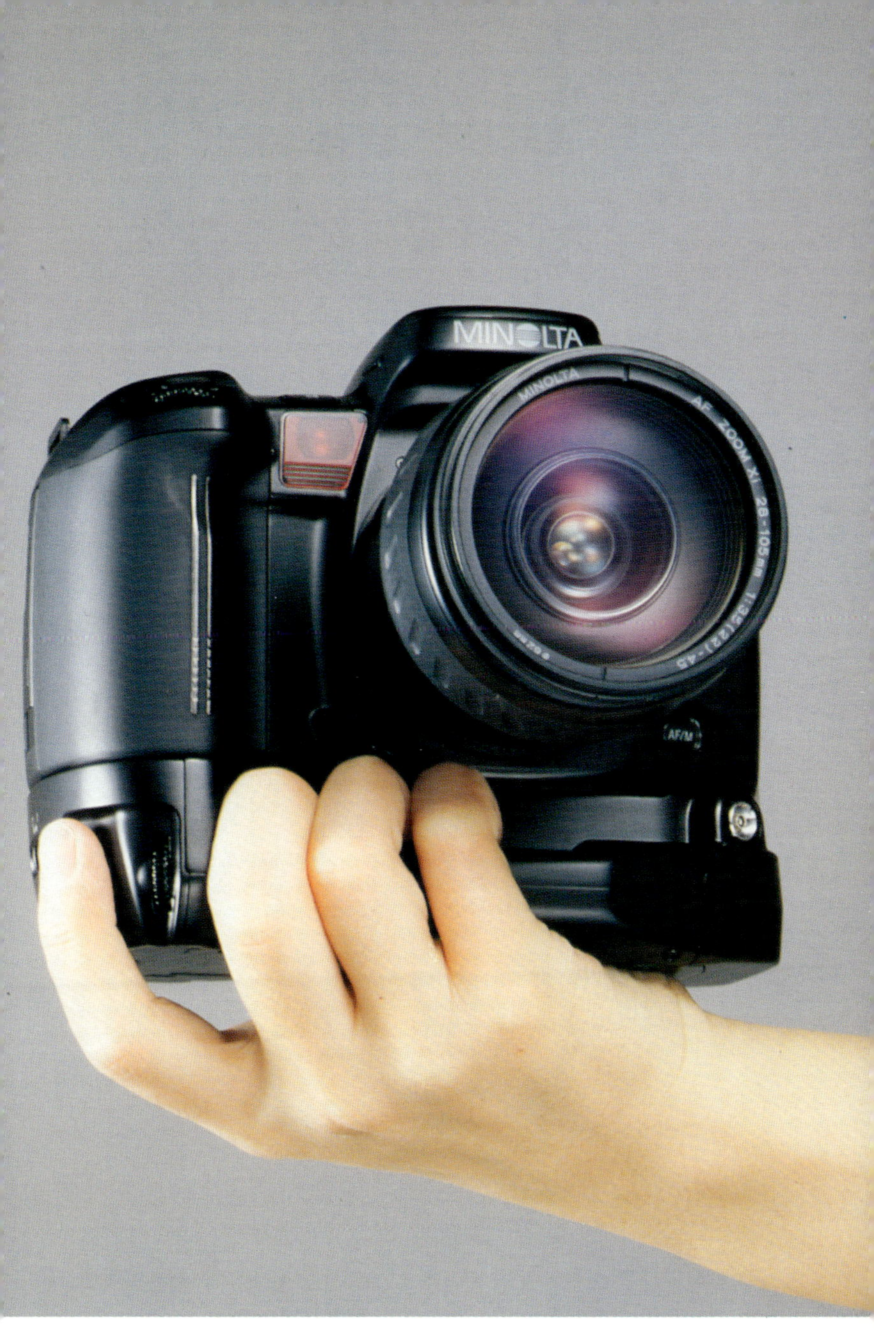

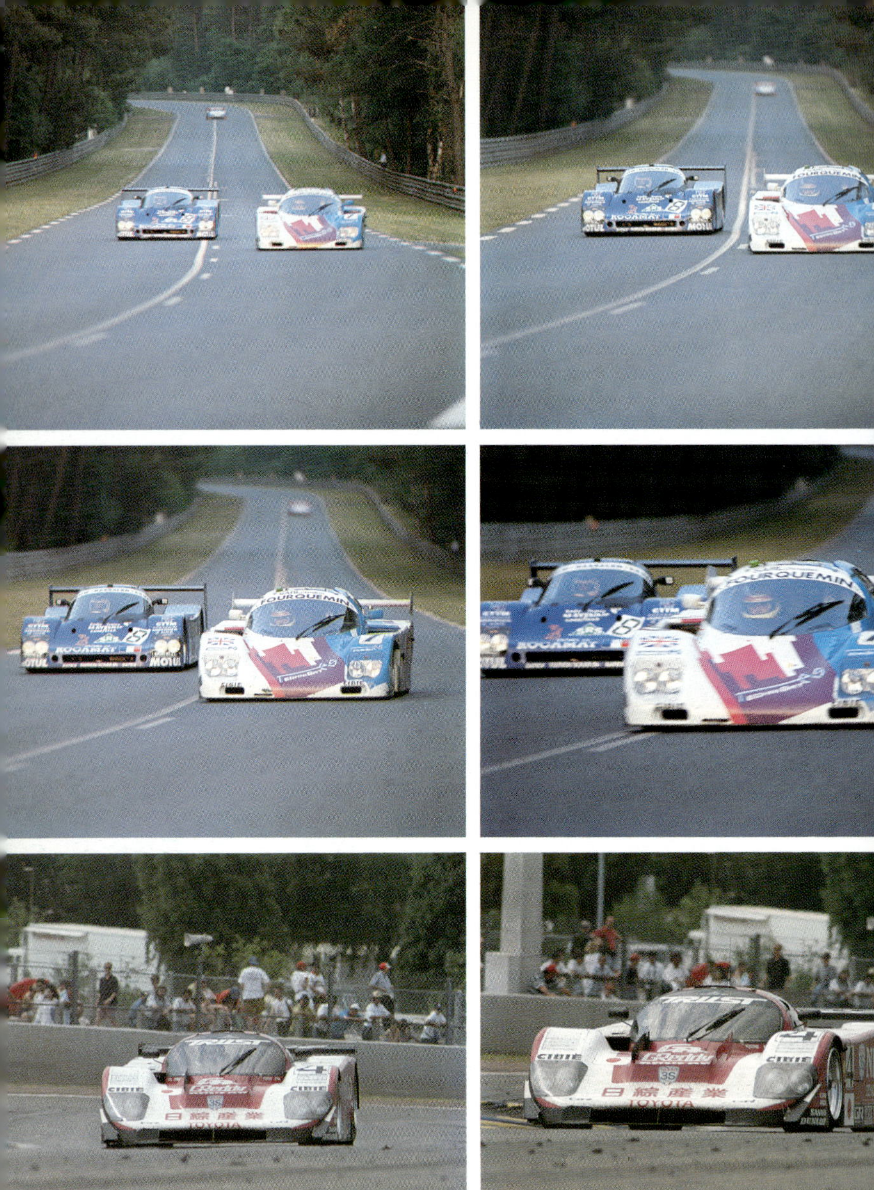

200mph The Minolta with 300mm f2.8 lens + 2x converter, hand held 1/125 sec. f5.6 3 frames per second. The sequence is still in focus in spite of camera shake.

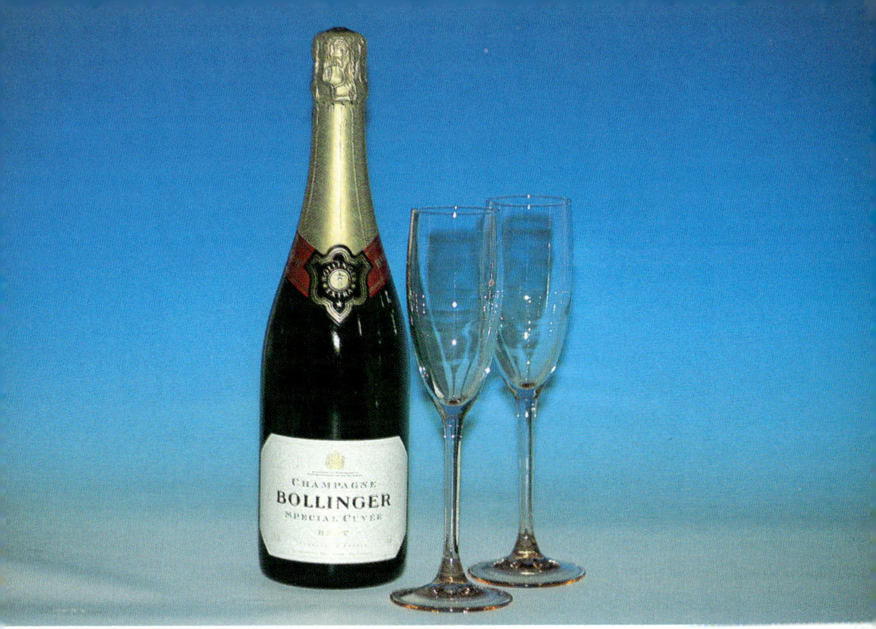

Built in Flash

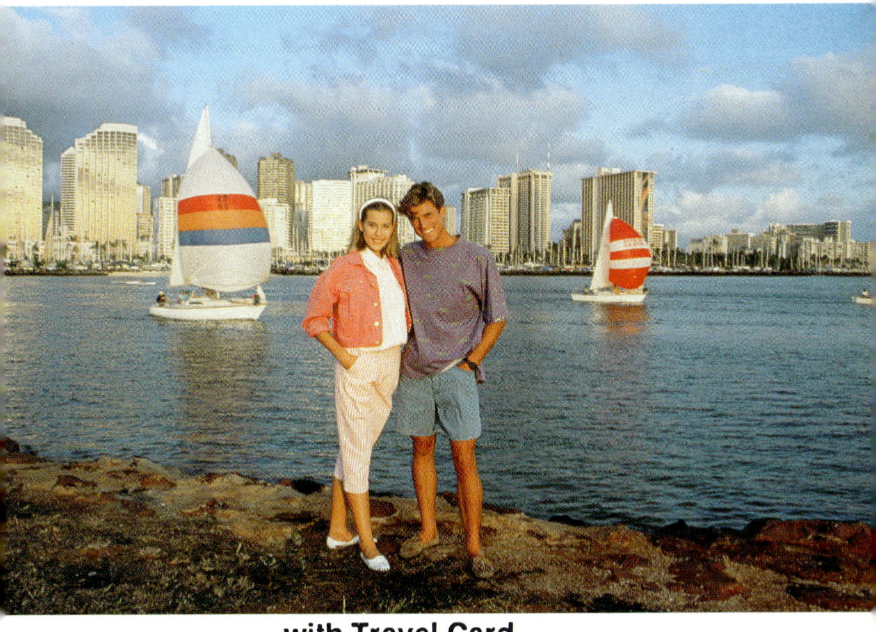

with Travel Card

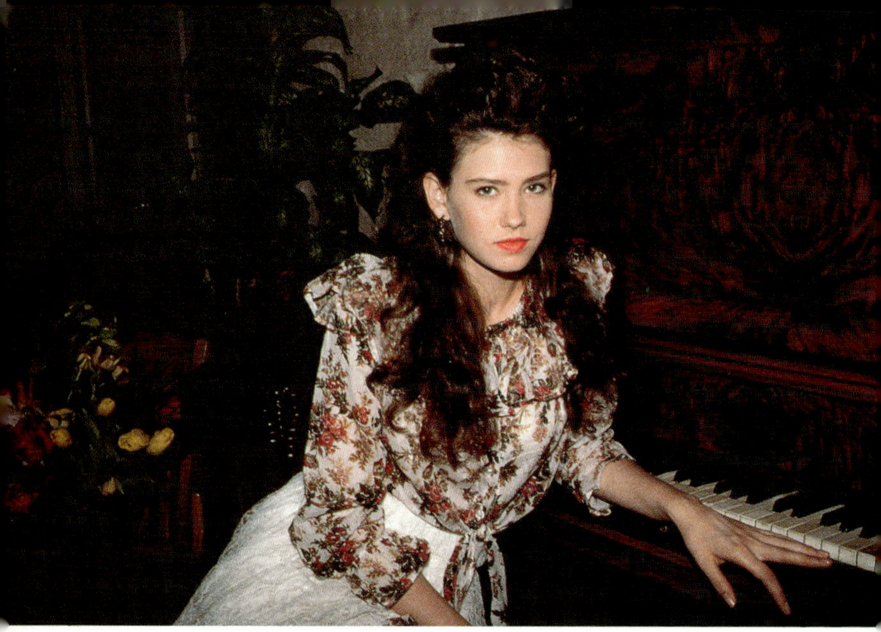

Exposure Flash Bracketing Card

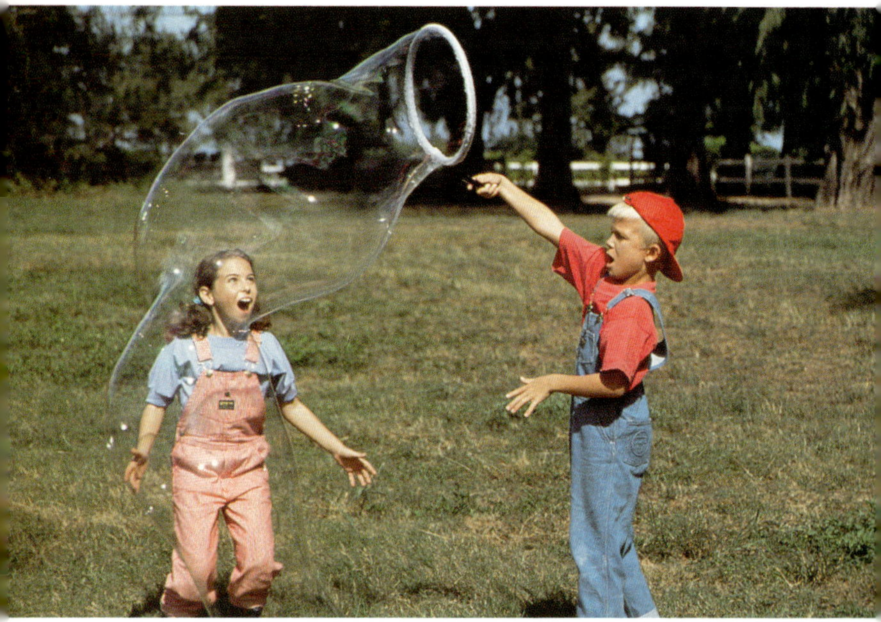

Child Card

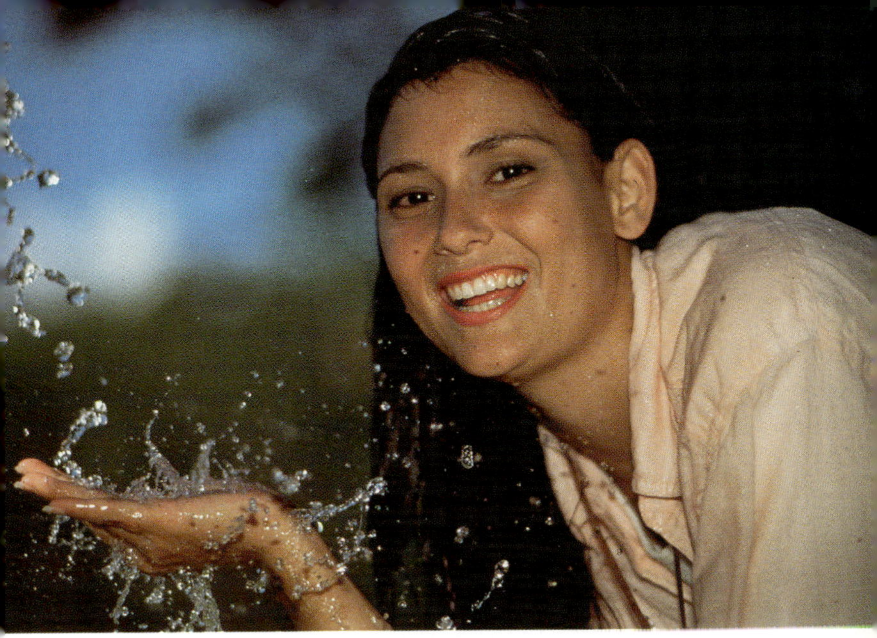

with High-speed Sync.

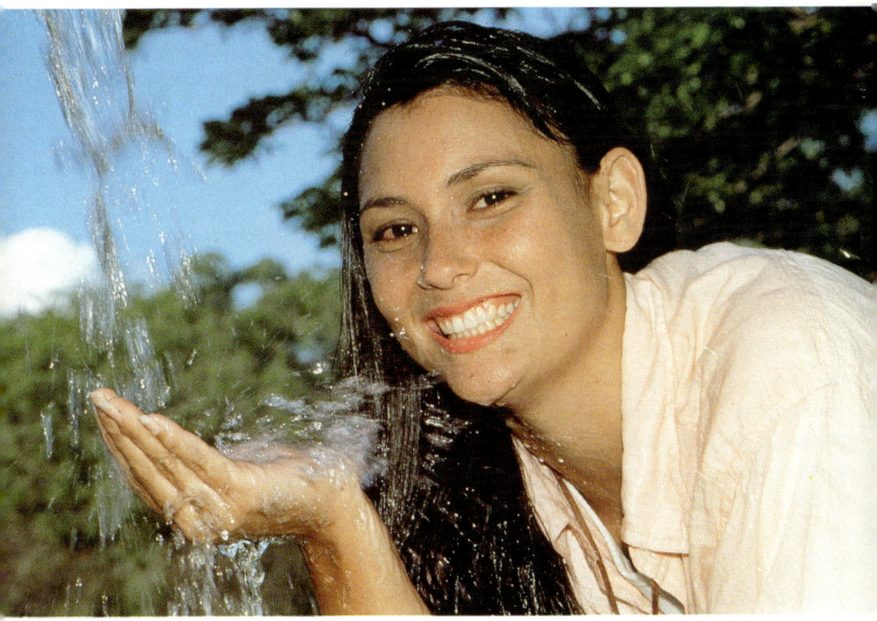

without High-speed Sync.

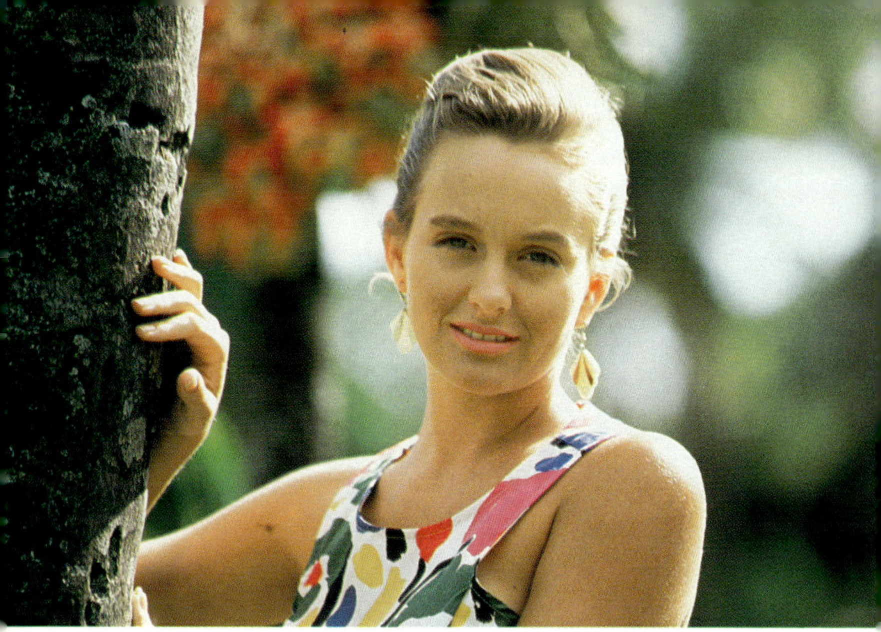

Portrait Card

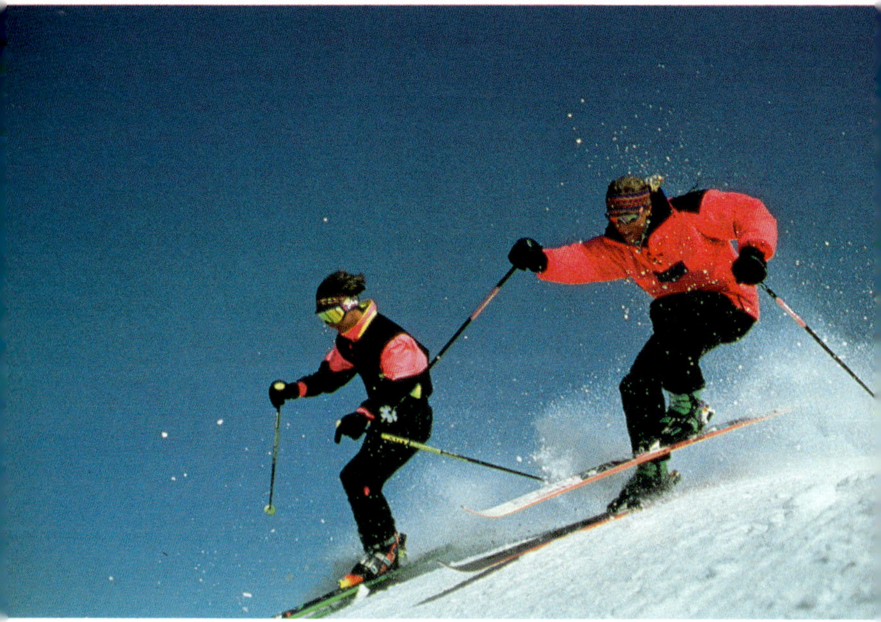

Sports Action Card

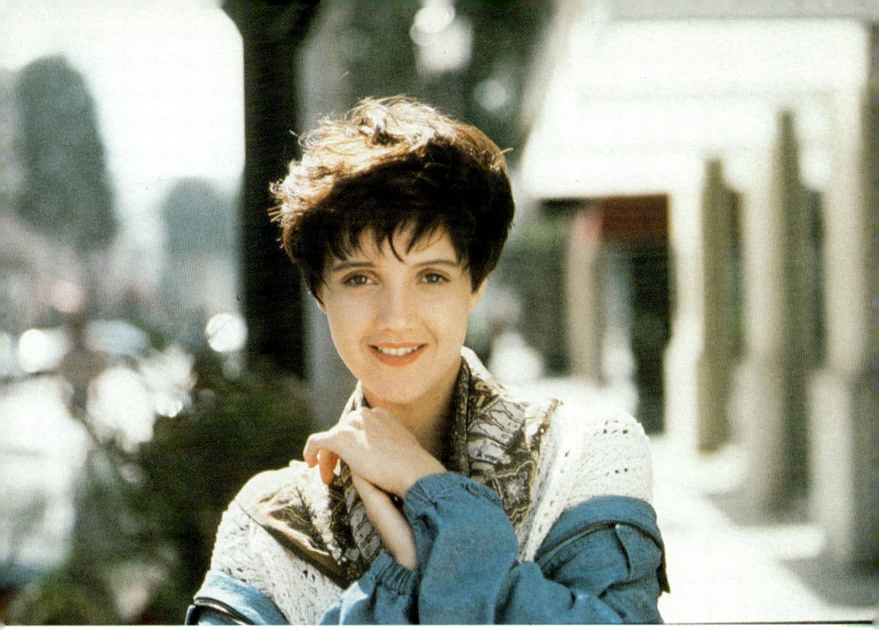

Multi Shift Card

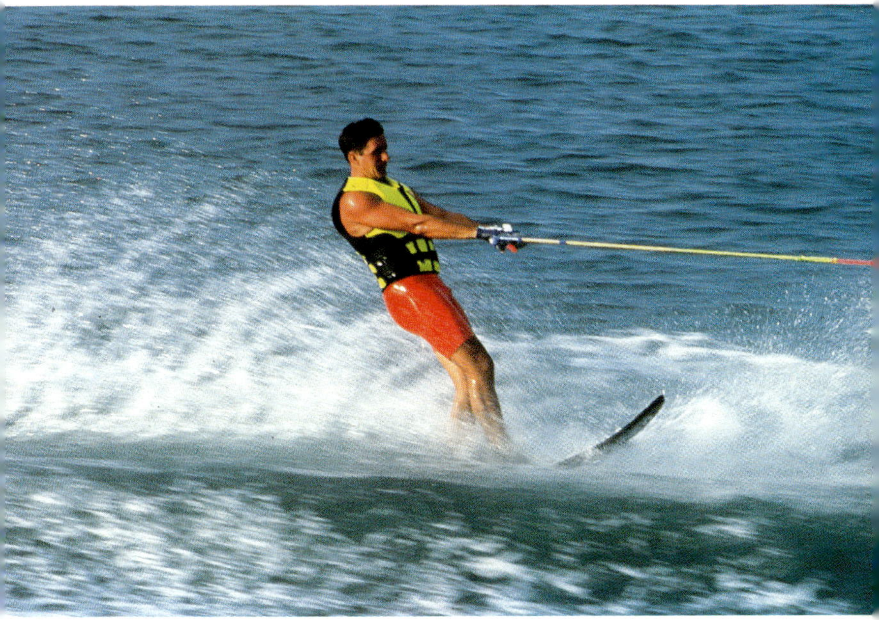

Background Priority Card

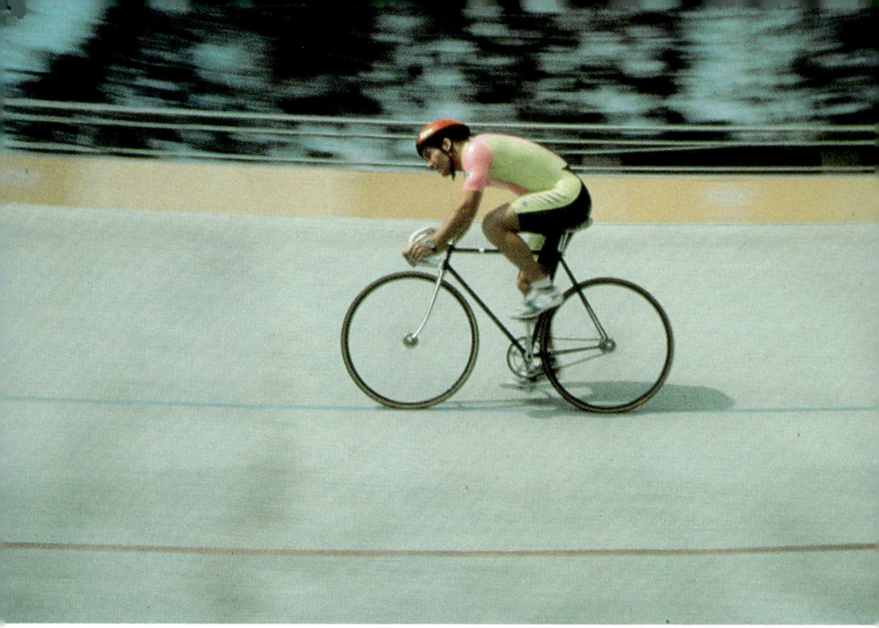

Panning Card

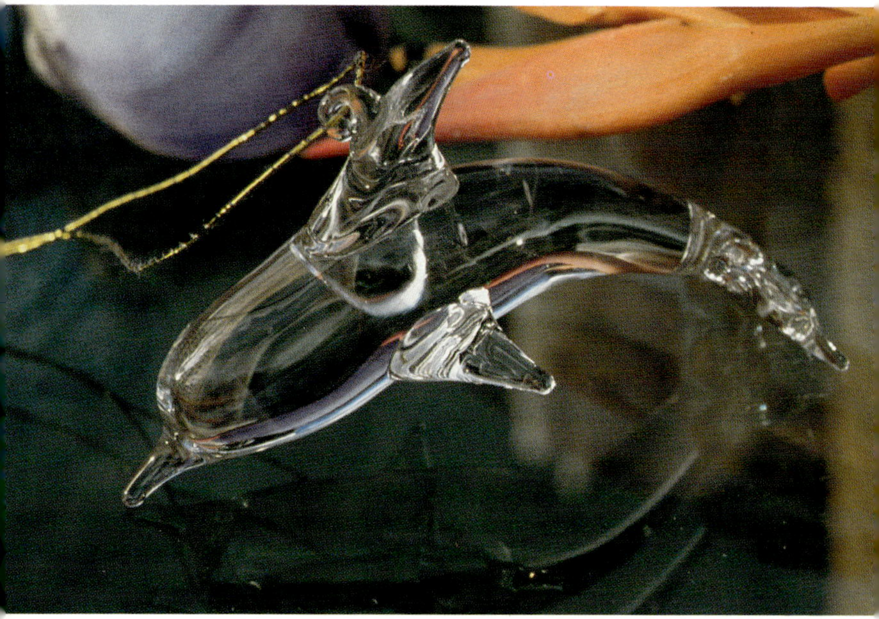

Close Up Card

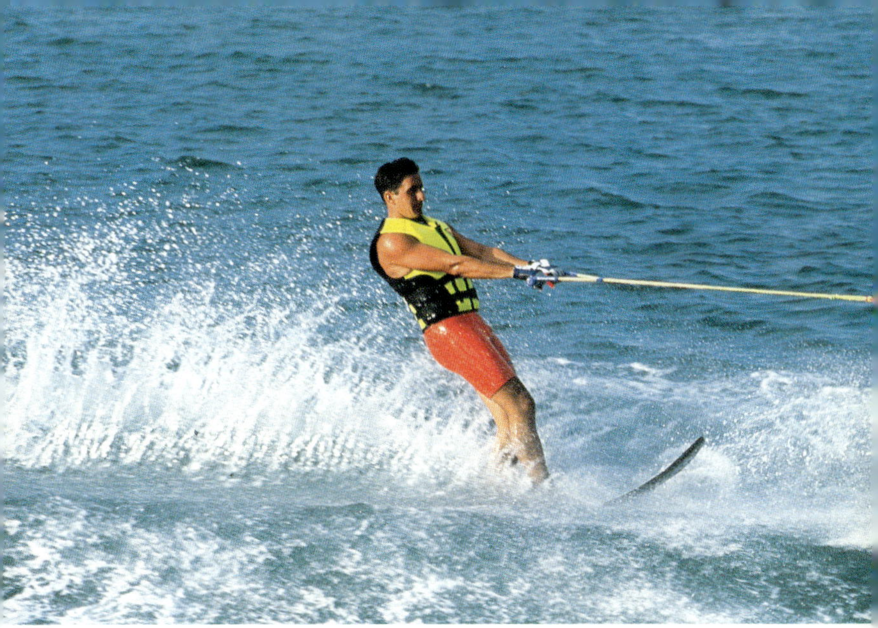

Automatic Program Shift Card

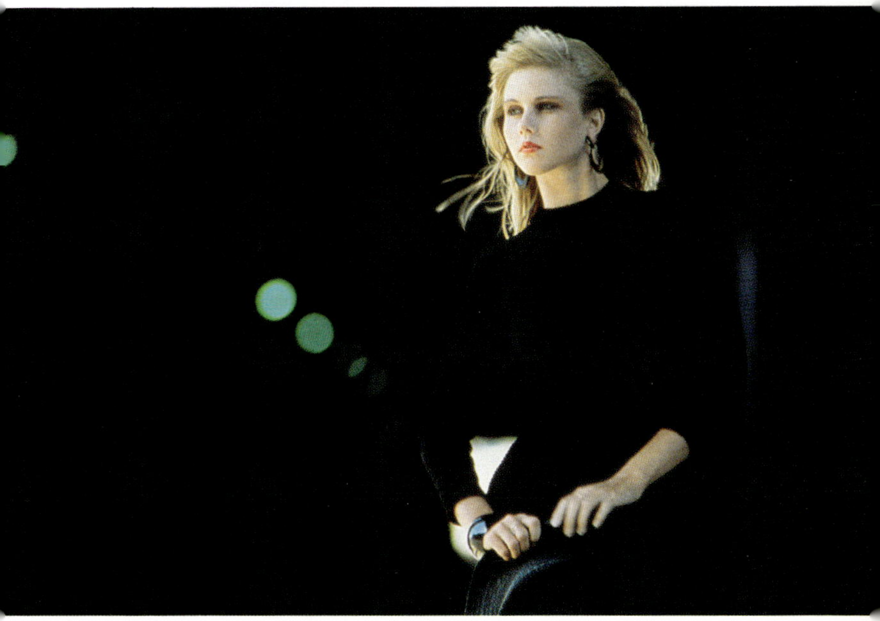

Highlight/Shadow Card

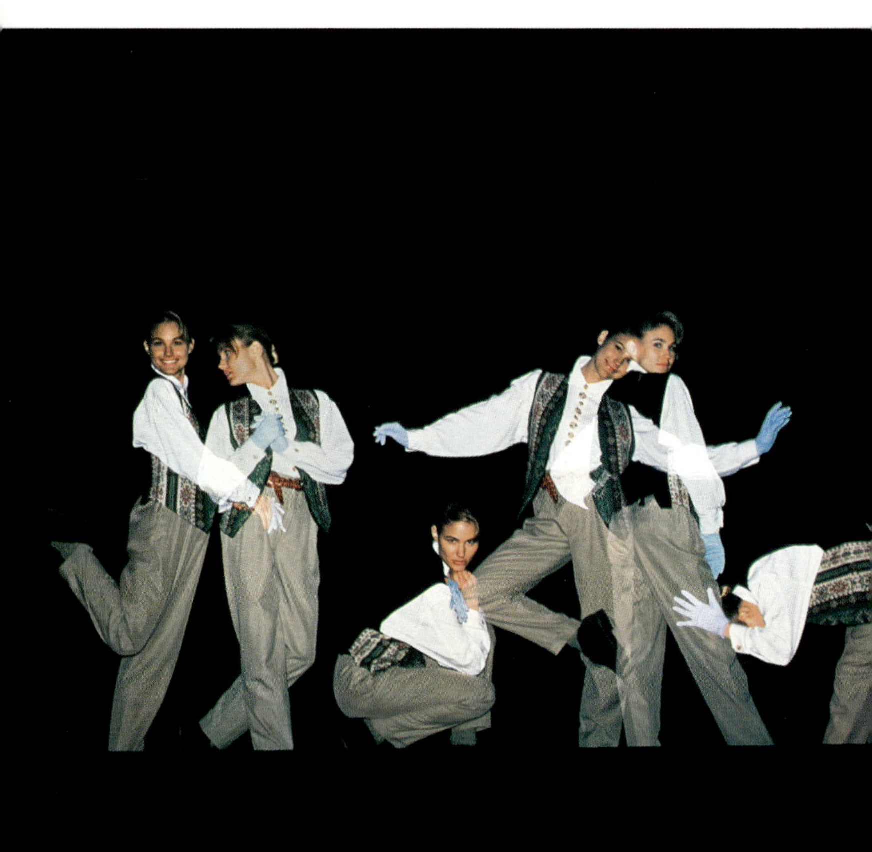

Multiple Exposure Card

FLASH - NO LIMITS

Since the introduction of the 7000, Minolta have only been thought of when discussing autofocusing systems. But Minolta have also had a great deal to do with the development of flash photography. TTL (through the lens) flash metering, one of the biggest, if not the biggest advance in flash photography was originally developed by Minolta (although admittedly Olympus were the first to use the system). More recently Remote off-camera TTL flash and TTL HSS (high speed sync) flash have been developed by Minolta. Yet still no one associates Minolta with having a good flash system on their cameras.

Well the 700si should put a stop to that. The Minolta engineers have looked at all of the limitations and problems associated with flash photography and come up with an answer to everything.

However, it doesn't have everything. In fact, there's no second curtain sync facility, this is where the flash fires at the end of the exposure rather than at the beginning, which is conventional. I'll have to wait until the replacement arrives!!!

No Limits

Many amateur photographers do not like to take photographs with flash. Why?

I personally believe this is because of a number of reasons. Not least that it is seen as too complicated. As far as the 700si and many other Minolta Dynax/Maxxum AF SLR's are concerned flash photography is as easy as photography without flash (ambient).

Literally all you need do is attach the flash to the camera, press the Program reset button and forget it is even there. The camera will sort everything out for you, and only fire the flash if it feels it is necessary. What could be easier?

Other reasons for photographers not making full use of flash are various associated limitations, such as the expense and inconvenience caused by using cables for off camera work, which then cause in most cases unsightly shadows, and being limited to shutter speeds up to a maximum of between 1/300 (Dynax/Maxxum 9xi) and 1/60 second.

The 700si, when used in conjunction with the 5400HS flash unit, overcomes all of these problems.

First, the basics:

TTL (Through The Lens) Flash Photography

Approximately 10 years ago if an SLR had TTL flash it was really something, it was the business! Now, as far as I am aware, all AF SLR's feature TTL Flash, it has become standard specification. Similarly to autofocus, if you cannot remember 10 years back, when all the manufacturers were using TTL flash as a major reason for buying whichever model in the range featured it, you probably cannot remember the basic principle and benefit behind it.

TTL flash measurement was developed to give more accurate exposure and to take into account different lenses in use, filters, bounce flash, reflectors and all 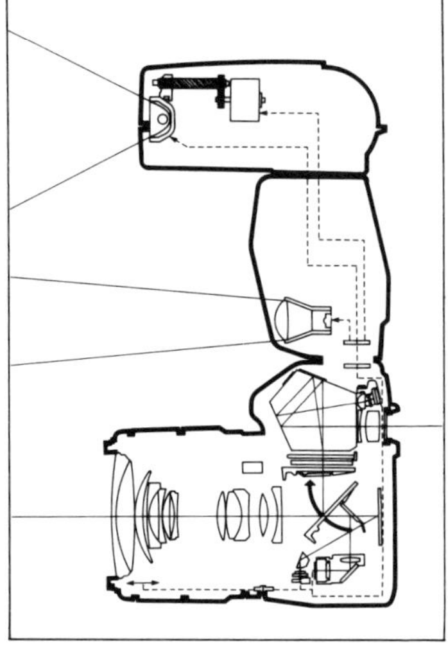 sorts of other accessories that you otherwise have to take into account when using flash guns.

This is the basic principle.

The camera starts off by calculating the amount of illumination required to correctly expose the subject. When the shutter opens the flash fires. Whilst the flash is firing the camera measures the amount of light the film has received. This is done by the light entering the camera being reflected off the film and into a small SPC (silicon photo cell) in the base of the camera. Once the film has received the correct amount of light the flash burst is instantly stopped, resulting in an accurate exposure.

Using this method, although using filters, bouncing flash, using reflectors and all sorts of other accessories reduce the effective output of the flash, the TTL system keeps the flash firing until the film has received the necessary illumination to give correct exposure.

This basic system has gradually been improved by using more and more sophisticated technology over the years to handle tricky lighting situations and to provide more natural illumination, specifically for fill-in flash - perhaps the most difficult form of flash photography.

The features that we shall be concentrating on in this section are as follows:

- **The 700si's TTL Flash Metering**
- **Auto-Switchover Flash (P-mode)**
- **A/S/M Mode Flash**
- **Slow Sync Flash**
- **Flash Compensation**

Before all of that, however, I think it wise to spend a bit of time on the built-in flash of the 700si.

The built-in unit provides illumination for lenses as wide as 24mm. This is currently the widest coverage of any built-in flash unit, most SLR's built-in units cover to either 35mm or 28mm focal lengths.

Guide numbers

The guide number of the built-in flash is 12 at 100 ISO in metres.

The guide number is a standard method of quoting the maximum possible output based upon ideal conditions. We can use the guide number to calculate the maximum possible flash range based on the lens in use. It is easily calculated by using the formula below:

Flash range   = Guide number/Max f.no.

Therefore the flash range for the 700si when used with a lens whose maximum aperture is f/4 is calculated as follows:

Flash range   = 12/4

           = 3m (100 ISO)

Therefore in ideal conditions the built-in flash is suitable for subjects up to 3m from the camera.

Effect of different film speeds on flash range

As we increase the film speed the flash range increases.

Flash range at 100 ISO = 3m
Flash range at 200 ISO = 4.5m
Flash range at 400 ISO = 6m

Here we can see quite clearly that using faster film has a noticeable effect on the flash range, and as the modern film emulsions improve even further it allows us to use faster film, without the drawbacks that were associated with film sharpness about 10 years ago. The modern 400 ISO films seem as good as the 100 ISO speed films that were being produced approximately five years ago.

Effect of shutter speeds and apertures on flash exposure

With flash photography, the apertures and shutter speeds affect the exposure in a different manner to that of photography when not using flash (ambient light).

The aperture controls the exposure and the effective flash subject range.

Shutter speeds have very little, if any in most cases, effect on the subject exposure level. However, do not think that changing the shutter speed will have no affect at all. The shutter speed is used to affect the background brightness. Fast shutter speeds will generally cause the background to appear dark, but the selection of a slow shutter speed can cause the background to appear equally well exposed as the subject, and in some cases we can even overexpose the background. As to how the background appears, this is obviously down to you, the photographer, it therefore becomes an important element of the overall composition.

Duration of power

With most flashguns the effective power or output is controlled by the duration of the flash and not the intensity, although the flash tube in a 5400HS is more powerful than say the tube in the 3500xi flashgun. The flash duration of these units is in the region of 1/600 to 1/50,000 second.

The 700si's TTL Flash Metering System

The 700si uses honeycomb, centre-weighted or spot metering (depending upon which is set as a **PERMANENT** metering mode) to evaluate how much illumination will need to be provided by the flash for correct exposure. The flash fires and the TTL flash metering system monitors the amount of illumination off the film. Once the TTL metering system detects that the film has received the calculated amount of illumination, a signal is sent to the flashgun, instantly quenching the burst.

Auto-Switchover Flash (Program)

With either the built-in flash (raised) or a Minolta i/xi/HS series flash fitted to the hotshoe (switched on), the flash will fire automatically in low light situations or if the camera's honeycomb metering system detects that the subject is backlit.

To ensure that an accessory flash fires in these situations, follow the operation below:

1. Attach the flash unit to the camera's accessory shoe.
2. Press the Program reset button.
3. Take pictures.

ATTACHING THE FLASH AND THEN PRESSING THE ON/OFF BUTTON TO SWITCH ON MAY CAUSE THE FLASH NOT TO FIRE WHEN IT SHOULD.

SELECTING EITHER SPOT OR CENTRE-WEIGHTED METERING DISABLES THE CAMERA'S ABILITY TO DETECT A BACKLIT SUBJECT.

With honeycomb metering in use, flash exposures will be extremely accurate in most situations due to the camera still taking into account the same information as if flash were not being used, i.e. subject distance, position in the frame, subject brightness and lighting condition, (e.g. spotlit, backlit etc).

Why use fill-in flash?

I briefly mentioned exposure latitude of films in the exposure section of this book. I stated that print film has a latitude of around 7 stops whilst slide film has a latitude of 5 stops. Rather than calling this range the film latitude, I should really refer to it as the contrast range; i.e. the difference between highlights and shadows where the shadows will not be blocked out and the highlights not washed out. However, I understand that when slides are printed or are used for publication, this contrast range is reduced to approximately four stops.

So what can we do?

As good as the Honeycomb system is, it can only try and balance the exposure between subject and background whilst emphasising the subject. This however will inevitably still lead to the background being overexposed in some situations.

The answer to the problem is, fill-in flash. By providing extra illumination for the subject which is in shadow for example, we can reduce the scene contrast by increasing the subject brightness so that it is closer to that of the background.

The 700si is capable of distinguishing between four different lighting conditions.

Backlight Fill-in Daylight situation where the subject is darker than the background.

Frontlight Fill-in Daylight situation when the subject's brightness is close to that of the background

Lowlight Fill-in Lighting condition where the light is low enough to cause camera shake.

Night Scene Fill-in Lowlight situation where the background is very much darker than the subject.

Listed below are the varying ways in which the flash output, subject's ambient level, and background brightness are controlled in each exposure mode depending on the lighting conditions. The various exposure compensations automatically made by the 700si's metering system are set to give the best balance of subject brightness, ambient level and background appearance, to give the most natural looking flash photographs possible in most situations.

Program Mode Flash

In program, as already explained, the flash fires automatically. Shutter speeds between 1/200 and 1/60 are set automatically, depending upon the focal length in use. The aperture is then controlled within the lens' working range depending on the ambient light level and the subject or scene characteristics.

In backlit conditions requiring flash, the ambient light exposure will be reduced by approximately one stop, whilst the flash exposure will be reduced by 3/4 stop to ensure a natural fill-in flash effect. The background exposure will be controlled by the setting of a shutter speed that will overexpose this area by 1.5 stops. This results in a fill-in flash ratio of 3:1.

In dark conditions requiring flash to overcome camera shake the ambient exposure is reduced by one stop.

Tip: DO NOT SWITCH TO SPOT OR CENTRE-WEIGHTED METERING IF YOU WANT AUTO FILL-IN FLASH.

Manual Fill-in Flash in Program

Should there be a situation where the 700si's metering system decides that fill-in flash is not needed and yet you would like to add some fill-in flash, simply hold the flash button in whilst taking the photograph. This will force the flash to fire and will be balanced as a fill-in burst. The flash level, ambient exposure and background exposure will all be reduced by one stop.

Note: If flash is required for fill-in, the flashgun symbol in the viewfinder will blink. In this case, raise the built in flash or attach an accessory flashgun.

Other flash symbols

Once the flash is charged the flash ready symbol will appear in the viewfinder to confirm this. This is represented by a single lightning bolt symbol or two lightning bolts when red-eye reduction is selected.

If exposure was sufficient the flash ready signal will blink confirming this.

Aperture Priority Mode Flash

When you wish to control depth of field with flash, set the aperture in the normal way. The camera will then set the shutter speed between 1/200 and 1/60 second depending on the ambient light level calculated using whichever metering mode is in use.

The ambient exposure is reduced by one stop by increasing the shutter speed, and, if possible, it is maintained at this level for backlit, frontlit and lowlight fill-in situations. In backlit and frontlit conditions the flash exposure is reduced 3/4 stop to ensure a natural appearance of the subject.

In dark conditions, when flash is needed to overcome the possibility of camera shake, the flash level is controlled to its normal level whilst the ambient exposure is reduced by one stop. Remember that the slowest shutter speed available is 1/60 second. Therefore, background ambient levels requiring slower shutter speeds will tend to underexpose. In this case refer to Slow Sync Flash.

Precaution:

If the aperture you set for fill-in flash is too large the shutter speed will blink. In this case select smaller apertures until the blinking stops.

If you own a 5400HS flashgun ensure the **HSS** flash symbol is shown on the flashgun's LCD panel, this will then allow the 700si to select a faster shutter speed to match the aperture setting.

Shutter Priority Mode Flash

With shutter priority, you can set any shutter speed between 1/200 and 30 seconds. The most appropriate aperture is then selected from the lens's working range depending on the lighting conditions.

In backlit conditions the subject's ambient exposure is reduced by one stop whilst the flash level is reduced by 3/4 stop. The background exposure will be increased by 1.5 stops. In frontlit situations both the flash level and ambient exposure are reduced by one stop.

This mode is best used when the ambient front or backlighting is equal to or greater than the subject's brightness. When this mode is used in low lighting conditions where the background is dark, the aperture will remain wide open until the ambient light level approaches a normal ambient light exposure level. This will provide the least amount of depth of field for the photograph. When the ambient level increases to such a level or the shutter speed is reduced low enough to produce an ambient exposure without flash, the metering system will treat the situation as a frontlit or backlit fill-in situation by reducing both the ambient and flash exposure by the amount already described above.

Precaution:

If the shutter speed you have selected is too slow, the aperture will blink. In this case set faster shutter speeds until the blinking stops.

Manual Mode Flash

Now you need to select both aperture and shutter speed (up to 1/200 second). The flash output necessary will be calculated by the 700si's metering system. It will be regulated to this level by the 700si's TTL flash metering system. The selection of the aperture and shutter speed will determine the ambient exposure, whilst the exposure compensation facility can be used to control the flash exposure.

Manual Mode Fill-in Flash

To adjust the flash output for fill-in flash follow the operation set out below.

1. Set the desired ambient exposure by observing the pointer on the metering index or the symbol in between the aperture and shutter speed display in the viewfinder. "0" is the meter's recommendation.

2. Whilst holding the exposure compensation button in, turn either input dials to control the flash level. E.g. -1 indicated in the display and on the index whilst holding the button in indicates the difference between the flash level and the ambient level. Therefore -1 indicates that the flash level will be one stop less than the ambient level.

3. When you release the compensation button the pointer will now indicate a +1 reading. This confirms that the ambient exposure will be one stop brighter than the flash exposure.

Personally I wouldn't waste my time with that operation, it is very much easier to use the flash compensation facility which has the same effect but is a lot easier and faster to set.

In Program, the flash fires automatically if the built-in flash is raised or an accessory flash is on. In A/S/M exposure modes the flash fires every time if the built-in flash is raised or an accessory flash is switched on. In all modes the built-in flash will not fire if lowered or if the accessory flash has been switched off.

Note: If you select a shutter speed greater than 1/200 second when taking flash photographs with HSS flash either unavailable or switched off, the shutter speed will automatically be reduced to 1/200 second or slower once the flash is charged or when the shutter release is pressed part way.

Slow Sync Flash

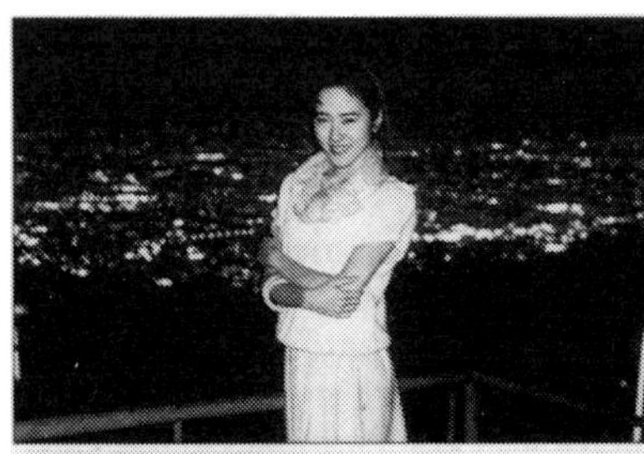

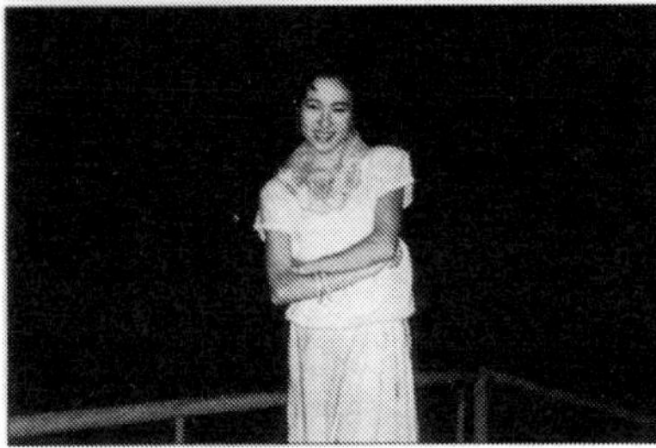

Top: With slow sync flash
Bottom: Without slow sync flash

This feature is available to use with either the built-in flash or an accessory flash. It can also be used in wireless/remote off-camera flash mode. Normally, when you photograph night scenes or subjects with very dark backgrounds, the subject will be correctly exposed by the illumination provided by the flash whilst the selection of a shutter speed to overcome camera shake, e.g. 1/60 second or faster will result in no distinguishable detail in the background.

This can also occur with macro flash photography when the shutter speed set is too fast to expose the background. In this case setting a shutter speed slow enough to allow the background to also form an image on film will overcome this problem.

The easiest method of achieving this is to use the 700si's Slow Sync Flash facility.

It is set by simply pressing the **SPOT/SLOW SYNC** button on the back of the 700si. The 700si's metering system is used to measure the background brightness. Based on this reading the 700si selects a shutter speed that will correctly expose the background. In some backlit conditions, when in aperture priority, the shutter speed may increase rather than decrease. This is because the shutter speed set for a backlit situation is set to overexpose the background by approximately 1.5 stops, whereas with slow sync flash there is no compensation made for the background. Therefore the background density should be similar to that of your subject. However, the flash output will be reduced by 3/4 stop to ensure that, due to the slower shutter speed used, the subject is not overexposed.

Precaution:

Slow Sync Flash is only recommended for use in aperture priority or program exposure modes. In shutter priority the aperture is adjusted to try and improve the background exposure and the flash output is reduced by 3/4 stop. However, if the aperture selected by the camera is already at maximum, it cannot of course be opened any further. Therefore it is best to only use Slow Sync Flash in the A and P modes.

Flash Compensation

The 700si is the first Minolta SLR to feature flash compensation. It allows you to tailor the TTL flash output to your own taste; e.g. if you photograph weddings frequently and you find for example the flash output is a little strong, flash compensation is the easiest method of adjusting the end result. The range is +/- 3 stops in half stop increments.

To set the required compensation press both the exposure compensation and manual fill-in flash buttons together. In the body LCD data panel the flash compensation symbol will be shown along with the amount of compensation set. With the buttons still pressed, turn either input dial to set the required compensation. When you release the buttons the flash compensation symbol will remain in both the

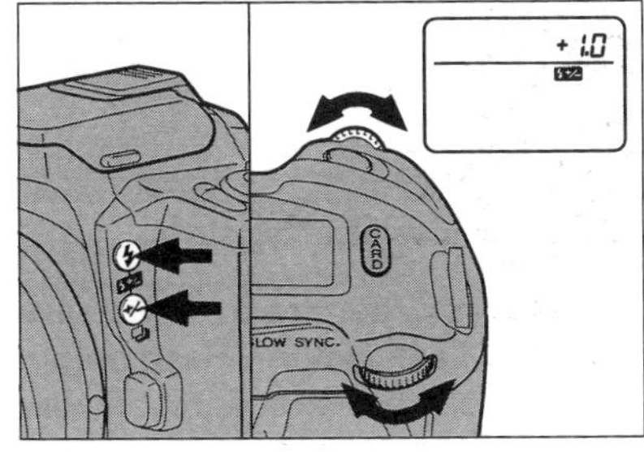

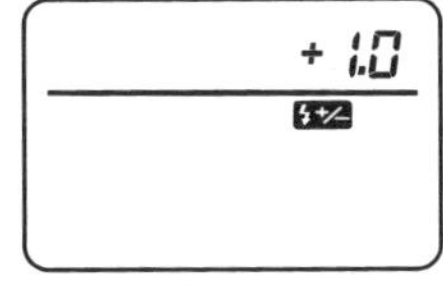

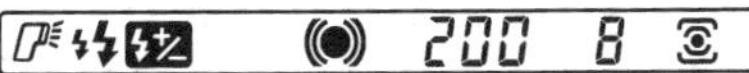

viewfinder and body LCD panels, to remind you that you have set flash compensation.

Incidentally, you can set flash compensation whilst looking through the viewfinder as the indicators are duplicated in the LCD display at the bottom of the frame. However, you will probably find that you need to know your way around all of the camera controls before being able to do this as it is a little tricky otherwise.

Remember that you can store flash compensation in the Memory, allowing you to recall the compensation factor instantly at any time.

Red-Eye

I think at this stage it is worth spending some time explaining how red-eye is caused and how it can be reduced or eliminated.

Light from a built-in flash or a separate flashgun illuminates the subject. This light is then reflected off the subject towards the film plane where the image is formed on the film. Red-eye is produced because the light from the flash enters the eye which is then reflected off the retina at the back of the eye. The retina contains red blood cells that cause the problem as the light reflected back to the camera is now red, and this is what you see on the film, a small red area in the centre of the eye.

How can we reduce or eliminate red-eye?

In dark areas the pupil, which operates in the same way as the aperture on a camera, opens and closes to control the amount of light reaching the retina. In very dark conditions the pupil is wide open and therefore more of the retina is exposed to the flash light. By reducing the size of the pupil opening we therefore reduce the area of the retina that is exposed to the flash. Although the red-eye effect may still be visible, the size of the red area will be much smaller. It is this principle that all camera red-eye reduction facilities work on.

The 700si's red-eye reduction works by firing the flash a number of times. However, it is only the first flash in the sequence that is used to reduce red-eye. The flashes between the first and final burst (the final flash being the one that is used to illuminate the subject when the shutter is open), are purely to maintain the attention of your subject.

To set red-eye reduction on the 700si, press the flash mode button inside the card door. The display will clear leaving only the feature to be changed. Now turn either of the input dials until the red-eye reduction symbol is shown. On the body LCD panel it is indicated by two lightning bolts and a small eye symbol. Once the symbol is shown, press either the same button again or part way on the shutter release to confirm the setting. You can also do this operation whilst looking through the viewfinder. Red-eye reduction is indicated by two lightning bolts. To carry out this operation whilst looking through the viewfinder you will need to know your way around the camera like the back of your hand. So I would recommend you select flash modes looking at the top display, until you are used to all of the controls.

Red-eye can also be reduced by increasing the ambient lighting level as much as possible, e.g. if shooting indoors turning all the room lights on. Using wide angle lenses and moving closer to the subject will increase the angle between flash and lens, the idea here being that when you get close enough to the subject rather than the light being reflected off the retina and straight back to the camera, the light is reflected off the retina at such an angle that it passes below the lens axis, therefore eliminating red-eye.

Therefore, the further the flash is from the lens axis, the less chance there is of red-eye occurring. A flash positioned off camera will increase the angle between flash and lens to such an extent that red-eye is unlikely to occur.

Getting the subject to look at a bright light source just before taking the picture will also help in reducing red-eye by causing the pupil to dilate, the same effect as the red-eye reduction facility of the 700si.

FLASHGUNS

There are currently five flashguns in the Dynax/Maxxum system. A fixed head type, three bounce head units and a macro ring flash.

Guide numbers

The first two numbers in the flashgun's model designation indicate the maximum guide number of that unit. Therefore:

2000xi has a guide number of	20 (in meters, 100 ISO)	
3500xi "	35	"
5400xi "	54	"
5400HS "	54	"
1200AF "	12	"

5400HS

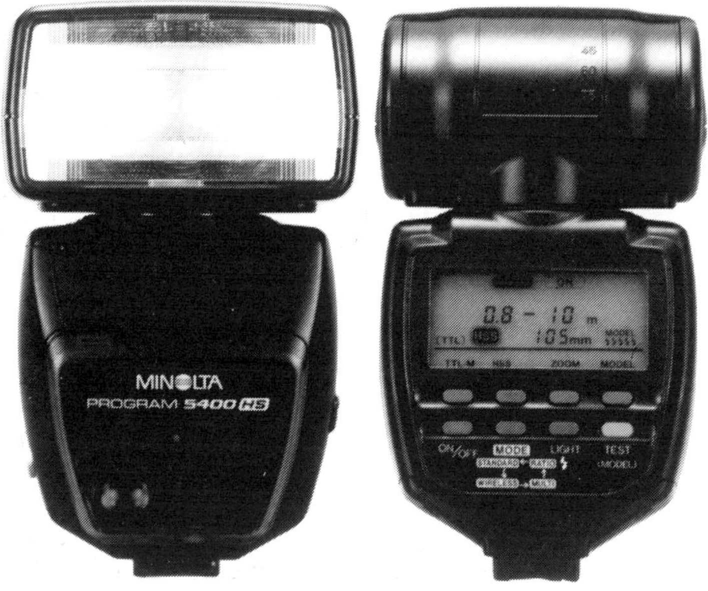

The main flash gun for use with the 700si has got to be the 5400HS. It is probably the most advanced flashgun on the market today. Its main features are as follows:

- Easy Operation
- Maximum Guide Number of 54 (in metres, 100 ISO at 105mm)
- HSS (High Speed Sync) Flash
- Wireless/Remote Off-Camera TTL Flash Control
- Modelling Light
- Multi-Burst Flash
- Auto Zoom Coverage (24 - 105mm)
- Full Bounce and Swivel Capability

Easy Operation

The 5400HS is based upon the 5400xi. If you were to remove all of the labels you would not be able to distinguish the two from one another. In addition to two extra facilities, HSS flash and a modelling light, the 5400HS offers greatly simplified operation. So easy in fact that I could run though the basic operation in just a few minutes, without the need for an instruction book, as you normally have to with an accessory as sophisticated as this.

The key to the ease of operation with the 5400HS are the four operating modes, **STANDARD**, **WIRELESS**, **MULTI** and **RATIO** and that only the relevant features to that operating mode are displayed on the LCD panel on the back of the unit.

Each mode is selected in the above sequence by pressing a single button, labelled **MODE**. There are two rows of four buttons. Working from left to right, they are, **ON/OFF**, **MODE**, **LIGHT** and **TEST (MODEL)**. The second row of button's functions depend on the current operating mode. In **MULTI** mode only three of the four buttons have functions assigned to them, and in **RATIO** only two have functions. By removing function displays that are not applicable to the current mode, operation is made much less daunting than having many buttons all of which are labelled, yet not seeming to have any function.

Standard Mode

As the name of this mode suggests this is the normal operating mode of the 5400HS. Features that are available are, **TTL-M** (Through The Lens) metering or Manual power settings (manual

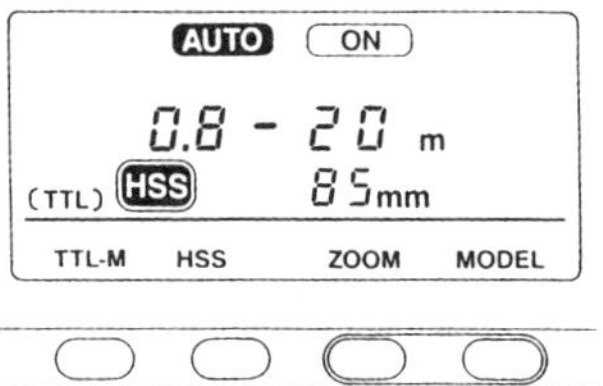

exposure mode only), **HSS** flash, **ZOOM** override and **MODEL**.

When the flash is fitted to the camera and the exposure meter is on, the display will show the current approximate flash range in meters. If you prefer to have the range indicated in feet instead of meters, move the small switch located in the battery compartment from **m** to **ft**. The range indicated takes into account the lens in use, the current aperture, and film speed as well as the lighting conditions.

When you attach the flash to the camera and you want to take advantage of flash in Program, remember to press the Program reset button on the camera to ensure that the flashgun is correctly initialized. This will not only reset the 700si's functions but also reset the flashgun to the Standard mode.

The display should now also indicate the focal length that the flash head is set to, along with the **AUTO** and **ON** symbols.

When you press the manual fill-in flash button on the 700si the **AUTO** symbol will disappear, indicating that the flash will fire every time, as long as the button is held in.

TTL-M metering

With manual exposure mode selected you can disable the TTL flash metering system by pressing the **TTL-M** button. The first press will show **M 1/1**. This confirms that TTL flash metering is switched off and that the current power setting is full power. Other power settings available are, 1/2, 1/4, 1/8, 1/16 and 1/32. The 1/16 and 1/32 power settings are especially useful when shooting high speed motor drive sequences.

The LCD display will indicate the distance that the subject should be from the camera to give correct exposure. Adjusting the power setting or aperture will alter this distance.

The main benefits of switching off the TTL metering system are, to use with manual settings whilst using a flash meter and by doing so overcoming the problem of high or low reflective subjects which could possibly fool the TTL system.

Note: When used on the low power settings, Minolta flash units can safely shoot off 40 frames at 3 FPS.

Autozoom flash head

The flash head of the 5400HS is normally adjusted automatically depending on the focal length of the lens in use. The range of focal lengths that are adjusted for are, 24 - 105mm. Whilst there is no problem using a lens whose focal length is greater than 105mm, you should not use lenses whose focal length is shorter than 24mm, otherwise vignetting may occur. With a zoom lens fitted the flash head will move automatically to match the coverage of the focal length in use.

Pressing the **ZOOM** button will allow you to override this setting, e.g. for use with a brolly (setting a narrower angle of coverage) or when shooting close-ups (setting a wider angle of coverage). With the first press **M ZOOM** will appear in the LCD panel and the flash head will move forward to the 24mm coverage setting. With each additional press you can select 28mm, 35mm, 50mm, 70mm, 85mm and 105mm settings. If you press the button once more the head will move back to its original position and return to autozoom.

Modelling Light

This is a fantastic feature for showing off your latest equipment at the local camera club meeting.

One of the biggest problems that has always been associated with flash photography are shadows. We know they are going to be there, but to what extent? Will they add to the overall effect or will they ruin it?

The 5400HS enables you to check for the size and position of any shadows that may occur in both wireless and standard flash modes. There are two modelling settings. The first is for portraits, the second for close-ups.

To select the modelling light press the **MODEL** button. The first press will select the first modelling mode (portraits), this is indicated by three lightning bolt symbols. Pressing the button again will select the second mode (close-ups), indicated by five lightning bolt symbols.

In the portrait mode the flash will fire three bursts at 2 Hz, each with a guide number of 5.6. This is ideal for portraits as the bursts are very much easier to see over a long distance.

In the second mode the flash will fire 160 bursts at 40 Hz for 4 seconds each with a guide number of 1.4. The frequency is so high in this mode that the burst will almost seem like one continuous burst of light. This makes it ideal for close-ups, allowing you to easily see the placement of the shadows. However, in dark conditions, this second mode may make it easier to check for shadows over a greater distance.

With the modelling light selected, firing the flash is achieved by pressing the **TEST** button when the flash is fitted to the hotshoe directly or through flash cables.

In wireless/remote mode the modelling light can be triggered by pressing the **SPOT** button on the back of the 700si.

Notes:

1. If the flash is not fully charged the bursts may be erratic.

2. With the flash attached to the camera the shutter will lock whilst the bursts are firing.

3. In Wireless/Remote Off-Camera mode do not release the shutter until the bursts have finished and the flash is charged.

4. Due to the fact that the output of the bursts is fixed they only serve to show the size and placement of the shadows and not the scene contrast, the relative brightness of two or more flash units, or the flash ambient ratio.

5. In the wired off-camera mode, the modelling light cannot be used because the photographer would have to press the **TEST** button on each unit simultaneously.

HSS High Speed Sync Flash

At the beginning of this section I mentioned that one of the biggest limitations of flash photography is the fastest sync speed that we can use.

All shutter units in 35mm AF SLR's have two curtains. A conventional shutter works by a number of blades moving across the film plane at very high speed, opening up the light path to the film. This first set of blades are referred to as the first curtain. The second set of blades, known as the second curtain then move across, closing the light path to the film. The shutter speed is the time between the first curtain starting and the second curtain starting.

Up to and including 1/200 second, the second curtain of the 700si's shutter starts to move after the first curtain has moved across the film plane exposing the entire area of film to the light. Above this speed the second curtain starts moving before the first curtain has stopped. Therefore the film is never completely uncovered at anyone time. Effectively the first and second curtains form a slit that moves across the film exposing it to the light entering the camera. The faster the shutter speed the smaller the slit. By the time the slit has moved across the entire film area the film has been evenly exposed, as not one area of the film is left uncovered for more or less time than any other area of film.

When taking flash photographs the flash is triggered when the first curtain stops and stops firing before the second curtain starts to move. This ensures that the entire area of film is evenly exposed.

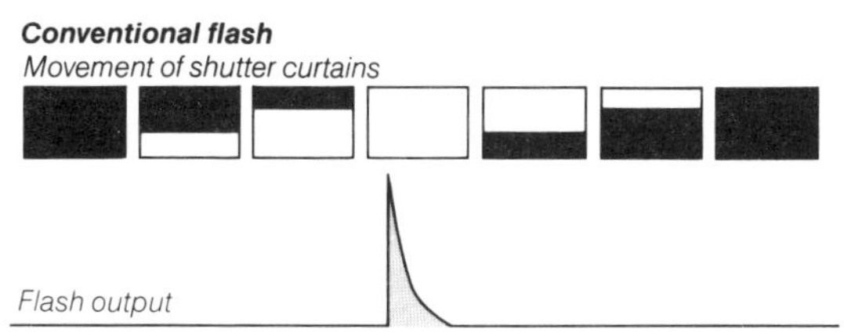

If however the second curtain starts moving before the flash has finished firing this will result in one area of the photograph not being evenly exposed.

This is where HSS flash comes in.

To overcome the above mentioned problem the flash fires an extremely high frequency flash burst. This burst starts prior to the first curtain moving and stops once the second curtain has stopped. Although not a constant light source, the frequency is so

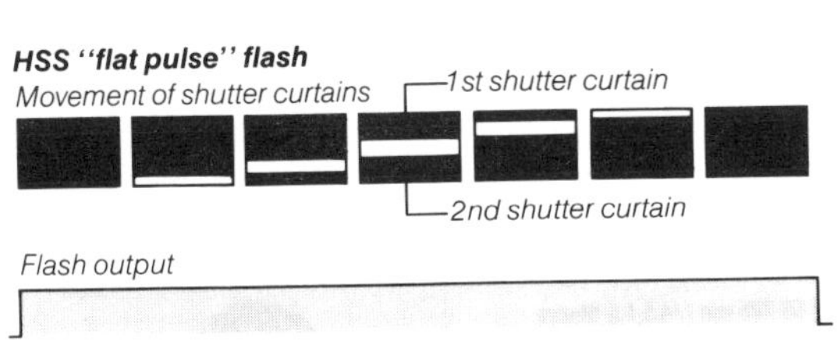

high (50,000Hz) that it can be used as such. Therefore, even at 1/8000 second, the film is evenly exposed.

As previously mentioned, the shutter speed normally has very little if any effect on the exposure. It is the aperture that affects exposure with flash photography. With HSS flash, because the output of the flash is constant throughout the duration of the exposure, (just like ambient light) the shutter speed now has an equal effect on exposure. Therefore as you increase the shutter speed the flash range decreases.

With conventional TTL flash the exposure is controlled by the duration of the flash being controlled during the exposure. With HSS flash, the flash output has to be set prior to the shutter opening as the duration is based upon the shutter speed, as proved in the above section.

So how do we get accurate exposure?

This is the beauty of Minolta's HSS system.Other manufacturers have had a facility similar to what has already been described above for a while, but all the settings and calculations have to be made manually, whereas using the Minolta HSS system everything is automatic. In fact in program you may not even notice that the feature is being used.

This is how it works, firstly in Program

Firstly the camera meters the scene and determines what shutter speed and aperture are most appropriate, and whether to use flash or not. If flash is required and the shutter speed needed to ensure correct exposure is higher than 1/200 second then HSS flash is automatically selected by the 700si.

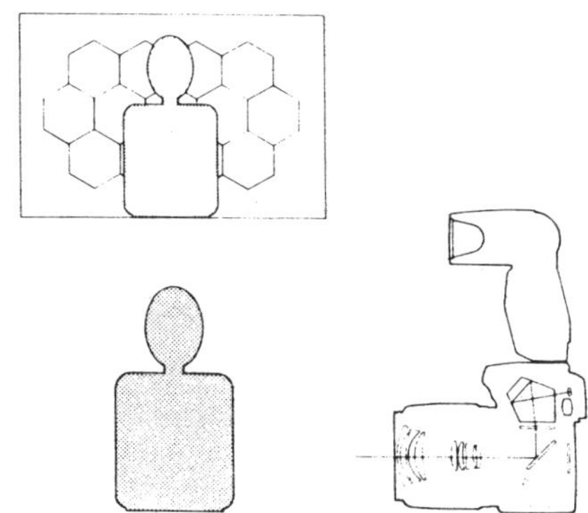

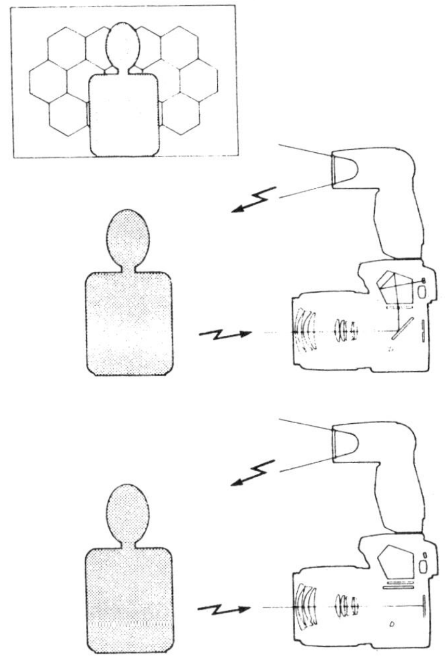

When the shutter release is pressed fully the flash fires a burst of light prior to swinging the mirror up. The 700si is then able to calculate, from the light reflected back off the subject, using the honeycomb metering system, the power of the burst needed by the 5400HS flash unit during the exposure.

The flash then fires and stabilises just before the first curtain starts moving. Once the second curtain stops, the flash also stops.

Aperture Priority HSS flash

If the aperture you have selected requires a shutter speed faster than 1/200 second, the 700si will select the necessary shutter speed and make use of the HSS facility (as long as it is available).

Shutter Priority/Manual HSS flash

With HSS available you can select any shutter speed between 1/8000 and 30 seconds.

Limitations of HSS flash

The biggest limitation is the flash range, which varies from 0.2 to 0.7 of the conventional output due to reasons already explained. Therefore, the use of large aperture lenses and fast film speeds is recommended.

In Program, HSS flash may not be selected if shooting under

florescent lighting. This is due to the peaks and troughs in the fluorescent light waveform causing interference.

Flash meters will not be able to give a correct reading. Ratio control cannot be used.

HSS flash will not function when the flash head is tilted or swivelled, this is because the output in HSS mode is unlikely to be powerful enough.

Why use HSS flash?

For several reasons. Mainly for fill-in flash photography, where the background is extremely bright. Using conventional shutter speeds for fill-in flash will lead to an overexposed background, with the result being loss of detail.

It also allows us to use large aperture lenses and therefore allows greater depth of field control for portraits. With conventional flash, the aperture may be quite small to ensure that the subject is not over exposed, which will then of course increase the depth of field.

Also, when we want to photograph action with fill-in flash, using a faster shutter speed will ensure that if the subject moves there will be no subject blur in the final result.

If you do not want HSS flash to be used and wish to rely purely on the full shutter opening sync speeds, press the **HSS** button, the **HSS** symbol will disappear from the display, confirming that this feature is no longer available.

Note: If HSS flash is in use, the flashgun symbol will appear along with a small H next to it, in both the viewfinder and body data panels to confirm this.

Pressing the Program reset button will not reset HSS flash mode.

When in manual exposure mode, with a shutter speed set faster than 1/200 second and the TTL metering disabled, the HSS pre-flashes will not occur as they are not needed.

Wireless/Remote Off-Camera TTL Flash Control

One of the many world's first features on the Dynax/Maxxum 7xi, launched in 1991, was wireless/remote off-camera TTL flash. I remember the day when I was first shown this feature working. I could not stop smirking all the way home.

Before this feature was introduced, if you wanted to take the flash off-camera, you would need to buy expensive flash cables that retained the capabilities of the TTL flash control system. The main restriction was not the price but the inconvenience of tripping over the cables and the limitations of the distance the flash could be removed from the camera. This feature solves all of the problems associated with the cable system.

To be able to make use of this feature you must have any of the following flash units:

     5400HS
     5400xi
     3500xi

This is how it works

The built-in flash sends signals to off-camera flash units controlling the time duration that they fire for.

When the shutter release is pressed all the way, the built-in flash fires two flash bursts. The time interval between them identifies which channel setting the camera is operating on. If the flash units are on the same channel they will be readied by this.

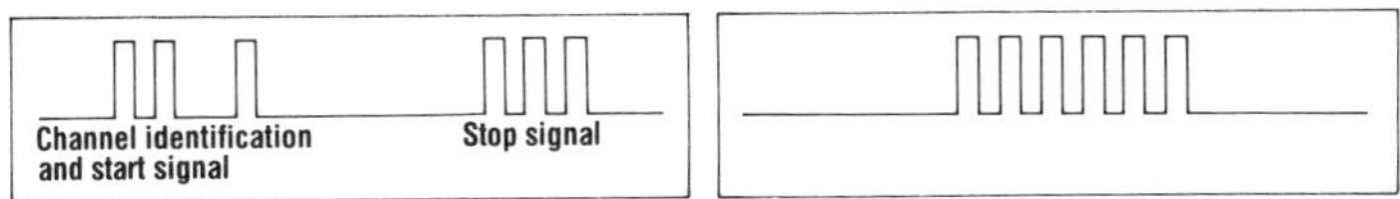

Flash output of control unit   ***Flash output of off-camera unit***

The camera then fires a third burst just as the shutter opens. This causes the off-camera units to start firing individual bursts. The bursts start at a guide number of 1.4 (in meters) and quickly increase to a guide number of 5.6. Once the flash has reached this output it will continue firing until the stop signal from the built-in flash is received, during which time the 700si's TTL flash metering system is continuously measuring the accumulative exposure. Once the correct amount of illumination has been received by the film the built-in flash fires three further bursts to stop the flash firing.

Exposure will be confirmed in the normal way in the viewfinder and on the LCD panel on the back of the 5400HS/xi flash units.

The control bursts emitted by the built-in flash are so weak in output that they will have no effect on the overall exposure, red-eye is also unlikely to occur because of this.

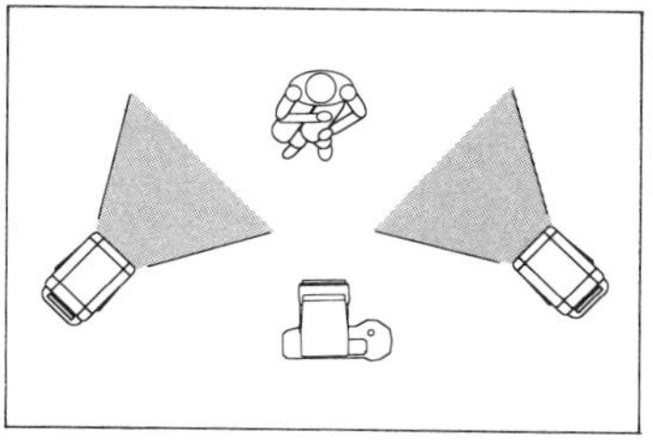

The off-camera units do not respond to visible light but to the infra-red part of the light spectrum which leaves the built-in flash. Although the control signals are infra-red their effective range is affected by the ambient light level, therefore reducing the ambient lighting level to as low a level as possible/practical.

How to set wireless/remote flash

The easiest method, is to firstly attach the flash to the camera. With the flash switched on, press the flash mode button inside the card door. Now turn either of the input dials until two alternating lightning bolt symbols appear in the display. You will notice that the wireless indication will appear on the back of the flash unit. Confirmation of the flash mode in use will also be shown in the viewfinder. Remove the flash from the camera and set it up in the required position. The AF-illuminator on the front of the flash will blink indicating that it is charged and in wireless/remote flash mode.

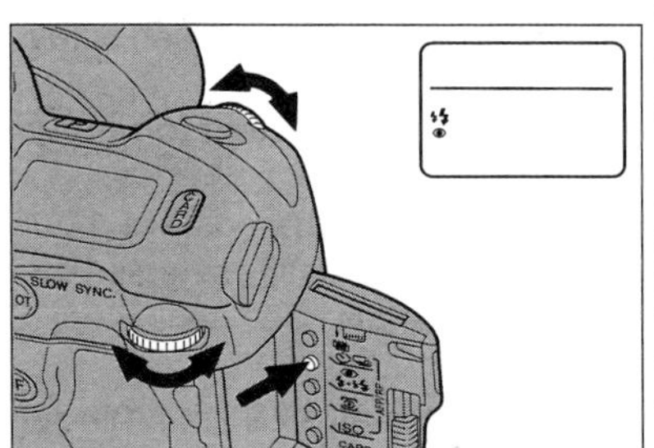

When the flash is removed from the hotshoe, the flash head will automatically zoom to its widest setting (24mm). This ensures that the flash should cover the scene or subject. Pressing the **ZOOM** button allows you to override this setting if you wish. For example, if you want to create a special effect by illuminating a small area of the scene only, set the flash head to the 105mm setting. You may also wish to set the zoom manually if firing the flash into a brolly or reflector.

Within Range Test Facility

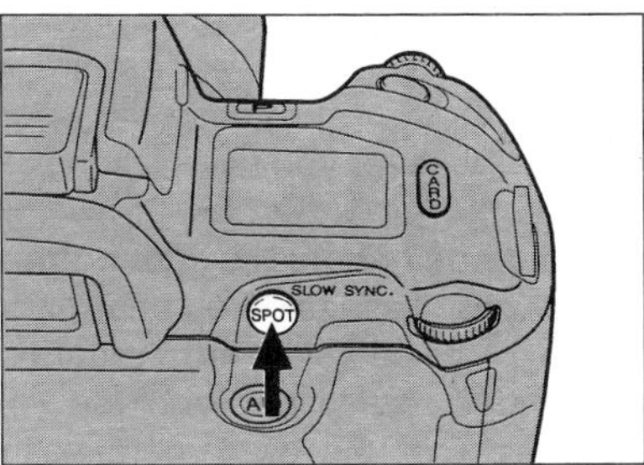

Before you take any photographs it is possible to check if the flash is within the control range or not. This is done simply by pressing the **SPOT** button on the 700si.

The built-in flash will fire a small test burst, the off-camera flash units should respond by also firing a small burst. If not, they are out of the system's control range. In this case move the flashguns closer to the camera and perform the operation again. You may also find that rotating the main body of the flash so that the AF-illuminator is pointing towards the camera may make the system more effective in this case.

As a guide, the flash to subject range is approximately 5m and the approximate camera to subject distance is also 5m. However, the lower the ambient light level, the greater the camera to flash range.

The system works equally well outside, although the control range may diminish of course, due to the high ambient light level. This allows the system to be used for close-up photography.

The flash units should still operate, even behind the subject. Ensure you check whether the units are within the control range by using the test burst facility.

If the modelling light is selected on the 5400HS, pressing the **SPOT** button will trigger the modelling light facility.

If you continue to keep the **SPOT** button pressed whilst releasing the shutter, SLOW SYNC flash will operate.

Mounting the flash in wireless/remote mode

The easiest method of mounting the flash unit is to use the supplied **MS-2 Mini Stand**. This allows the flash to be positioned on any flat surface. In addition, it features a standard tripod bush, allowing it to be mounted on a tripod, flash stand or bracket.

Wireless/Remote Ratio Control

As previously explained, the built-in flash will have very little, if any, effect on the overall exposure. If, however, you would like to light the subject from the camera as well as the off-camera unit(s), you can select a 2:1 lighting ratio. This will boost the power of the built-in flash to provide one third of the total exposure, whilst the off-camera unit(s) will provide, as a total, the remaining two thirds.

This is achieved simply by pressing and holding the manual fill-in flash button whilst taking the photograph.

Channel Settings

If you are using the wireless/remote flash system in the same environment as another user who is also using the same system, you can set your flashguns to operate only with your camera by selecting a new channel setting. The flashguns are set to operate on channel one from the factory.

To change the operating channel

Inside the battery compartment of the 5400HS flash gun are three switches, one of which as previously mentioned is for changing the flash range indication readout from metres to feet. The two 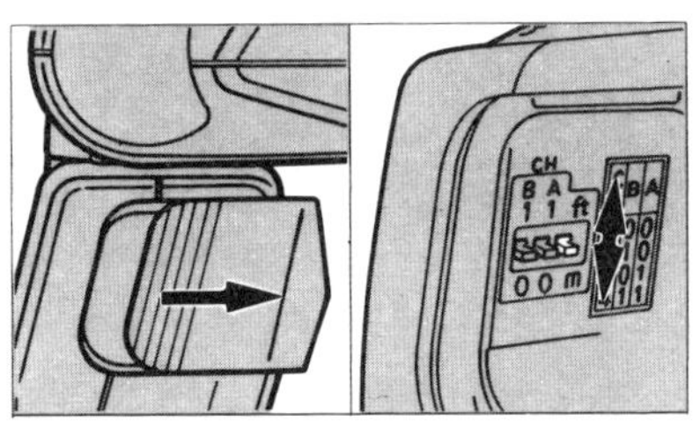 other switches are for changing the channel setting. The two switches are labelled **B** and **A**. Each switch has two settings, labelled **1** and **0**. the position of each switch determines the channel setting that the flash is operating on.

There are four channel settings in total. The switch position for each channel is as follows:

Channel	Switch B	Switch A
1	0	0
2	1	0
3	0	1
4	1	1

Note: Once the channel setting has been changed the flash unit must be attached to the 700si's hotshoe and wireless/remote flash selected again on the camera. If you own a number of units ensure that you set each flash unit to the same channel setting. On the back of the 5400HS the display will confirm the channel setting by displaying **CH** - and then the channel setting.

Pressing and holding the **OPT** (option) button for approximately four seconds selects **WIRELESS CONTROL** mode. This allows the 5400HS to be mounted on the 700si and used as the control unit, in place of the built-in flash. The flash head will be fixed at 24mm coverage to ensure even illumination and to improve the reliability of the control signals.

Press the **OPT** button again, the display will now indicate **WIRELESS CONTROL RATIO 2:(1)**. This is the same as pressing the manual fill-in flash button whilst releasing the shutter when using the built-in flash as the control unit. The brackets around the 1 confirm that this flash unit will provide one third of the exposure whilst the off-camera units provide the remaining two thirds.

Pressing the **OPT** button again will now display **WIRELESS RATIO (2):1**. This feature is purely for use with the **Wireless Flash Controller**. Pressing the **OPT** button once again moves the brackets to the 1.

If the brackets are shown around the 2 this flash will contribute/provide two thirds of the overall exposure. If the brackets are shown around the 1, this flash will now contribute/provide one third of the overall exposure.

Pressing the **OPT** button again sets the flash to normal off-camera mode.

Note: The maximum sync speed useable in wireless/remote flash mode is 1/60 second.

Wireless/Remote Off-Camera Flash using the Wireless/Remote Flash Controller

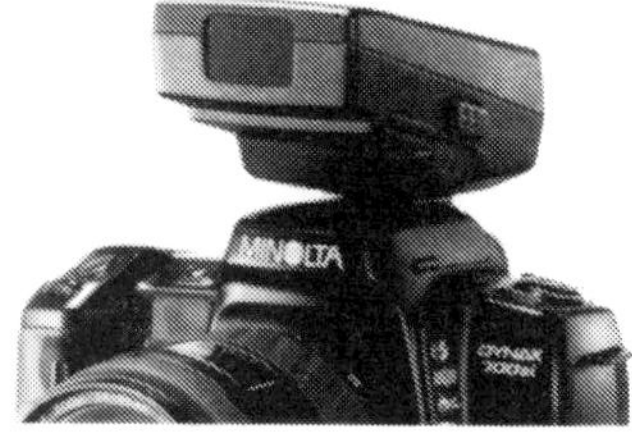

This accessory was originally introduced for use with the Dynax/Maxxum 9xi, as this model has no built-in flash to provide the control signals. It works purely on infra-red signals. This leads to a number of benefits.

1. No reflections from shiny surfaces caused by direct light from the camera position.

2. All illumination provided by the off-camera units only.

3. Red-eye virtually eliminated.

4. Off-Camera Ratio Control.

The fourth benefit listed above is the most interesting. I remember being at a meeting long before this accessory was introduced and being told about this feature. To say I was impressed would be an understatement.

Basically, it allows, say, two flashguns to be used off camera, but controlled independently to one another, resulting in one flash providing two thirds of the overall exposure and the other unit providing the remaining one third.

This is how it's done:

The Wireless/Remote Controller first fires two bursts to identify the channel setting to the off-camera units. If they are set to the same channel setting they will ready themselves for the start signal. The third signal starts the flash set to (2):1 firing. Once the 700si's TTL flash metering system detects that the film has received two thirds of the total exposure required, the Controller fires a fourth signal stopping this unit. Eleven milliseconds after the initial start signal, the flash set to 2:(1) starts firing. Once the 700si detects that the remainder of the exposure has been supplied, a second stop signal is fired by the controller to stop it firing. Now, that is clever!

How to set Wireless/Remote Off-camera Ratio

First attach the wireless/remote controller to the 700si's accessory shoe. Repeatedly press the **ON/OFF** button on the controller until a light appears against **RATIO**.

Turn each flashgun on and select wireless mode.

Hold the **OPT** button for approximately four seconds until the display changes. Press the **OPT** button twice. The display panel should indicate **WIRELESS CH** - (channel setting in use), **RATIO (2):1**. This indicates that this flash will provide two thirds of the exposure.

With the second flashgun, in addition to the above operation, press the **OPT** button again so the brackets are displayed around the 1 rather than the 2. This confirms that this flashgun will provide the remaining third of the exposure.

When you fire a test burst the unit/s set to **(2):1** will fire first, followed by the unit/s set to **2:(1)**.

Ensure that the Wireless/Remote Controller is set to the same channel as the flashguns.

Note: Maximum sync speed in off-camera ratio mode is 1/30 second.

Cancelling wireless/remote flash

IMPORTANT

After using the wireless/remote controller in the RATIO mode, ensure that you select **WIRELESS** on the back of the controller, press part way down on the shutter release and then remove the controller, otherwise you will be limited to 1/30 second flash sync for normal wireless/remote operation.

Pushing the built-in flash down will only temporarily cancel wireless/remote flash until the flash is raised again. This is worth remembering should you wish to take some ambient only shots and then return to wireless/remote flash later.

Otherwise, to permanently cancel wireless flash, press the flash mode button inside the card door and then turn either input dial to select any other flash mode.

Cancel wireless/remote flash mode by simply pressing the **MODE** button repeatedly until you return to the **STANDARD** mode.

Auto power off

In all modes, except for wireless/remote flash, the 5400HS will switch off after 4 minutes and enter a standby mode. As soon as the shutter release is pressed part way down the flash will come back on, instantly. The capacitor holds its full charge for some time, so, even if you haven't used the camera for some time, the flash will be ready to fire the instant you press the shutter release.

If you switch the 700si off and let the flash turn itself off, the flash will come back on the instant you switch the camera back on.

In wireless/remote flash mode the flash will not switch off automatically until one hour after the last operation. This ensures that if you leave the system for a while to make an adjustment, you will not have to switch each unit back on again.

What makes it all possible?

Something called the IGBT (Insulated Gate Bipolar Transistor) system. It was first introduced by Minolta in 1988 and has been progressively developed to allow HSS, 100Hz Multi burst flash and Wireless/Remote flash control possible. When compared with conventional thyristor circuitry designs, the IGBT allows faster switching speeds for more precise TTL flash control and the above mentioned features. In addition, it uses 30% fewer parts which allows the units to be smaller, lighter and more reliable.

Multi flash mode (strobe flash)

There is no automation to this mode whatsoever, so those of you who do not like manual operation, skip to the next section. Only joking, it's not that difficult. This mode makes it possible to photograph motion studies by firing a number of flashes at a high frequency on a single frame.

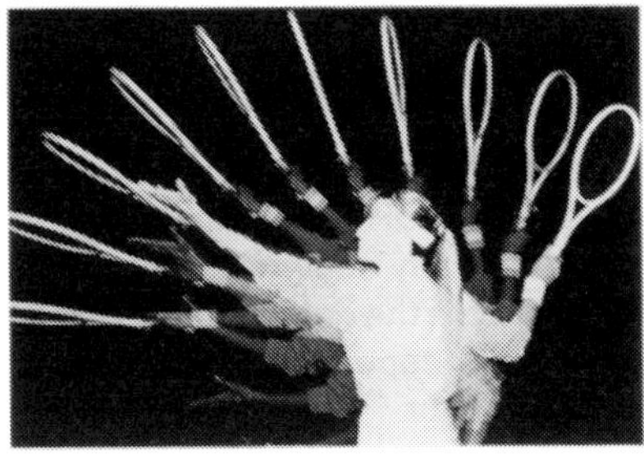

How to set Multi flash

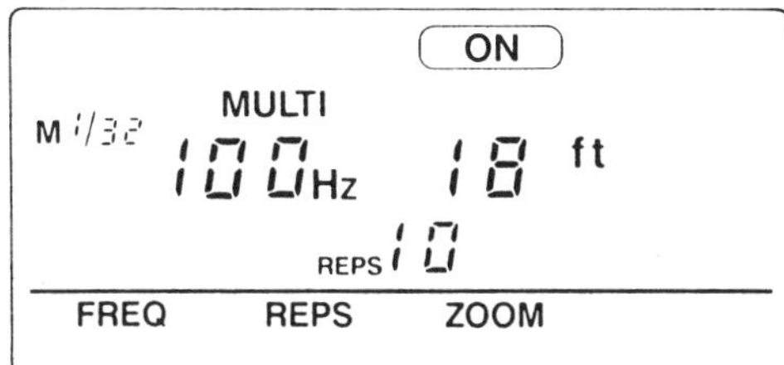

Firstly you must set the 700si to manual exposure mode, otherwise you will not be able to set multi flash.

Turn the flash on and select **MULTI** mode by pressing the **MODE** button repeatedly.

The number of flashes (**REPS**, short for repetitions) that you wish to fire depends on the composition you wish to have, or the number of images on the frame you wish there to be. The number of flashes than can be selected are 10, 7, 5, 4, 3, 2, --. The -- symbol indicates that the flash will continue firing until the capacitor is discharged or the shutter closes, whichever is sooner. Set the number of flashes by repeatedly pressing the **REPS** button until the desired number is reached.

The frequency (**FREQ**) of the flashes depends on the time that you either want the shutter to be open or the time it will take your subject to perform the operation being photographed. The frequencies that can be selected from are, 100Hz, 50Hz, 30Hz, 10Hz, 5Hz, 3Hz, 2Hz, 1Hz. 50 and 100Hz are beyond the frequency of the human eye, and so I doubt if you will be able to count them or check the number of flashes that are fired!? Press the **FREQ** button repeatedly until the required frequency is shown.

Hz stands for Hertz which means cycles per second, therefore 1Hz = 1 cycle (flash) per second.

Focus on the subject and read off the distance scale on the lens the subject distance, make a mental note of this.

Press part way down on the shutter release to activate the 700si's exposure meter.

Adjust the aperture until the distance on the flashgun's LCD panel equals the subject distance.

Set a shutter speed that is longer than the time it will take for the sequence to be completed. This can be calculated using the following formula:

reps/freq < time.

e.g.10 reps/50Hz = 1/5 second

Therefore the shutter speed set will be 1/4 second.

If the shutter speed needed could cause possible camera shake, mount the camera on a tripod.

Take the picture.

Note: The distance indicated on the flash is the distance at which a single burst of the sequence will correctly expose the subject. Therefore, areas of the image which overlap during the sequence, may be overexposed.

The output is fixed at 1/32 power level.

Ratio Mode

Pressing the **MODE** button again selects the final mode available, **RATIO** mode.

This feature is mainly for previous Minolta SLRs which do not feature the wireless/remote flash system but use the cable system to retain full dedication and TTL flash.

In this mode the flash can either be attached to the 700si's hotshoe or connected using one of the cables such as the cable OC-1100.

I am not going to spend too much time going through the use of all the cables and the many different combinations, because of the already mentioned easier to use and cheaper wireless/remote flash system. If you already own these cables from previous Minolta systems I take it that you already have an understanding of how they function. However, here are just a few reminders.

All cables are coiled and 1 metre in length when uncoiled.

Cable OC-1100   This attaches to the camera's hotshoe and plugs directly into the terminal on the side of the 5200i/5400xi/5400HS.

Cable EX   Acts as a 1 metre extension. It is also used to connect flash units to the TC-1000.

Cable CD   This is used to bridge two terminals, e.g. two flash units together.

TC-1000   Allows up to three units via Cable EX to be connected to a master unit or the hotshoe of the camera.

OS-1100   This is used to provide a terminal to allow the cables to be connected to the flash units.

FS-1100   Allows pre-Dynax/Maxxum flash units to be used on Dynax/Maxxum bodies.

FS-1200   Allows Dynax/Maxxum flash units to be used on pre-Dynax/Maxxum bodies.

The maximum number of cables that can be used in one system is six.

With ratio selected and one flash connected to the 5400HS it allows you to select two thirds of illumination from one unit and the remaining third from the other unit.

To select the desired ratio, press the **RATIO** button. With the brackets shown round the 2, the 5400HS will provide the two thirds contribution. With the brackets round the 1, the 5400HS will provide the one third contribution.

The only other feature that can be changed in this mode is the zoom head position.

Note: The fastest sync speed available is 1/60 in ratio mode.

Bounce/Swivel Head

The flash head can be tilted 90° vertically with click stops at 45°, 60°, 75° and 90°. It can also be rotated 90° clockwise with click stops at 30°, 45°, 60°, 75° and 90° and rotated counterclockwise through 180° with click stops at 30°, 45°, 60°, 75°, 90°, 120°, 150° and 180°.

Bounce flash softens and gives more natural lighting effects than with direct flash. Because the light is indirect, it also eliminates red-eye.

The flash head can be rotated to allow bouncing the flash off a wall or when using the camera vertically.

To achieve optimum results, the reflector surface that is used to bounce the flash should be of a light tone and matte. An ideal portable solution to a 'perfect' white is the range of LUMIQUEST flash accessories to control and soften the light from the flash. A shiny surface will produce harsh shadows that bounce flash is generally used to prevent. When using colour film, ensure that the surface is of a neutral colour, preferably white or light grey. Otherwise the light reflected off this surface will have the same colour. E.g. if the surface is blue, in the final result there will be a blue cast to the scene.

When bouncing the flash, the angle of the flash head should be set so that the subject does not receive any direct illumination. To prevent direct illumination, set the flash head angle at a minimum angle as indicated in the table below.

Focal length	Vertical angle
Greater than 70mm	45°
28-70mm	60°
24-28mm	75° or 90°

With the flash head rotated rather than tilted, you should set the angle to at least 90° from the direct position to ensure no direct illumination falling on your subject.

AF-Illuminator

Refer to the section under the same title in the autofocus section.

5400xi

The 5400xi has the same specification as the 5400HS except for the HSS flash and the modelling light facility. Operation is slightly different. Rather than having four modes, the 5400xi has two main menus. In each menu there are four functions that can be changed. The first menu displays **TTL-M**, **ZOOM**, **LEVEL** and **WIRELESS**. The second menu displays **MULTI**, **FREQ**, **REPS** and **RATIO**.

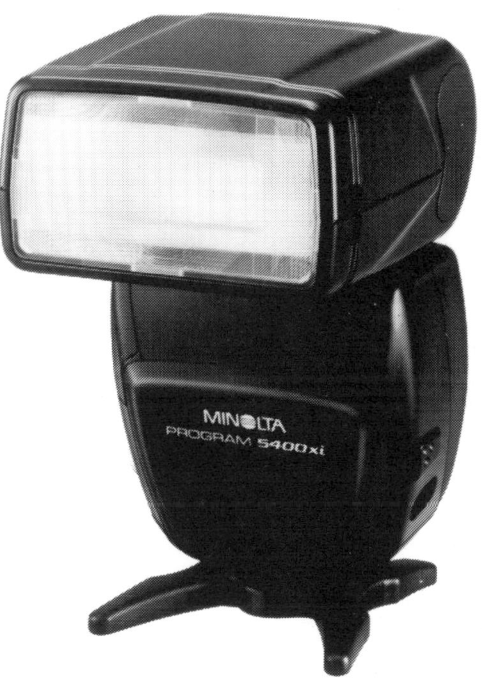

With the exception of **WIRELESS** and **MULTI**, simply pressing the button repeatedly sequences through the available settings relevant to that function.

The first press of either the **WIRELESS** or **MULTI** buttons selects that mode of operation.

Once the **WIRELESS** button has been pressed once, the display will show **W.L - F.1** (channel setting). This indicates that this flash is set to function as an off-camera flash unit and is set to channel one. Pressing and holding the **WIRELESS** button will now change the display to **W.L. - C.1**. This indicates that the flash is now set to act as a control unit, for use on the camera hot shoe, instead of the built-in flash. Pressing the **WIRELESS** button again will now select wireless/remote off-camera ratio control. In addition to the previous display, **RATIO 2:(1)** will be shown. This confirms that rather than just being used for the control signals, the 5400xi will now provide one third of the exposure whilst the off-camera units will provide the remaining two thirds.

Pressing the **WIRELESS** button again will change the display to show **W.L. - F.1** and **RATIO (2):1.** This indicates that the flash is now set to operate as an off-camera unit and provide two thirds of the overall exposure. Pressing the button again will change the ratio to one third of the overall exposure. This is indicated by **RATIO 2:(1)**.

To return to normal wireless/remote flash, press the button again.

Multi flash operation

Pressing the **MULTI** button will select the multi-flash mode. The operation is now exactly the same as that mentioned in the description of the 5400HS using the **FREQ** and **REPS** buttons.

3500xi

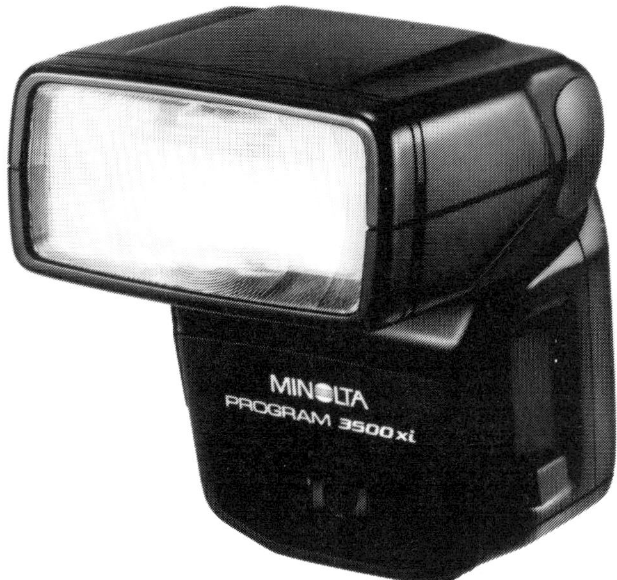

The main features of this unit are:

- Guide Number of 35 (in metres at 100 ISO)
- Autozoom flash head (28-105mm coverage)
- Wireless/Remote off-camera flash control
- Bounce flash head
- Easy operation

This flashgun is ideal for use in low light and fill-in flash situations. It also features the wireless/remote flash system.

To set wireless operation

Attach the flash to the 700si and select the wireless/remote flash mode using the flash mode button in the card door.

Remove the flash and attach it to the supplied **MS-2** stand for easier positioning. Check if it is within range by pressing the **SPOT** button.

If you have more than one unit you may find it easier to select the wireless/remote flash mode on each individual unit without having to attach each unit to the camera to set this mode. To do this, press the **ON/OFF** button, repeatedly if necessary, until a confirmation light is lit next to **OFF**. Press and hold the **ON/OFF** button until the **WIRELESS** indication is lit.

Using the 3500xi with other off-camera units in ratio mode

If the Wireless/Remote flash controller is being used in the **RATIO** mode, any 3500xi will provide the two thirds contribution as you cannot select **RATIO** mode on these units. The 5400xi/5400HS must then be set to **2:(1)** to ensure that they then provide the remaining third.

LO power setting

The 3500xi has a **LO** power setting. This should be set when using flash in high-speed motordrive sequences. It cannot be selected in Program.

Channel Settings

The 3500xi has only two channel settings unlike the 5400 guns which have four. The switch is clearly labelled inside the battery compartment.

Remember to attach the flash to the 700si and to re-select wireless/remote flash mode after changing the channel or removing the batteries.

Manual Zoom Operation

The flash head is normally adjusted automatically to suit the lens focal length in use. In wireless/remote flash mode the head is automatically set to 28mm (its widest setting). Pressing the far right button will allow you to select one of three manual settings, 28mm, 50mm and 105mm.

Faster Recycling

Minolta flash units feature two capacitors which are used to store the flash charge. Once the subject has been focused the 700si calculates the guide number required for correct exposure using subject distance information from the lens, film speed and the aperture setting. Once the charge is sufficient for correct exposure, charging stops and the flash ready signal appears in the viewfinder and on the flashgun's rear panel. This allows recycling in approximately half the time of conventional flash units.

2000xi

This small unit has a guide number of 20 (in meters at 100 ISO). It is suitable for lens focal lengths as wide as 28mm (when used with the wide-angle adaptor). If you do not take many photographs with flash, but you would like something small and a little more powerful than the built-in unit then this is ideal.

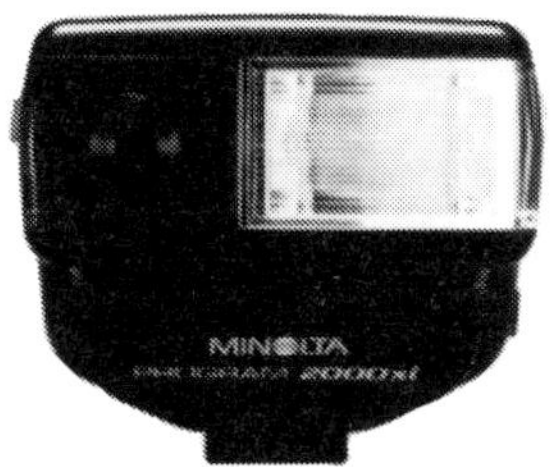

AF-Illuminator

All Minolta flash units feature an AF-illuminator, and with the exception of the 2000xi (which is a single beam), are three beam illuminators. This ensures that they cover the camera's entire focusing area, whereas the 700si's illuminator only covers the central AF sensor.

Low Battery Power

When the battery power drops to a very low level you may find that the flash operation is intermittent. This is not a fault but a further indication that the batteries need replacing immediately.

1200AF Macro Flash

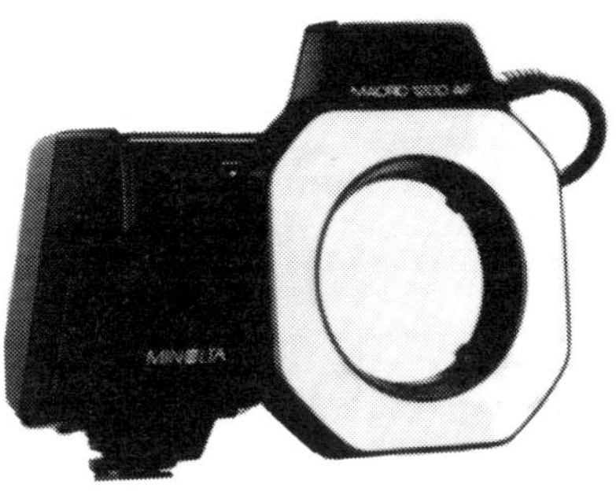

Although the 1200AF macro flash can be used for normal flash photography, its primary function is of course for extreme close-up work. It is comprised of two units, a flash head with four flash tubes which form a ring around the lens, and a control unit which is attached to the 700si's hotshoe using the supplied FS-1100 adaptor. The two units are connected by a cord that is permanently attached to the flash head but plugs into the control unit.

Attaching the flash head

The set is supplied with two adaptor rings, 49mm and 55mm. These are screwed into the filter thread of the lens. The flash head has two spring loaded lugs which locate in a groove on the outside of this ring.

Note: The 3x-1x zoom macro lens has this grooved ring built-in.

Each individual flash tube can be switched on or off at will and in any combination depending on the desired effect. This is simply controlled by the position of four switches on the back of the flash head.

In each of the four corners of the flash head is a lamp which comes on (if required), when the exposure meter is on. These lamps illuminate the subject to provide sufficient light for the AF system to function and also to allow you to see the subject. When shooting at very close distances, it becomes very difficult to see the subject due to the light being obstructed by both you and the camera. They are switched off automatically prior to the shutter opening.

The benefits of using the macro flash are, that it allows you to hand hold the camera, although this is not ideal for very high magnifications, and allows you to counteract the problem of extremely shallow depth of field by using very small apertures.

FLASH ACCESSORIES

External Battery Pack EP-1

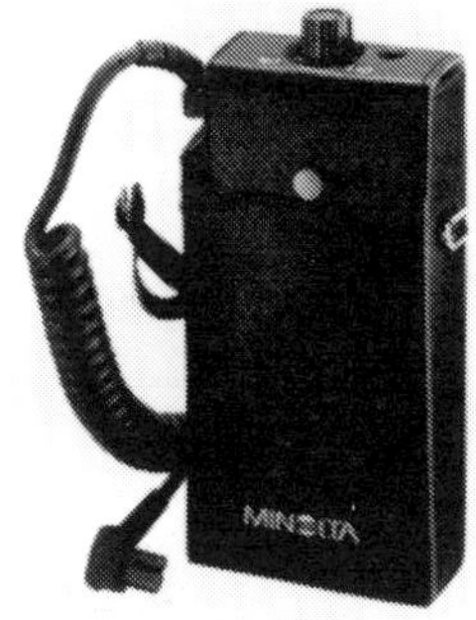

This is for use exclusively with the 5400xi/HS flashguns. The EP-1 houses 6 C-size batteries, either Alkaline or Rechargeable. By converting this into the equivalent of 330 volts, very fast recycling times in addition to a greater number of flashes are made possible.

The set is supplied with a case, which allows attachment to a belt, and a connecting cord, between the pack itself and the side of the flashgun.

Below is a table of the recycling times when the flash is set to full power.

Battery Type 5400xi/HS	EP-1	Flashes	Recycling Time (seconds)
Alkaline	Alkaline	600	4
Alkaline	Ni-Cd	300	3
Ni-Cd	Ni-Cd	250	3

Note: In cold temperatures the use of Ni-Cd batteries is recommended. If alkaline batteries are used in the EP-1, the flash must also be fitted with alkaline batteries.

Once the flash is charged the EP-1 turns itself off automatically.

Bounce Reflector Set III (5400xi/HS) / IV (3500xi)

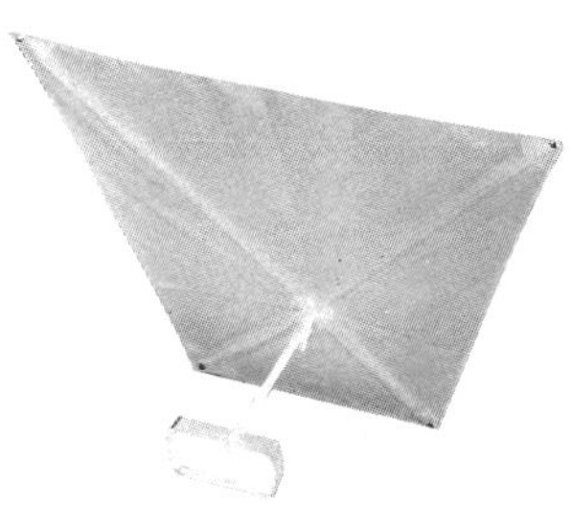

This collapsible, lightweight reflector attaches to the flash head via an adaptor. It allows soft, natural bounce lighting anywhere - even out doors. The white reflective surface ensures that the colour rendition is unaffected. It is ideal for those situations where a bounce surface is not available or if the colour of the bounce surface could cause a colour cast.

Although the effective flash range is reduced, the 700si's TTL flash metering system will ensure that correct exposure is maintained.

As a guide, multiply the normal flash range by 0.6 to determine the actual flash range.

The bounce reflector is identical in Set III and Set IV. The difference lies in the adaptors, which are available separately. This allows you to use the reflector on different Minolta bounce flash units, by simply using a new adaptor.

Close-up Diffuser CD-1000

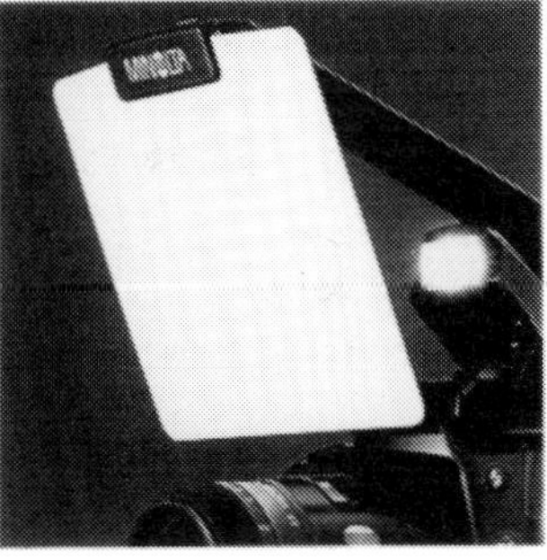

This new accessory is specifically for Minolta Dynax/Maxxum cameras which have a built-in flash. It allows you to use the built-in flash for subjects closer than 1 meter, where the built-in flash on its own could cause overexposure. Not only does it reduce the output of the flash by acting as a diffuser, but it also reduces shadows and softens the illumination.

The diffuser cannot be used with the following lenses as their minimum focusing distances are greater than 1 meter:

        70-210mm f/4
        70-210mm f/3.5-4.5
        70-210mm f/4.5-5.6
        75-300mm f/4.5-5.6
        80-200mm f/2.8
        80-200mm f/4.5-5.6
        100-200mm f/4.5
        100-300mm f/4.5-5.6

It also cannot be used with the following lenses due to shadowing:

        200mm f/2.8
        300mm f/2.8
        500mm f/8
        600mm f/4

Macro 3x-1x
16mm f/2.8
20mm f/2.8

Shadowing may also occur with the following lenses:

28-85mm f/3.5-4.5 (within macro range)
28-70mm f/2.8
28-135mm f/4-4.5

When using the 24mm f/2.8 you should shoot at distances greater than 35cm and with the 50mm f/2.8 macro greater than 23cm.

CREATIVE EXPANSION CARD SYSTEM

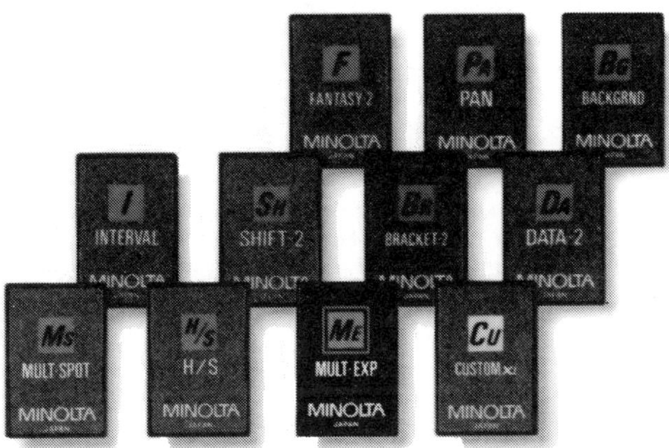

The expansion card system is probably the most controversial system accessory ever launched by a camera manufacturer. There are a number of reasons for this. Firstly, some photographic magazines, in their initial test reviews, heavily criticised the system and stated that you had to buy the full range of cards to be able to use the cameras. This is quite honestly complete rubbish. There has never been a claim by Minolta that says that you **have** to buy a single card.

So where's the problem?

The problem lies in the understanding of the card system, what each card does and how it does it. In some respects this is probably the fault of Minolta in not supplying enough information to the users and the magazine journalists. However, in defence of Minolta, one of the main reasons for the system was to make available a range of features that are not necessarily difficult to perform but are very time consuming to achieve. The card system was developed to make these operations very fast and easy to use, there is no doubting their success in this area.

Let us look at another reason for introducing the card system. Quite often I hear the comment from some photographers, "I wouldn't buy a Minolta because you have to use those cards." OK, so you don't want the card system, fine, we'll take it off the next range. But wait a minute, that would then mean that we no longer even have the option of that feature. And, that is what one has to understand.

IT IS PURELY AN OPTION!

I feel much better now that I have got that out of my system.

Let us take another viewpoint. Assume we were to build in to the 700si the functions provided by all of the cards. How easy do you think it would be to operate the camera, bearing in mind what we have already covered so far? Once you have completely read this section I almost guarantee that there will be at least one expansion card that you will want to buy and try out.

There are three types of cards:

1. The blue cards are known as the Special Application Cards. They provide automated processes for specific photographic situations. With the exception of the Travel Card, the benefits of these cards are somewhat limited on the si and xi series due to the extremely sophisticated Expert Program Mode. They were originally introduced for the Dynax/Maxxum i series.

2. The red cards are known as the Feature Cards. They are by far the most useful as they add features to the camera. Make sure that you read this section carefully.

3. The final group only has one card. It is the yellow card and is known as the Customized Function Card xi. It is also useful but because of the nature of the card it is one which you may not use that often.

When you wish a computer to take on a new task you load it with new software to manipulate the hardware. The card system operates in exactly the same manner. Each card contains a ROM IC (Read Only Memory Integrated Circuit) which interfaces with the 700si. The card is not simply a way of activating a pre-programmed feature. As long as the hardware in the 700si can be manipulated to give a new feature a card can be introduced to add that feature after the camera's original development. This of course allows you to add features at will in the future even though they may not have originally been available.

This brings me on to another benefit of the card system, and that is that it allows you to tailor the specification of the camera to your own requirements.

The cards are inserted into a small slot in the top of the card door. The button labelled **CARD** on the right of the body LCD panel allows you to switch the card function off and on, thus allowing your favourite card to be left in the camera and only used when required.

When the card is initially inserted or switched on, an abbreviation of the card's name will appear in the body LCD panel for a few seconds, to confirm the card is correctly inserted.

SPECIAL APPLICATION CARDS

This group consists of five cards:

1. Portrait Card

2. Sports Action Card 2 (previously known as Sports Action)

3. Close-up Card

4. Travel Card (previously known as the Depth Control Card)

5. Child Card

The basic function of the portrait, sports and close-up cards is to modify the program line so that a suitable aperture/shutter speed combination is selected.

With all of these cards, program is the only available exposure mode, PA and Ps modes cannot be selected.

Portrait Card

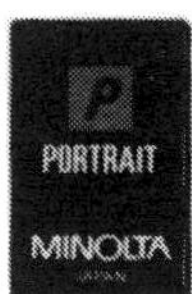

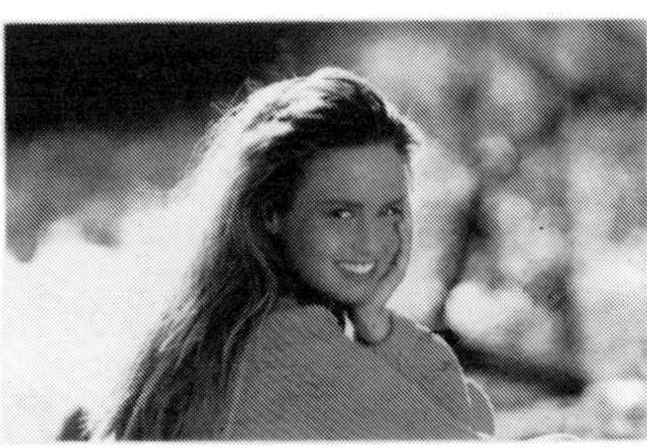

By using subject distance information and the lens focal length in use, the camera is able to calculate the image magnification. Once this has been achieved the aperture and shutter speed are set to give the optimum amount of depth of field.

The lens aperture is controlled to blur the background, whilst still maintaining sufficient depth of field to ensure that all of your subject is in focus.

When using telephoto lenses and shooting close to the subject the aperture in some cases may be as small as f/11.

Sports Action Card 2/Sports Action Card

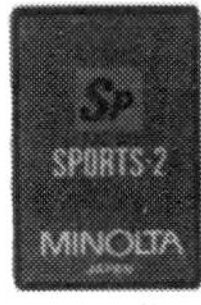

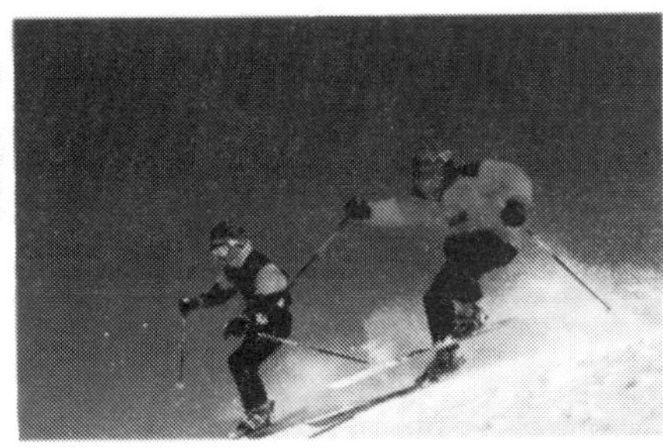

The sports action card is designed to give faster shutter speeds to freeze subject movement based on the image magnification. The higher the magnification the faster the shutter speed.

Continuous AF is selected permanently, and because of this the AF illuminator will not function.

When the card is initially inserted, the flash is switched off. Although the flash can be switched back on, this is not recommended as it will limit the shutter speeds to 1/200 second.

The functions listed above are the same for both the first and second generation Sports card. The additional feature of the second generation card is APZ (Advanced Program Zoom). This feature is only available in use with the five xi zoom lenses.

With the card switched on the camera will control the focal length of the zoom lens to frame the subject, based on its measured distance. There are five programs available which cause the card to set either higher or lower magnification settings.

As the subject moves the lens is continually controlled to frame the subject accordingly. The closer the subject, the higher the magnification. As the subject moves away from the camera, telephoto focal lengths are used but these will include more of the subject's surroundings.

In continuous drive mode, the 700si will try to adjust the focal length within the time available between frames.

If you change the focal length, APZ will be deactivated. To reactivate APZ press the program reset button. If eye-start has not been activated for 30 seconds APZ will be restored. To cancel APZ completely, press the **CARD ADJ** button inside the card door and then turn the front input dial so that **OFF AP** is shown in the body LCD panel.

With the exposure meter on turning either of the input dials will change the APZ program. The program number will be shown in place of the frame counter and will disappear approximately one second after you have made your selection.

The easiest method of selecting the best program for your subject, is to look through the viewfinder and turn either of the dials. As you do this you will see the framing change for each click stop of the dial.

Program	Zoom Setting
1	wide
2	
3	
4	
5	tele

Close-up Card

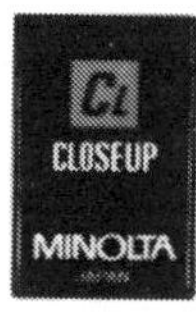

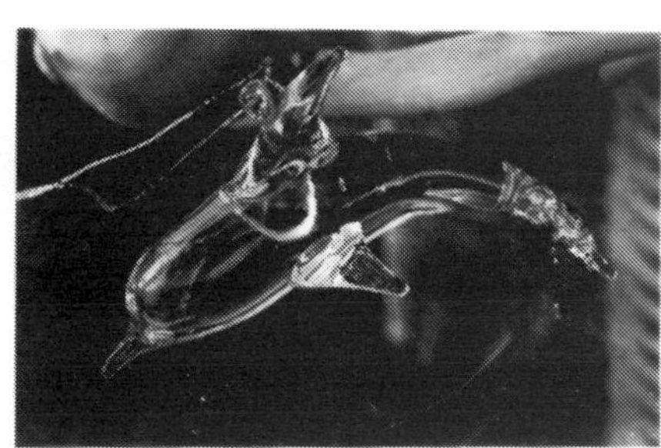

This is the reverse of the portrait card. Rather than reducing depth of field, this card is designed to increase it depending on the image magnification.

Therefore, the higher the magnification, the smaller the aperture and hence greater depth of field.

Up to magnification of 1:4 (1/4 lifesize), the 700si will use aperture settings of f/5.6. As the magnification increases, smaller apertures will be selected to compensate for the reduction in depth of field.

Beware: The card assumes that you are hand holding the camera, therefore faster film speeds may be necessary.

Travel Card/Automatic Depth Control Card

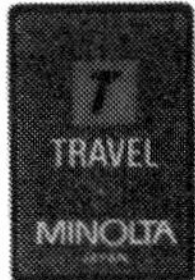

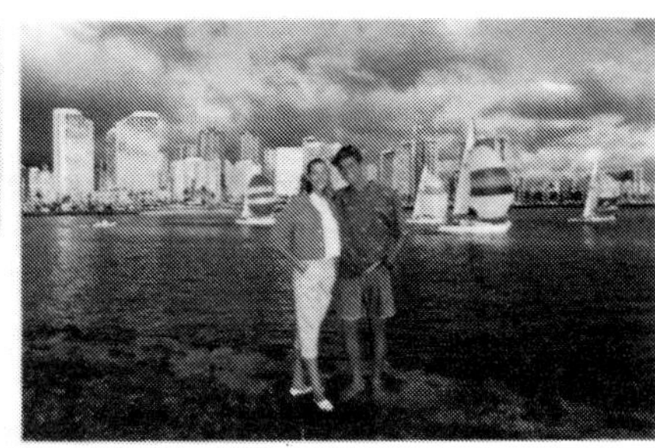

The main function of the card is to increase the depth of field to an absolute maximum.

This is achieved, firstly, by setting smaller apertures, as long as there is sufficient available light, and secondly, controlling the focus point, to ensure that from the subject to the background is in focus. This second feature is achieved by utilising the hyper focal distance.

The camera calculates the available depth of field using the subject distance, lens focal length, and aperture setting. Once this has been calculated, if the TOTAL amount of the depth of field is large enough to cover the subject to the background, the camera will then control the focus point at the time the shutter release is pressed fully.

E.g. If the available depth of field is say, 10m to 40m (just short of infinity) and the subject is 20m away, when the shutter release is pressed fully the lens will be refocused at approximately 30m, thus utilising the depth of field in front of the subject to keep the subject in focus. This will now cause infinity to appear in focus as the depth of field has been extended sufficiently. Because this feature is designed to get both the subject and background in focus, when shooting at closer distances, where there is insufficient depth of field to make this possible, the lens will not be controlled.

Remember that if the lens is refocused, the subject is the closest object that will appear in focus.

This feature is on both the Travel and Depth Control cards. The Travel card's additional feature is used when taking pictures from a moving platform.

Imagine you are photographing a scene through the window of a moving coach or car. If the camera was to use the normal depth of field program, which results in slower shutter speeds being selected, the scene will appear blurred. In this case, the 700si will detect this movement and override the depth program and automatically select a fast shutter speed - clever!

Note: When taking photographs of still subjects and you wish depth of field to be the priority, ensure that you hold the camera steady, otherwise the camera may select fast shutter speeds/large apertures, which will result in reduced depth of field.

Child Card

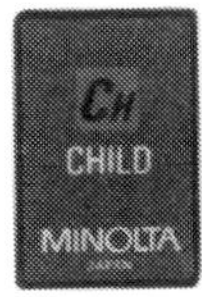
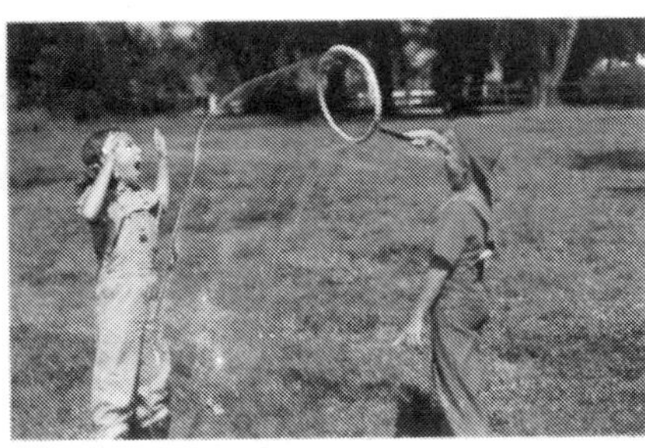

No laughing please!

This card is for use with the xi zoom lenses.

The card is intended to allow the camera to be given to someone who does not normally use the camera, and yet not have to worry about not only focus and exposure, but also framing as well.

The operation is exactly the same as the Sports Action Card 2. The lens focal length is controlled based on the subject distance. As the subject moves towards the camera, image magnification is increased, when the subject moves away from the camera, telephoto focal lengths are used but the lens is controlled to show more of the background.

Changing the APZ programs is once again done by turning either of the input dials.

Program	Zoom Setting	Subject Height
1	wide	approx 1.4m/4'9"
2		
3		
4		
5	tele	approx 0.6m/2"

In continuous drive mode the focal length is fixed on the first frame and the shutter will lock after three frames, just in case you get carried away!

The program used with this card is designed to give fast shutter speeds whilst still giving sufficient depth of field control.

Continuous AF is selected for full time operation.

FEATURE CARDS

The feature card group is made up of the following cards:

1. Multi-Spot Memory Card

2. Highlight/Shadow Control Card

3. Multiple Exposure Card

4. Data Memory Card 2 (previously Data Memory Card)

5. Bracketing Card 2 (replaces both Exposure Bracketing and Flash Bracketing Cards)

6. Intervalometer Card

7. Automatic Program Shift Card 2 (previously Automatic Program Shift card)

8.   Background Priority Card

9.   Panning Card

10. Fantasy Effect Card 2 (previously Fantasy Effect Card)

Multi-Spot Memory Card

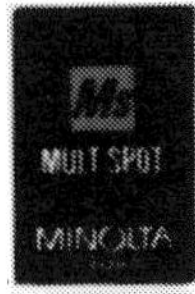

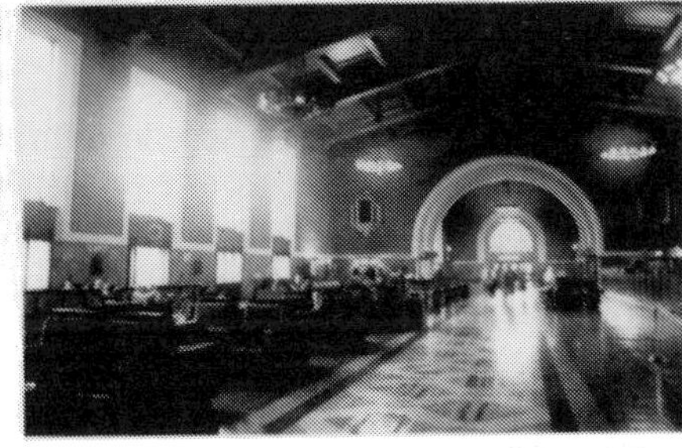

This is probably one of the most popular cards available. As soon as the card is inserted, spot metering is automatically selected and the spot metering measuring area is shown on the screen. The basic function of this card is to allow you to take up to eight spot readings, the camera will then set an average exposure for all of the selected areas.

To take readings:

Position the area to be metered within the spot metering area shown in the viewfinder and press the **SPOT** button to measure that area. Continue to take readings up to a maximum of eight. After each reading, the 700si will display the aperture/shutter speed combination for the average calculated so far.

Operation in each exposure mode

In program the 700si sets both the aperture and shutter speeds according to the calculated average. PA/Ps can be used to adjust the 700si's chosen combination.

In aperture priority, after you have selected the aperture the 700si will set the shutter speed. However, once the readings have been taken and averaged, the shutter speed required may be out of the camera's shutter speed range. In this case the 700si will automatically set a new aperture to ensure correct exposure. Although the final selected shutter speed may blink, the exposure will still be correct.

In shutter priority, the 700si will select the correct aperture once you have selected the shutter speed. Similar to the operation in aperture priority, if the aperture required for correct exposure is out of the range of the lens the 700si will automatically adjust the shutter speed until an available aperture for correct exposure is found. Although the final aperture may blink, the exposure will still be correct.

In manual exposure mode you set both the aperture and shutter speed. Once the average exposure has been calculated, the 700si will display the difference between this exposure and the set exposure.

As the readings are stored in the card's memory, you can not only take successive shots with the same readings without having to repeat measurements, but you can also change the exposure mode, aperture and shutter speed without affecting the overall exposure.

IMPORTANT

AS THE EXPOSURE READINGS ARE STORED IN THE CARD'S MEMORY, YOU MUST ENSURE THAT THE CARD IS EITHER SWITCHED OFF, OR REMOVED, IF YOU NO LONGER WISH TO TAKE PHOTOGRAPHS USING THE CALCULATED AVERAGE EXPOSURE.

Extra Information:

Flash cannot be used. The built-in flash or a Minolta i/xi/HS series flashgun will automatically be switched off. If you own a flashgun other than that listed above, ensure that it is switched off, otherwise the card will not function.

It is not necessary to refocus on each area that you measure unless the focus point is very different to that of the main subject.

If you make a mistake you must ensure that you either remove the card or turn it off and start again.

Tip: If you continue to hold the **SPOT** button in after taking a measurement, the metering index will display the difference between the measurement taken and the calculated average exposure.

Taking more than one reading of the same area will bias the average towards that area. However, I would recommend that you limit the number of readings of the same area to 2 or 3.

Highlight/Shadow Control Card

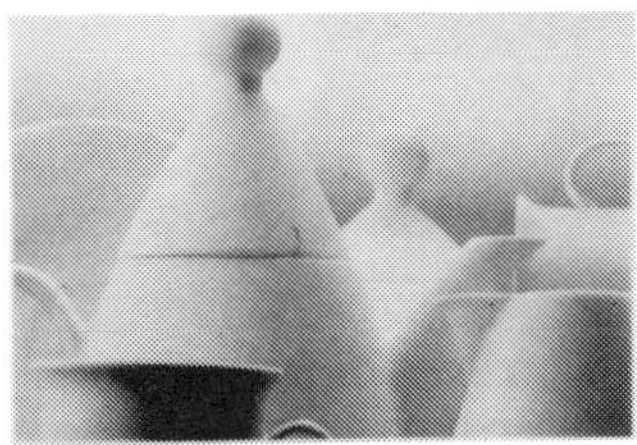

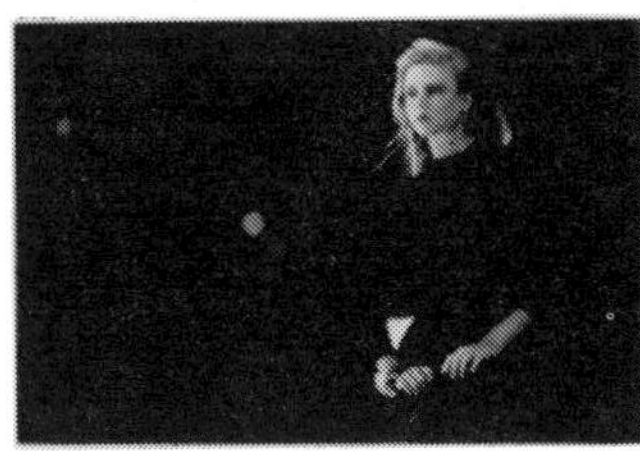

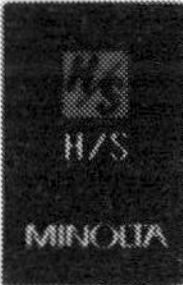

The basic function of this card is to overcome the problem of incorrect exposure metering of high or low reflectance subjects. When highlight readings are taken the exposure is increased by 2.3 stops to ensure that white or light areas are exposed as highlights, whilst with shadow readings the exposure is decreased by 2.7 stops to ensure that dark or black areas are exposed as shadows.

As with the Multi-Spot Memory Card, the camera will automatically be set to spot metering and the spot meter measuring area will be shown on the viewfinder screen.

Taking readings

Firstly, select the required mode, highlight or shadow. This is achieved by pressing the **CARD ADJ** button. The display will now indicate either **HIGH** or **SHAD** depending upon the mode currently selected. To change the mode, simply press the **CARD** button on the 700si's top plate.

Press the **CARD ADJ** button again to confirm the setting.

To take readings, simply position the spot metering area on the light or dark area (depending on the selected mode) and press and hold the **SPOT** button to lock the reading. The 700si will now automatically compensate for the reading and set the new shutter speed to ensure correct exposure.

Extra Information:

Flash cannot be used. In aperture or shutter priority exposure modes, if the aperture (A mode) or shutter speed (S mode) set are outside the 700si's range then an aperture/shutter speed is selected within the camera's range.

With the **SPOT** button held in, the metering index will display **APPROXIMATELY** the exposure adjustment made by the card.

IMPORTANT

Ensure that the **SPOT** button is kept pressed whilst releasing the shutter, otherwise the 700si will not adjust the normal exposure.

Multiple Exposure Card

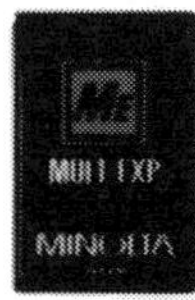
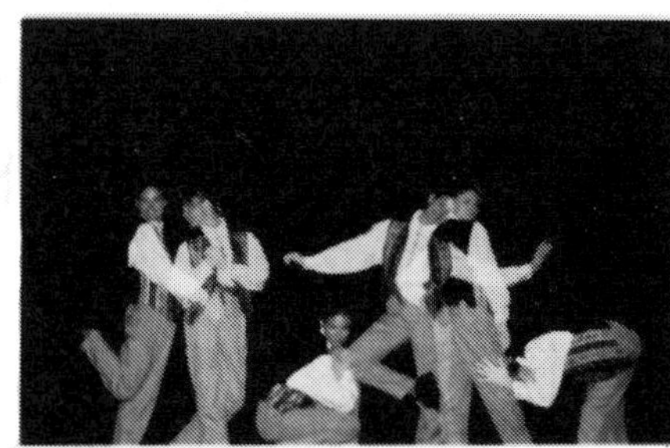

Earlier in this book I explained how to do straightforward multiple exposures without the need for this card. However, this card does have one thing up its sleeve, and that is the unique Fade In/Out feature. Fade in mode gradually increases the exposure for each frame in the sequence, reaching correct exposure for the last frame. Fade out mode gradually decreases the exposure from the first frame which is correctly exposed. The change in exposure between frames is adjustable, with a choice of 0.3, 0.5, 1.0 EV steps.

Operation

When the card is installed, the 700si will confirm the card in use as well as the multiple exposure mode, number of frames in the sequence, and the exposure adjustment step between frames (fade in/out only). E.g. **ME - I 0.5**
3

This indicates that the fade in mode is selected with an exposure adjustment between frames of 0.5 EV with three frames to be taken in the sequence.

Press the **CARD ADJ** button in the card door. Turn the front control dial to select the desired mode, Fade In, Fade Out or Normal. If you select the fade in or fade out mode you will need to select the required amount of exposure adjustment required between frames. This is done by pressing the **CARD** button on the top plate and then turning the front dial to select the desired setting.

If you are using print film I would suggest that you set 1.0 EV steps. If you are using slide film I would suggest that you use either 0.3 or 0.5 EV steps. This is due to the film type and exposure latitude.

If you were to use 0.3 or 0.5 EV steps for print film the adjustment will be well within the film latitude and you may not notice the fading effect in the end result. On the other hand 1.0 EV step adjustments for slide film may be too great, resulting in some of the frames at the far end of the sequence not appearing on the film.

Pressing the **CARD** button again will allow you, by turning the front input dial, to select the number of frames to be taken in the sequence, up to a total of nine.

Once you have done this you can now press the **CARD ADJ** button again which will store your settings.

You can use any exposure mode. When using the fade in/out effect, for best results use manual exposure as this will ensure that you have a constant base exposure. To set the base exposure, first turn off the card and set the aperture and shutter speed that you wish to use for the base. Turn the card on and take pictures.

When using the 700si in continuous frame advance and with the shutter release pressed fully, the shutter will lock after the sequence has been completed. If you continue to keep the shutter release pressed fully the sequence will be repeated after two seconds.

To cancel the sequence before the programmed end, press the **CARD** ON/OFF button. The film will advance to the next frame.

Tips for exposure adjustment

Multiple exposure is one of the most difficult photographic

techniques to master. Here are a few pointers that I can give to help you towards better multiple exposure photographs.

If the subject will overlap in the sequence or the background is bright, exposure adjustment is recommended. Refer to the table below for adjustment factors.

Number of exposures	2	3	4	5	6	7	8	9
Exposure Adjustment	-1	-1.5	-2	-2.5	-2.5	-3	-3	-3

If the subject will not overlap in the sequence and the background is dark no exposure adjustment is needed.

Note: If the total change in exposure adjustment is less than -2.66EV, the exposure may be below the exposure latitude of the film and therefore may not appear.

The best advice I can give you is, experiment.

Data Memory Card 2/Data Memory Card

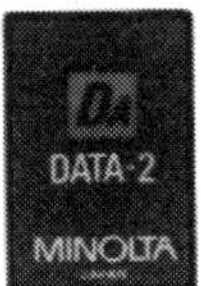

Each expansion card automates a photographic technique or process. This does not necessarily mean that it completely removes the creative process, in some cases it simply means that you are still part of the creative process, but it takes out most of the guess work. On the other hand you may see that as part of the process which you would like to feel part of.

There are three cards in the entire range which perform operations which you could not possibly perform. One of those is the Data Memory Card 2.

This card is used to store the information applicable to every frame for four films. Information stored is as follows:

- Shutter speed and aperture
- Exposure mode
- Exposure adjustment
- Film speed
- Lens focal length used
- Maximum aperture of lens in use

Okay, so you could write all that down, but at three frames per second?!

How to use the card

Insert the card, the display will confirm the card in use by displaying **dAtA** and **F1**, F refers to the film area. Information for each film is stored in a film area, of which there are four. When the card is new, the 700si will automatically use the first film area. When a new film is loaded, information will automatically be stored in the second film area. Once all four film areas have been used, information will then over write the information in the first film area, then the second area etc. However, before information is over written on film area 1 after the fourth area has been used the 700si will warn you of this by displaying **ArEA** and **F1**.

If at this point you wish to save the information in film area 1 and would rather store new information in a different film area, this can be achieved as follows:

1. Press the **CARD ADJ** button, this will display the film speed and film area in the body LCD data panel.

2. Press the self timer/drive mode button, the display will now show **ArEA** along with the film area number which will be flashing.

3. Turning the front control dial will allow you to select a new film area for the information to be stored. Selecting **Fr** will erase the information in all film areas.

4. Press the **CARD ADJ** button. At this point, if **Fr** was selected the information in all the film areas will be erased.

You may wish to clear all the information to make it less confusing when recalling the information later.

To recall data

Recalling data is easy. Firstly press the **CARD ADJ** button in the card door. The film speed and the film area will be shown. Turning the front dial will allow you to select a new film area.

Press the **CARD** button on the top plate. The display will now show the exposure mode, shutter speed and aperture used for that frame. Turning the front dial at this point will allow you to check this same information for the remaining frames taken on that film.

Each press of the **CARD** button will change to the next display. The next display will indicate the amount of exposure compensation set. The final display indicates the focal length used and the maximum aperture of the lens that was used

When you have finished checking data, press the **CARD ADJ** button.

You can view data mid-roll, including data relating to the film in use. When you press the **CARD ADJ** button after viewing data the card will continue to store data from where it left off.

Extra Information:

When using the 700si's double exposure facility, only data for the last frame will be stored.

The card can only store information when it is in the camera.

When using the 70-210mm f/3.5-4.5 at focal lengths close to 70mm, 75mm will be stored in the memory.

Only the film speed value for the last frame is stored in the card's memory.

Data will not be stored if there is no film in the camera.

Information for up to 40 exposure per film can be stored.

If the card is removed, the information is still retained in its memory.

Difference between series 2 and series 1 Data Cards

The original series 1 card would only store one roll of information and will not store the film speed as in the series 2 card.

Exposure Bracketing Card 2

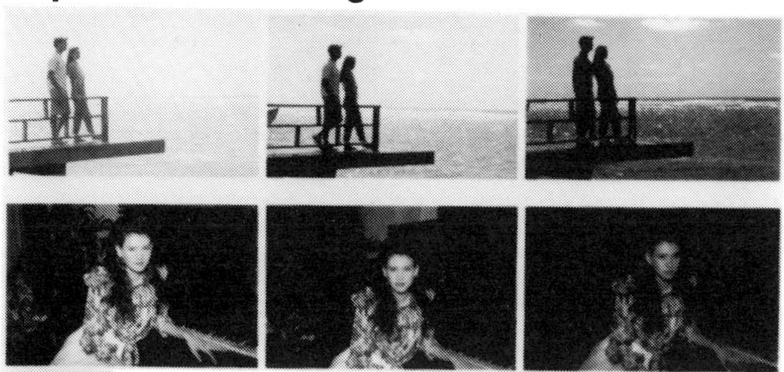

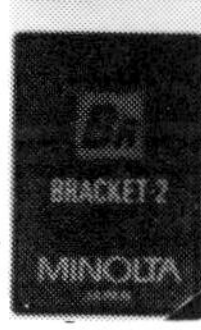

The 700si features both flash compensation and exposure bracketing. However, the bracketing function is really only suitable for slides as the exposure shift is only 1/2 a stop either side of the normal exposure value. Flash compensation is really only suitable for adjusting the flash level based on your own personal preference.

Bracketing allows you to quickly shoot a sequence of shots, each one at a different exposure level.

The Exposure Bracketing Card 2 features both exposure and flash bracketing. You can select the number of exposures in the sequence, 3, 5 or 7. The exposure adjustment in between frames is also adjustable. With exposure bracketing selected the increments available are, 0.3EV, 0.5EV, 1.0EV. In flash bracketing mode the increments are 0.5EV and 1.0EV.

In exposure bracketing mode the exposure is changed by adjusting the shutter speed and aperture either separately or together. In flash bracketing mode it is the flash output that is controlled to give the change in exposure.

To change the card settings

Insert the card, the card indicator and bracketing mode will be displayed.

Press the **CARD ADJ** button in the card door. The card indicator and bracketing mode will now blink. Turn the front control dial to set the required bracketing mode. **brAc** is the display for exposure bracketing, whilst **F br** is the indication for flash bracketing.

Press the **CARD** button. The exposure adjustment increment value will now blink. Use the front input dial to select the desired exposure increment (0.3*, 0.5 or 1.0 EV).

[* 0.3 EV increment only available in exposure bracketing mode.]

Press the **CARD** button again, the frame counter will now blink, this is the number of frames to be taken in the bracketing sequence. Turn the front input dial to select the number of frames(3, 5 or 7).

Once you have made the required adjustments press the **CARD ADJ** button to confirm the changes.

Taking pictures in Exposure bracketing mode

The drive mode will automatically be set to continuous and cannot be changed.

The built-in flash, if raised, will not fire. If a Minolta i/xi/HS series flash is attached it will automatically be switched off and cannot be switched on. If you have a flash other than those mentioned above, you should ensure that it is switched off. If you do not do so, **OFF FL** will appear in the viewfinder and body LCD displays, warning you of this when you lift your finger off the shutter release.

Focus will be locked after the first frame in the sequence. In program both the aperture and shutter speed will be adjusted. In P_A and aperture priority modes the shutter speed will be adjusted to give the change in exposure. In Ps and shutter priority modes the aperture will be adjusted to give the change in exposure. In manual the shutter speed will be adjusted to give the change in exposure.

IMPORTANT

Ensure that you hold the shutter release down for the entire sequence. The 700si will stop automatically at the end of the sequence. Lifting your finger off the shutter release during the sequence will cancel the operation.

Taking pictures in Flash Bracketing mode

The drive mode will be set to single frame advance and cannot be changed.

If you are using the built-in flash ensure that it is raised. If a Minolta i/xi/HS series flash is attached it will automatically be switched on and cannot be switched off. If you are using a flash other than those mentioned above, ensure that it is switched on. If not, **ON FL** will appear in the viewfinder and body LCD displays warning you of this when you lift your finger off the shutter release.

Wait for the flash to fully charge and then take the picture, the flash ready signal will blink after the exposure to confirm that the subject was within range.

When you lift your finger off the shutter release the exposure increment and frame number for the next frame in the sequence will appear in the data panels for approximately five seconds.

Once the flash has recharged, take the next picture. Continue until **END** appears in the display panels.

To cancel the series before the end, press the **CARD** ON/OFF button.

Single frame advance will remain set when the card is switched off.

If you are using a 5200i, 5400xi or 5400HS flash unit in manual exposure mode with TTL flash metering switched off on the flash unit, the aperture will be adjusted to give the change in exposure rather than the flash output.

Exposure adjustment sequence:

	Frame 1	Frame 2	Frame 3	Frame 4	Frame 5	Frame 6	Frame 7
0.3	Normal	+0.3	-0.3	+0.6	-0.6	+0.9	-0.9
0.5	Normal	+0.5	-0.5	+1.0	-1.0	+1.5	-1.5
1.0	Normal	+1.0	-1.0	+2.0	-2.0	+3.0	-3.0

Flash range

The range of the built-in flash or an accessory flash will change depending on the exposure adjustment increment set. When the exposure is increased (+EV), the flash range will decrease because the flash cannot overexpose subjects beyond its normal flash range. If the exposure is decreased (-EV), the flash range will increase because it can underexpose subjects beyond its normal range.

Calculating the new flash range

For an overexposed frame the approximate flash range can be calculated by multiplying the range by 0.7 for every +1 EV increase. Therefore, if the normal flash range is 10m, the new range becomes 7m for a +1 EV increase. For a +2 EV increase the range will become 4.9m.

To calculate the approximate flash range for an underexposed frame, multiply the normal range by 1.4 for every -1 EV decrease. Therefore, if the normal flash range is 10m, the new range for a -1 EV decrease will be 14m and for a -2 EV decrease, the range becomes 19.6m.

The minimum flash distance will be unaltered.

The 5200i, 5400xi and 5400HS data panels will indicate the new flash range for the adjusted exposure when you press halfway on the shutter release.

Note: Bracketing is really only suitable for slide films. With print film the exposure latitude is so large that you will probably have to set the maximum exposure adjustment and number of frames. Even then, you may only notice the change in exposure on the frames at the two extremes of the sequence, e.g. +/- 3.0 EV, and that is only if the processor has not tried to correct the exposure so that they all end up looking the same! When using slide film, a change in exposure of 0.3 or 0.5 EV may not increase or decrease the exposure dramatically, but it is enough to affect the visible detail.

Therefore when using slide film set 0.3 or 0.5 EV increments and limit the number of frames to 3 or 5.

On the other hand for print film set 1.0EV increments and the number of frames to 5 or 7.

As the settings are stored in the card's memory, you can safely switch the card off or even remove it from the camera and the settings will be unchanged until you change them again. This allows you to set the card up to a "favourite" bracketing sequence and to simply recall it when required, rather than having to reset the entire sequence as on some other cameras which have a more limited bracketing function built-in. Yet another advantage of using the card system rather than a built-in feature.

Difference between Bracketing Card 2 and Exposure/Flash Bracketing Card

Before the introduction of the Bracketing Card 2, you would need one card for exposure bracketing and another for flash bracketing. The series 2 card combines the features of both cards.

Intervalometer card

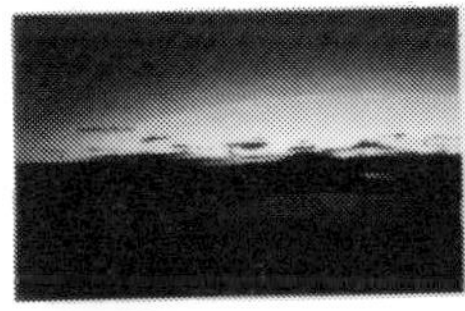 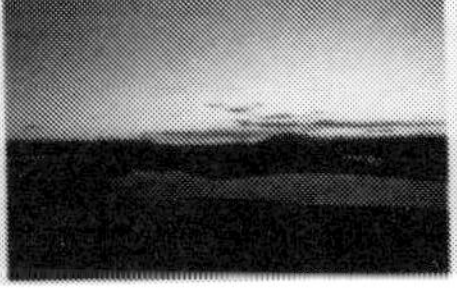 

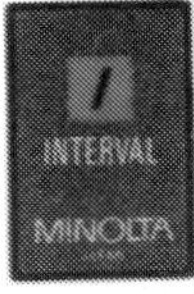

In the past Minolta have had extremely advanced program backs for their AF SLR's. The most advanced of these was without a doubt the Program Super Back 70/90 for the 7000/9000 cameras. There was nothing that they did not do. They were bristling with so many features that the price ended up being extremely high (as much as the camera itself) and of course the instruction book resembled the thickness of an encyclopaedia! Through the card system, it is possible to add any of those features offered by the Super Backs (except data imprinting) whilst still allowing it to be affordable and easy to use.

The Intervalometer card is one of these. It is also one of those cards that allow you to perform an operation that is otherwise impossible.

It enables you to set the camera for independent operation, and allows you to record events that will occur over a long period of time by taking a photograph at a set interval. This is known as time-lapse photography. Good example applications for this card are, the sun rising or setting, a flower blossoming or an insect emerging from its pupa stage.

There are three parameters. Interval time (the time elapsing in between frames), start time (the time elapsing between the shutter release being pressed fully and the first exposure of the sequence) and the number of frames (the total number of frames in the series).

Let us look at an example series.

Suppose we want to take 5 photographs every 30 minutes starting one hour from the time we press the shutter release.

Insert the card; **InVL** will appear in the 700si's body LCD data panel for approximately five seconds to confirm the card in use.

Press the **CARD ADJ** button in the card door, **In** will appear, indicating the interval time and three figures. From left to right, they represent hours, minutes and seconds. Initially the hour will blink. Turn the front input dial to set the hour to 0, then press the **SPOT** button on the back of the 700si. This will cause the minutes to blink, once again use the front input dial to change the setting, in this case we need 30 to be indicated. Press the **SPOT** button. The seconds indicator will now blink, turning the input dial will change the settings, we require 0 to be indicated.

The interval time can be set between 0 hours, 0 minutes, 1 second and 24 hours, 0 minutes, 0 seconds.

Press the **CARD** button on the top of the 700si. The display will change to Fr and a number. This is the display for the number of frames. Turn the dial to set this to 5.

The number of frames can be set between 1 and 40.

Press the **CARD** button once more, the display will now show **St** and two numbers. This is the start time. Initially the hours will blink. Turn the front input dial to set this to 1. Press the **SPOT** button, the minutes will blink. Turn the front input dial to change this setting. We require 0.

The start time can be set between 0 hours, 0 minutes and 24 hours, 0 minutes.

Once you have set all three parameters press the **CARD ADJ** button.

Press the shutter release button all the way down.

The result will be that in one hour the first photograph will be taken. 30 minutes later the second will be taken, and so on until five photographs have been taken. **InVL** will be indicated in the body LCD panel until the sequence has finished.

Extra Information:

The settings will be stored in the card's memory until you change them again, even if the card is removed.

Approximately five seconds prior to each photograph being taken, autofocus and autoexposure will be activated automatically.

Approximately one minute prior to each photograph the flash will automatically begin charging. If the start time is less than one minute, charge the flash before pressing the shutter release.

If autofocus is selected and the 700si is unable to focus, the photograph will not be taken and the 700si will proceed to the next frame in the series. To prevent this, set the 700si to release priority.

The interval time must be at least five seconds longer than the exposure time. If it is equal to or less than the exposure time, the operation will be cancelled.

You can still take photographs normally without affecting the interval sequence at any time.

Do not adjust the interval settings during the sequence, otherwise the operation will be cancelled.

P$_A$/P$_S$ modes are not recommended.

To cancel intervalometer operation at any time press the **CARD** on/off button or switch the camera off.

Ensure that the subject is centred in the AF area before pressing the shutter release button all the way when autofocus is selected. If manual focus is selected, ensure that you focus accurately on the subject prior to the series.

Auto Shift Card 2/Automatic Program Shift Card

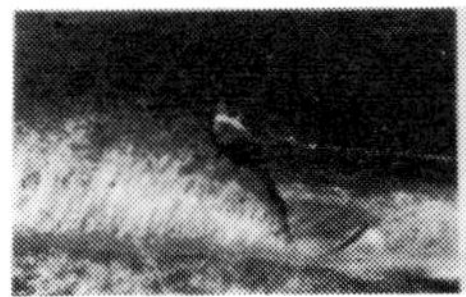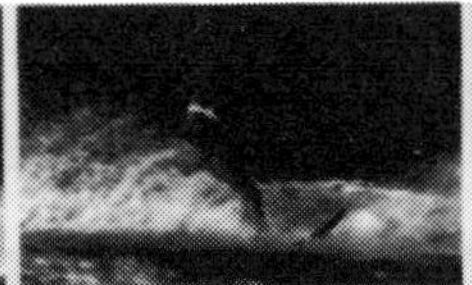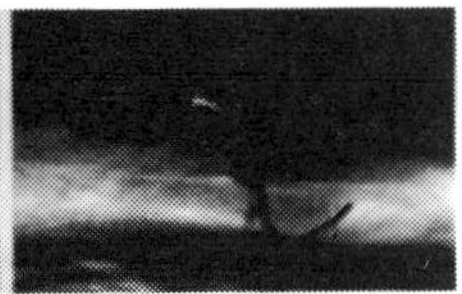

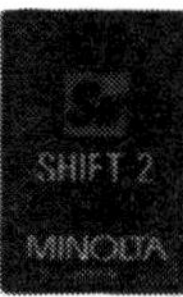 This card is ideal for those situations when you are not sure which aperture to use to create a certain amount of depth of field, or how much depth of field is required, or which shutter speed to use to create a certain action effect.

The shift card will take three photographs, each with the same overall exposure level, but using different shutter speed/aperture combinations for each frame to create varying effects.

The size of the shift between frames can be set to 1, 2 or 3 stops.

All exposure modes can be used including PA/Ps. The base exposure is the second frame. This is automatically set in program and manually set in PA/Ps, aperture priority, shutter priority and manual exposure modes. The first frame will have a higher shutter speed/larger aperture, whilst the third frame will have a slower shutter speed/smaller aperture.

Operation

Insert the card. **SHFt**, the shift size and number of frames (fixed) will be indicated in the body LCD panel for five seconds confirming the card and value set.

Press the **CARD ADJ** button in the card door. The shift size will now blink. Turn the front input dial to select the shift size (1, 2 or 3 stops). Press the **CARD ADJ** button to confirm the setting.

Press and hold the shutter release button down for the entire three frame sequence. Releasing the shutter will cancel the series.

Extra Information:

Continuous drive mode is automatically set and remains set after the card is removed or switched off.

If a Minolta i/xi/HS series flash is fitted it will automatically be switched off and cannot be turned on. The built-in flash will not fire.

Focus will be locked after the first frame in the series.

When eye-start activates, the base exposure (second frame) will be indicated in the viewfinder and body display panels. When you press half-way down on the shutter release the exposure for the first frame will be indicated in the displays.

In aperture or shutter priority exposure modes, if the aperture or shutter speed display flashes, correct exposure is not available. Therefore change the aperture/shutter speed until the display stops flashing.

If the desired shutter and/or aperture required for the desired shift size are beyond the 700si's range, the exposure will be adjusted as follows:

In program, the shift size (or the aperture/shutter speed combination for the base exposure) will be adjusted to provide equal shift sizes between all three frames to ensure that all three combinations are within the correct exposure range.

Difference between series 2 card and series 1 card

The series 1 card could only be used in Program exposure mode. The series 2 card can be used in all exposure modes.

Background Priority Card

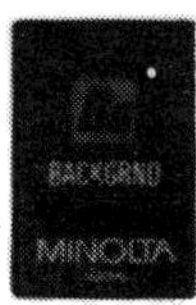
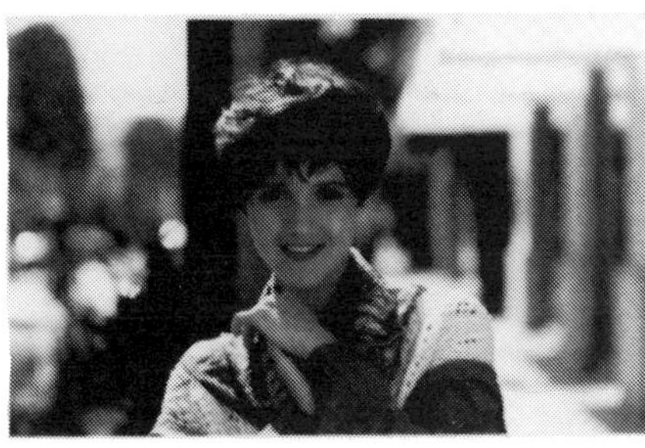

This card allows you to specify a set level of background sharpness. The 700si will then control the aperture accordingly to try and maintain the same level of background sharpness as the subject distance changes and the lens focal length is adjusted.

Operation

Insert the card. **bKnd** will appear in the body LCD panel for five seconds to confirm the card in use.

The metering index will appear on the viewfinder screen. A pointer at the +3 position indicates that the background will be in focus. A pointer at the -3 position indicates that only the subject will appear in focus.

To set the required level of background sharpness turn either input dial. The pointer will move either up or down the scale to indicate the background sharpness set, to one of five positions which are, +3, +1.5, 0, -1.5 and -3.

When you press part way down on the shutter release the 700si will confirm whether the depth of field you have selected can be accommodated based on the lens focal length set, the subject distance and lighting conditions by keeping the pointer position the same. If the required depth of field is not available the 700si will position the pointer to indicate the nearest level of depth of field available to that set.

Extra Information:

If a Minolta i/xi/HS series flashgun is fitted to the 700si, it will automatically be switched off. If you are using a flash other than those listed above, ensure that it is switched off.

Manual focus cannot be selected when this card is in use.

Tips: When you want the background to appear as blurred as possible, use telephoto lenses, shorten the camera to subject distance, and use slower speed films.

When you want to increase the background sharpness, use wide angle lenses, increase the camera to subject distance and use faster speed films.

Panning card

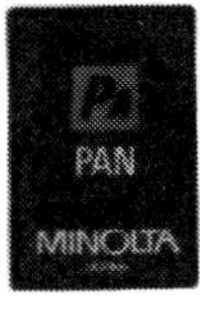
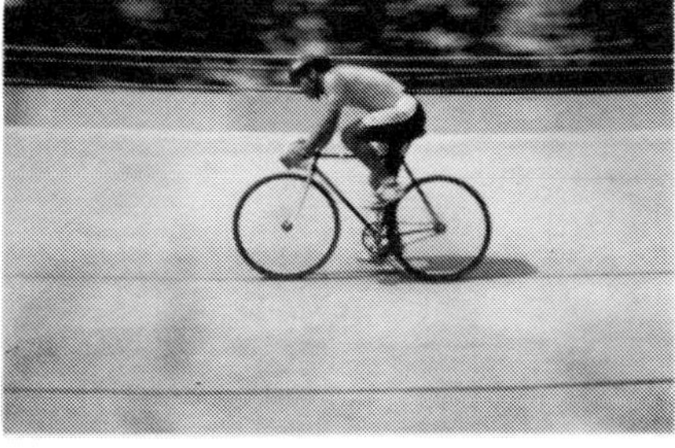

My favourite card in the entire range.

By simply inserting the card, the metering index will appear on the viewfinder screen. A pointer will move up and down the scale to one of five positions (+3, +1.5, 0, -1.5 and -3) as you pan a moving subject to indicate the accuracy of your panning technique.

A pointer toward the +3 position indicates smooth panning.

If you think that is clever, read this! Based upon the accuracy of your panning, the 700si will select the most suitable shutter speed to give the best possible panning photograph!

The better your panning technique, the slower the shutter speed set and therefore a flowing/blurred background results, yet your subject will still appear sharp. However, if your panning is not very accurate a faster shutter speed is set to maintain a sharp subject.

So, not only does it help you to improve your panning technique, it also improves your photographs.

How does it work?

Once the 700si has focused on your subject a waveform is produced for that subject and is memorised by the 700si. It will now monitor the placement of that waveform across the CCD (focusing sensor) as you pan. Ideally the waveform should not move at all across the CCD, therefore the subject is kept in exactly the same position in relation to the viewfinder area. However, if the waveform moves erratically across the CCD the 700si will therefore know that panning is not smooth.

What will they think of next?

Extra Information:

Program exposure mode is automatically set and cannot be changed.

The built-in flash will not fire and if a Minolta i/xi/HS series flashgun is attached it will automatically be switched off. Should you have a flash other than that listed above attached you should ensure that it is switched off.

If you have selected manual focus the 700si will flash **ON AF** in the body LCD panel. AF is recommended for use with this card.

Tip: Use the Panning card to full effect by first practising panning moving subjects and by using the index to improve your technique, this allows you to practise without wasting film.

Fantasy Effect Card 2/Fantasy Effect Card

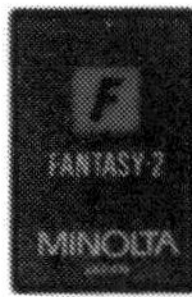

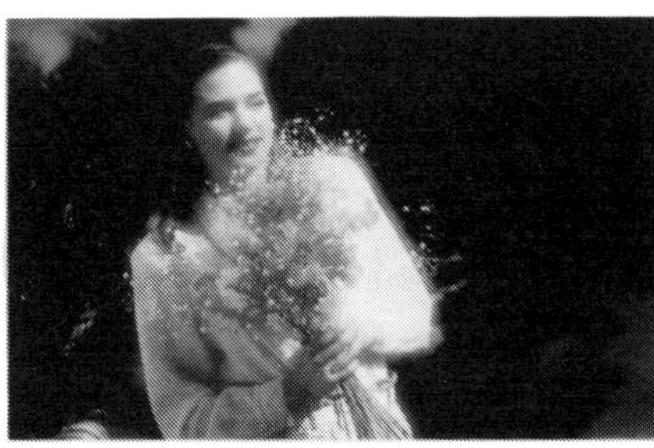

The Fantasy Effect Card 2 allows you to obtain soft focus, dream-like halo effects or zooming effects. There are two modes available. With the first mode selected the 700si will decide which method for creating the effect is most suitable, based upon the ambient light levels. The second mode exclusively uses the double exposure method for creating the effect.

Focus shift mode

For the first portion of the exposure, focus is locked. For the remaining portion of the exposure the focusing lens is driven at high speed. It is this focus shift that creates the "Fantasy Effect". In this mode the effect will be either a soft focus or a zooming effect.

Although you cannot select the type of effect, you can increase the chance of the desired effect being obtained by using a certain type of lens.

In general, the soft focus effect will be produced when the depth of field is small, such as when using a telephoto lens or when the lighting level is low, requiring larger apertures.

The zooming effect is likely to be produced when depth of field is large, such as when using wideangle lenses or when photographing in bright conditions, requiring smaller apertures.

Double Exposure Mode

This mode will create a soft halo around the subject. It works by taking two photographs on the same frame. The first photograph is taken in focus. The second is taken with the subject out of focus. The subject is thrown out of focus between the first and second frames.

Operation

Simply insert the card, **FAnt** will appear in the body LCD panel for approximately five seconds to confirm the card in use. To set the mode press the **CARD ADJ** button in the card door. Along with the card name will appear a number, either 1 or 2. Select 1 for focus shift mode and 2 for double exposure mode. Press the **CARD ADJ** button again. Frame your subject, ensuring that the 700si focuses on your subject. Press the shutter release all the way down to take the photograph.

HI or LO warning

The first fantasy effect mode is reliant on certain aperture/shutter speed combinations to obtain the "Fantasy effect". If the lighting conditions are such that one of these combinations cannot be used a **HI** or **LO** warning will be displayed in the viewfinder and body display panels when you press halfway down on the shutter release.

HI indicates there is too much light, whilst **LO** indicates there is insufficient illumination.

If the **HI** warning is displayed attach a neutral density filter to the lens or use a slower speed film (though this may not be practical).

If **LO** appears, use a faster speed film (once again, not always practical).

Also try recomposing the subject, e.g. when **HI** is indicated point the camera down slightly, so that there is less of the sky in the frame affecting the exposure reading. In situations when **LO** is indicated point the camera up slightly so that there is more of the sky in the frame.

DO NOT ALTER THE FILM SPEED SETTING, as the 700si reads the exposure latitude off the DX coding on the film and utilises the latitude to try and get the aperture/shutter speed combination to obtain the Fantasy Effect.

Therefore, when using print films, the likelihood of the **HI/LO** warning appearing is less than when using slide film as the exposure latitude is greater.

Using flash

The flash is automatically switched off. In which case switch the flash on. The flash will now fire every time. Because the flash fires during the time that focus is fixed, the subject, exposed by the flash illumination, will be sharp, but the background which is exposed for by the use of a slow shutter speed, will feature the Fantasy Effect.

When you press the shutter release part way, and if the **HI** or **LO** message appears, if you then press all the way down on the shutter release the card will automatically default to the double exposure mode to give an effect for that photograph.

Extra Information:

The card will automatically set the 700si to autofocus. Do not select manual focus. Do not lock focus with the **AF** button or the focus lock button provided on some lenses, otherwise the shutter will not release.

If using one of the macro lenses, ensure the limiter is set to **FULL**.

When using the 200 f/2.8, 300 f/2.8 or 600 f/4 lenses ensure that the focus range limiter is not set.

The card works most effectively between approximately EV 5 and EV 13 (100 ISO).

When using wideangle zoom lenses, such as the xi 28-80mm or xi 28-105mm, you may find using the telephoto end of the zoom yields a higher success rate.

Difference between series 1 card and series 2 card

The series 1 Fantasy effect card only features the focus control mode, whilst the series 2 card also features the double exposure mode.

Customized Function Card xi

The Customized Function Card xi is in a group of its own.

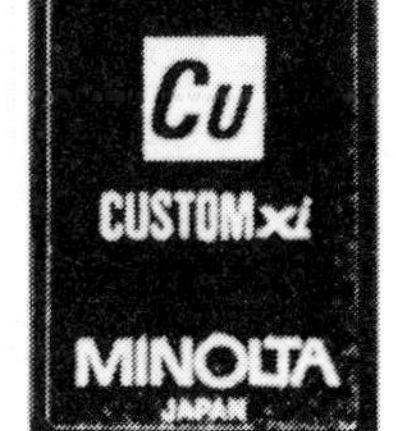

It allows you to re-program certain camera functions, depending upon your personal preferences.

The following features can be re-programmed:

Personal Program Mode

This feature allows you to re-program the following default settings of the program reset button:

Exposure Mode	P/A/S/M (initially P)
Exposure compensation	+/- 3 EV in 0.5 EV increments (initially 0.0)
Focus Area	Wide or centre focus area (initially wide)
Metering pattern	Honeycomb or centre-weighted (initially honeycomb)

Film Counter

Rather than the frame counter counting up, you can re-program so that it counts down, thus showing you the number of frames remaining.

Note: If using non DX coded film the counter cannot display the remaining frames.

Although the counter may display 0, it may be possible to shoot one or two more frames before the film is rewound.

Film Rewind

You can re-program the 700si so that the film will not automatically rewind at the end of the roll. It is recommended that you set this if using films with an unusual number of frames for which there is no DX code, e.g. 27 exposure film.

To rewind the film, press the film rewind button situated at the back of the camera below the 700si's back cover.

Film Leader

The film leader is normally rewound back into the cassette to prevent confusion as to which films have been used. However, this is inconvenient if you process your own films or if you wish to rewind the film and to re-load the same film at a later date. Therefore, with this card you can reprogram the 700si to leave the leader out after rewinding has completed.

DX Override Memory

When you override the film speed the 700si will remain set at that speed for the remainder of that film, unless the film speed is changed once again. However, if you tend to use the same film and you up-rate/down-rate the setting, when you override the film speed, the 700si will remember this setting. If the next film used has the same DX film speed code, the 700si will automatically set it to the overridden speed rather then setting the DX coded speed.

You can disable this feature using this card to reprogram the 700si.

Program Flash Control

In program, if the built-in flash is raised or if a Minolta i/xi/HS series flash is attached, the 700si will fire the flash automatically only if necessary, unless you force the flash to fire by holding in the manual fill-in flash button.

Re-programming allows the auto flash feature to be disabled. Therefore, if the built-in flash is raised or if a Minolta i/xi/HS series flash is attached and switched on, the flash will always fire.

Focus Lock button

The following lenses feature a focus lock button:

28-70 f/2.8 Dynax/Maxxum/G
70-210 f/4.5-5.6 Dynax/Maxxum
70-210 f/3.5-4.5 Dynax/Maxxum
80-200 f/2.8 APO Dynax/Maxxum/G
100-300 f/4.5-5.6 Dynax/Maxxum
100-300 f/4.5-5.6 APO Dynax/Maxxum
50 f/2.8 Macro Dynax/Maxxum
100 f/2.8 Macro Dynax/Maxxum
85 f/1.4 Dynax/Maxxum/G
200 f/2.8 Dynax/Maxxum/G
300 f/2.8 Dynax/Maxxum/G
600 f/4 Dynax/Maxxum/G
500 f/8 Mirror Dynax/Maxxum

Its normal function as already described in the autofocus section is to lock focus.

The function of this can be re-programmed, so that pressing the button will activate continuous AF or select the centre focusing area.

Eye-Start Grip Sensor Override

Normally eye-start is activated by the combination of the grip and eye-piece sensors. However, if you are wearing gloves, using the camera on a tripod, or if you suffer from dry skin you can re-program the eye-start system so that it is activated by only the eyepiece sensor.

Re-programming

Insert the card, **CUSt** will be indicated in the body LCD data panel for approximately five seconds to confirm the card in use.

Press the **CARD ADJ** button. All of the settings available for re-programming the program reset button will appear in the LCD panel. Press the **MODE** button. Only the exposure mode and exposure compensation will now be displayed. Turn the front dial to set the exposure mode and the rear dial to set the amount of exposure compensation required. Press the **MODE** button again. Now turn the front dial to set the focus area and the rear dial to select the metering mode.

Press the **CARD** button. The display will now show **CUSt**, the function number (1 to 7) and the present setting (1,2 or 3).

Use the **CARD** button to select the function number and the front dial to select the function setting. Once you have re-programmed the desired settings press the **CARD ADJ** button. The settings are now stored in the 700si and the card.

Function	Control	Setting	Action
1	Film counter	1	Displays number of frames shot
		2	Displays number of frames remaining
2	Start of rewind	1	Automatic
		2	Manual
3	Film leader	1	Wound into cassette
		2	Left out of cassette
4	DX memory	1	Off
		2	On
5	Program flash	1	Auto switchover
		2	Manual switchover
6	Focus lock button	1	Focus lock
		2	Centre area selection
		3	Continuous AF
7	Eye-start activation	1	By grip and eye-piece sensor
		2	By eye-piece sensor only

Initially, all settings are set to 1, except for function number 4, which is set to 2.

Extra Information:

If you own a second camera, when the card that was used to program the first camera is inserted into the second camera, it will function (as long as the **CARD** symbol is shown in the data panel) in the same way as the first camera was programmed. Taking the card out of the second camera or switching the card off will cause the camera to return to its original settings.

To reset the camera and card settings all to 1, perform the following operation:

1.   Press the CARD ADJ button

2.   Press the Program reset button

3.   Press the Drive mode button

Note: Ensure that the card is installed in the camera.

Card Case 1 and Card Case 2

Minolta produce two accessories in which to store your expansion cards when they are not in use.

Card Case 1 stores three cards in a credit card style holder, whilst the Card Case 2 is used to store up to 10 cards, which can then be attached to a strap or belt.

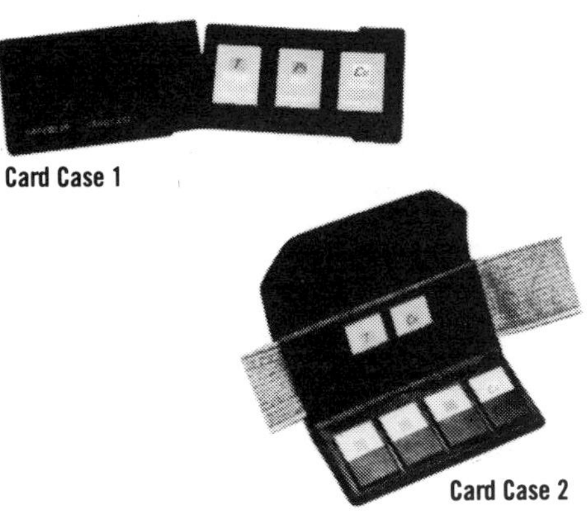

Card Case 1

Card Case 2

AF LENSES

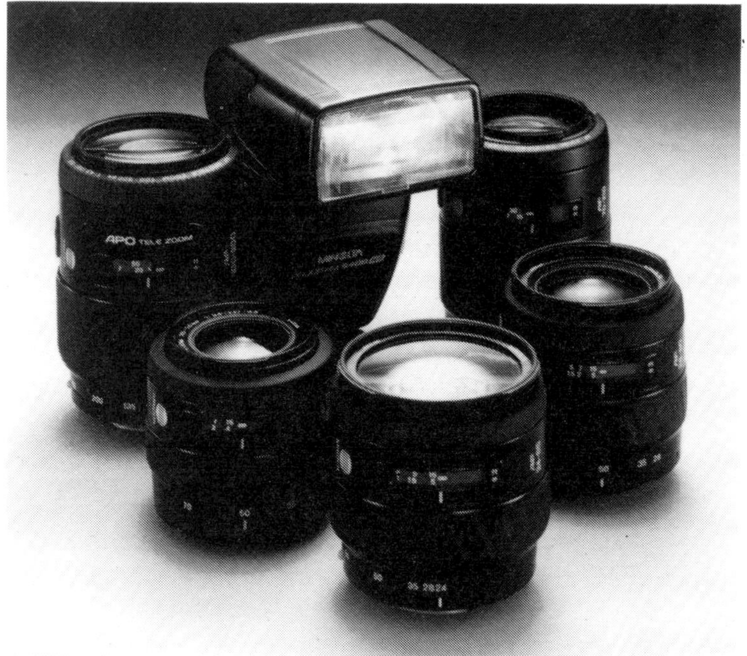

This section describes briefly the range of Minolta lenses currently available for use with your 700si and answers some of those questions which you have always wanted to ask.

Choosing the right lens

So many people once they have purchased their new camera skimp on the lens. You spend so much time in deciding which camera body to buy, you end up not paying as much attention to the lens. Ok, so I accept it is important to get the right camera body, but at the end of the day, it is the lens that delivers the goods.

The APO lenses are by far the most expensive in the range, but my advice to you is, if you are serious about your photography and you can possibly afford one of these lenses, **GO FOR IT!** You will not believe the difference in image resolution, contrast and colour rendition.

If I could afford it, I would go out and buy the 200mm f/2.8 and both convertors today, without any hesitation whatsoever. Admittedly the 300mm f/2.8 and 600mm f/4 I personally would find a little more difficult to justify for my photography.

There are currently 38 lenses available ranging from 16mm fisheye to 600mm telephoto.

Minolta are one of very few manufacturers to produce their own lenses from the raw elements right through to the final marketed product.

With over 150 different types of optical glass, many of which are unique to Minolta, and over fifty years of experience in lens making, Minolta have introduced many new lens designs to reduce the size and weight of lenses over the years. Wider and wider zoom ranges have also been introduced. In addition new optical designs have been introduced to increase focusing speed with autofocus lenses.

However, Minolta never introduce a new lens that compromises picture quality.

The famous Minolta Achromatic lens coatings were introduced in 1956 as the world's first multi-layer lens coatings.

Lens coatings are designed to reduce internal reflections and therefore light loss, as well as flare and to increase image contrast. A multi-coated lens can increase light transmission by up to 20%

Aspherical lenses

Minolta have made extensive use of aspheric lenses since the introduction of the AF 35-70mm f/4 lens in 1985 by introducing these special lenses into not only most of their interchangeable lens range, but also into their zoom compact cameras.

A conventional spherical lens surface is of even curvature. An aspherical lens surface, however, changes curvature across its surface.

Lenses can be made using only one or two elements, but this results in various lens aberrations, such as distortion, low contrast, soft image, poor colour rendition, etc. The lens designer then introduces extra lens elements to correct for these faults (aberrations). Aspherical lenses perform the same job of two or three lens elements. The advantage therefore is less glass, therefore increasing light transmission and image contrast and maintaining high image resolution. Of course less glass also results in lighter and more compact lenses.

Apochromatic lenses

All of Minolta's APO (Apochromatic) lenses and convertors use AD (Anomalous Dispersion) glass, designed, manufactured and tested by Minolta. This special low-refraction, low dispersion glass minimizes lateral and longitudinal chromatic aberrations which tend to occur with telephoto lenses. Chromatic aberration is a lens fault where only one or two of the three primary colours are focused sharply at the film plane. The term apochromatic is the cure for this lens fault (aberration). Therefore all three primary colours are focused sharply at the film plane, resulting in higher contrast, resolution and improved colour rendition.

Focusing Range Limiters

The 200mm f/2.8, 300mm f/2.8, 600mm f/4, 50mm f/2.8 macro and 100mm f/2.8 macro lenses feature focus range limiters.

With the above lenses due to the wide focus range and large apertures, resulting in small depth of field, there is a potential problem where the 700si may be unable to focus.

If your subject is close to, or at one end of the focusing range and the lens focus position is at the other end of the range the image appears so far out of focus that the signal generated by the CCD (focusing sensor), replicates that of a low or zero contrast subject, therefore causing the 700si not to focus because it believes that focusing is impossible from this position. In this case, the use of the focus limiter can be set so that the subject never falls so far out of focus for this to occur.

Lens Hoods

All Minolta lenses, with the exception of the 35-70mm f/3.5-4.5 and 35-80mm f/4-5.6 Power zoom, are either supplied with a lens hood or have a hood built-in. The lens hood is specially designed to reduce lens flare as much as possible by shielding the lens from stray light outside of the picture area, without causing vignetting in the corner of the photograph.

G-Series Lenses

The G-Series lenses are as follows:

    35mm f/1.4
    85mm f/1.4
    200mm f/2.8
    300mm f/2.8
    600mm f/4
    28-70mm f/2.8
    80-200mm f/2.8

The G-Series lenses represent the highest possible optical performance available from Minolta. By purchasing one of these lenses you can be assured that you will obtain the highest possible performance available for your Minolta camera.

They all feature large apertures which are also of circular design to produce a more natural background.

Dynax/Maxxum Specification Lenses

In 1988 when the Dynax/Maxxum 7000i was introduced, Minolta launched a range of new zoom lenses which where known as Dynax/Maxxum lenses. Not only were new optical lens designs used to make the lenses smaller and lighter, but the AF speed on these lenses was upgraded considerably by incorporating various improvements. Over the last couple of years Minolta have been updating some of the original prime (fixed focal length) lenses to Dynax/Maxxum Spec. Almost all lenses have now been upgraded to Dynax/Maxxum Spec.

Upgrading an original lens is achieved by:

1. New appearance, easily noticeable by the improved rubber focusing ring rather than the original serrated ring.

2. High Speed processing ROM IC in each lens. This is so the lens communicates faster with the camera body.

3. The rotation distance between infinity and close focus settings is reduced, therefore the lens has less distance to travel to bring the image into focus.

4. Reduced friction gearing etc, therefore less torque is required to turn the lens.

5. On some lenses, the addition of a focus lock button on the lens barrel, which can be re-programmed to allow selection of continuous AF or centre focus area.

Wideangle lenses

One of the strengths of the Minolta range of lenses is undoubtedly the range of wideangle lenses available. Wideangle lenses are normally associated with landscape photography, but are also ideal for indoor photography where large apertures are needed due to low lighting levels, and where large depth of field is also required. Many professional photographers use wideangle lenses for grab shots and when shooting in tight, crowded conditions. They are also suitable for group shots and architecture.

16mm f/2.8 Fisheye

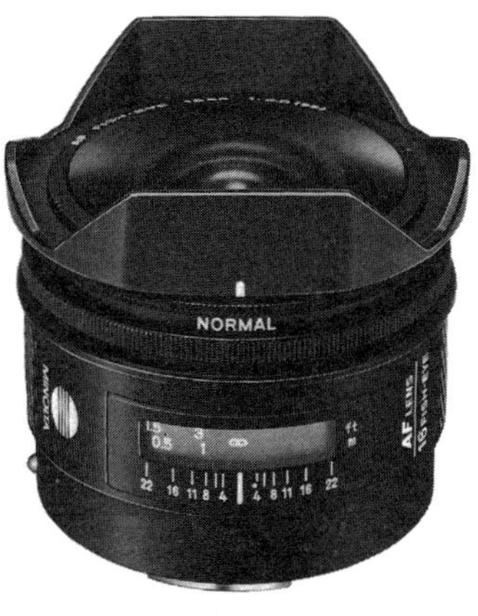

This lens covers a full 180° diagonal field of view. Four filters (normal, O56, FLW, B12) are built-in and selected by turning a ring at the front of the lens. Incidentally, it does not require much focusing beyond approximately 2m as at maximum aperture with the lens set to infinity. The depth of field extends down to 2.87m!

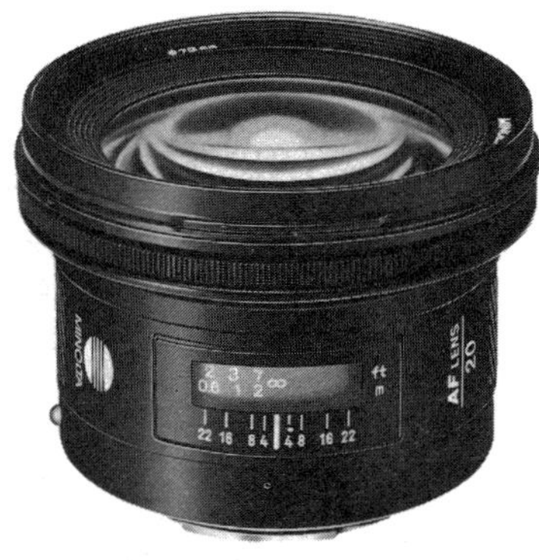

20mm f/2.8

One of my favourite lenses in the entire range. It offers extremely high image resolution whilst offering the perspective control of a super-wideangle lens without the distortion normally associated with lenses as wide as this. The use of a floating element lens design virtually eliminates close focus aberrations.

A rear focusing optical design also allows for very fast and precise autofocusing.

Recently updated to Dynax/Maxxum specification, but using the same optical design as the original.

In addition, the use of a seven bladed aperture produces a circular opening to provide more natural background highlights.

24mm f/2.8

A lightweight and compact super-wideangle lens employing a similar optical design to the 20mm, rear focusing with a floating element.

Recently updated to Dynax/Maxxum specification, but using the same optical design as the original.

The use of a seven bladed aperture produces a circular opening to provide more natural background highlights.

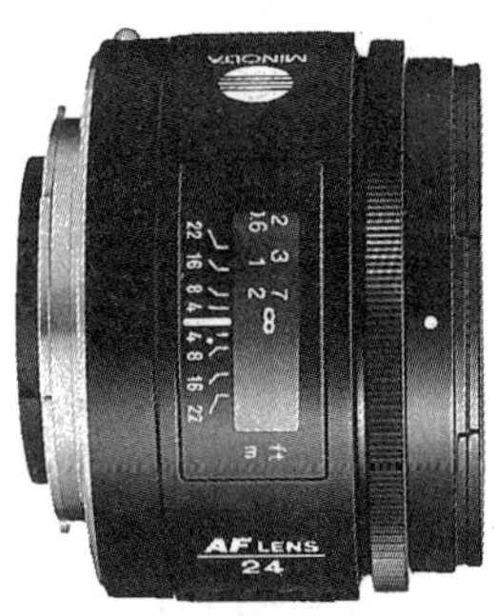

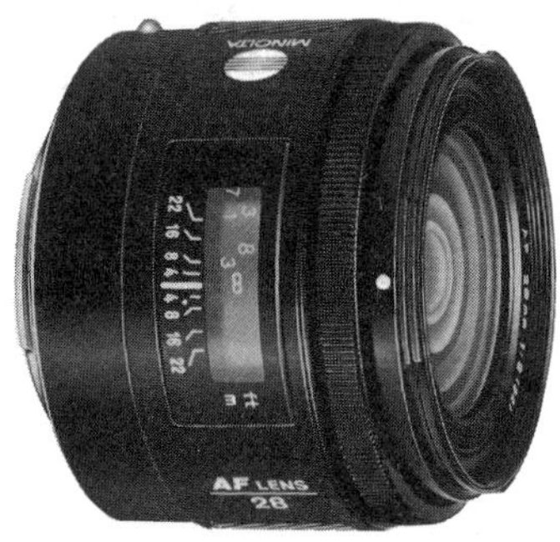

28mm f/2

A fast aperture wideangle lens suitable for working in dark conditions.

28mm f/2.8

An excellent cost performance lens which is lightweight and compact, ideal when travelling. Features a built-in lens hood.

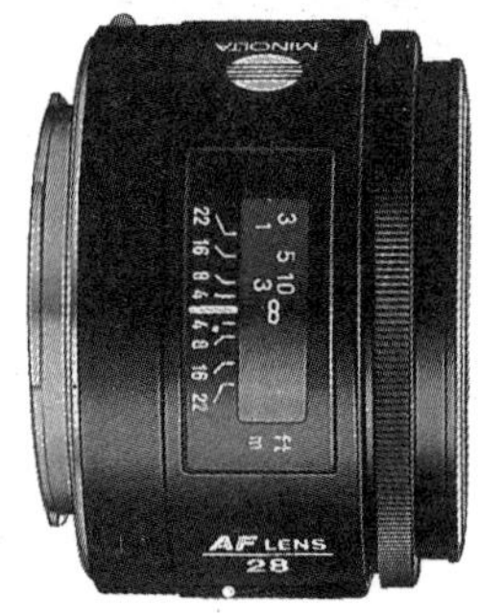

35mm f/1.4 G

A unique lens. The large aperture produces an extremely bright viewfinder image and makes the lens ideal for very dark lighting conditions.

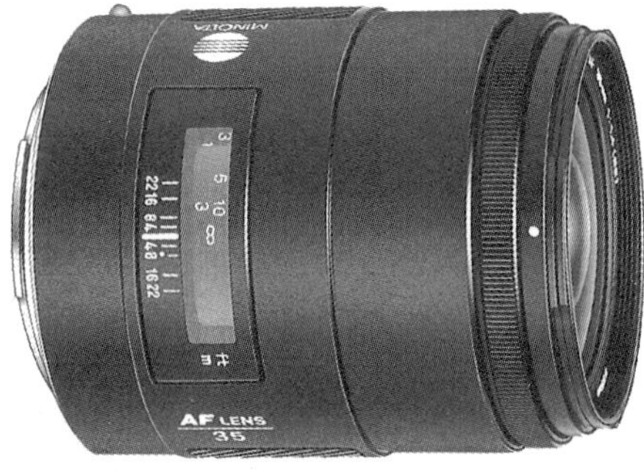

An aspheric element and rear focusing system contribute to the superb sharpness and extremely high contrast.

35mm f/2

35mm focal length lenses tend not to be that popular these days. However, a number of photographers prefer this to the 50mm lenses as their standard lens.

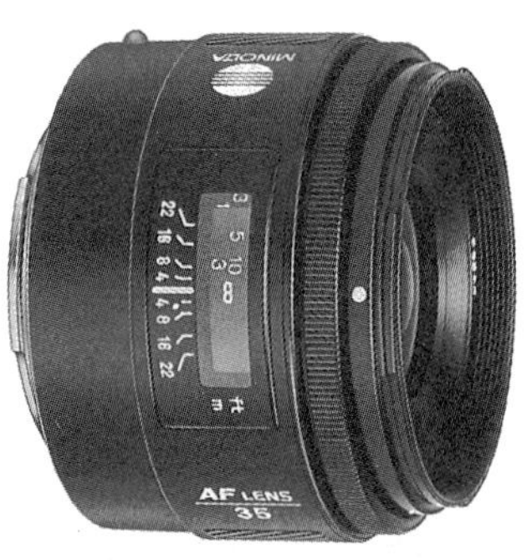

Standard lenses
50mm f/1.4 and 50mm f/1.7

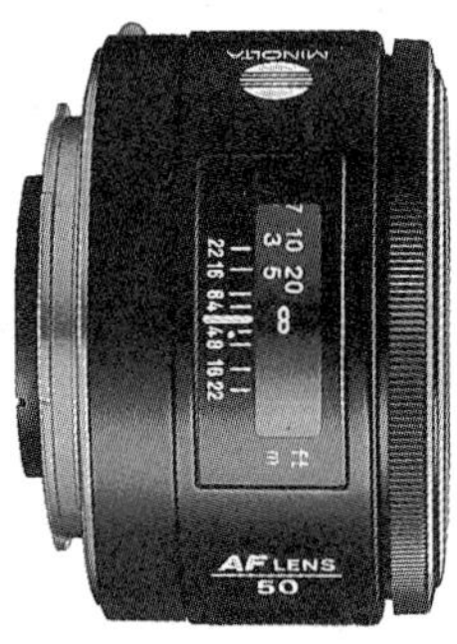

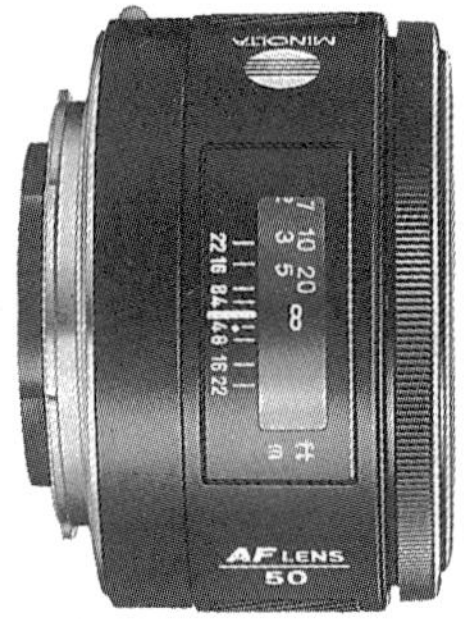

Standard lenses offer a natural angle of view close to that of the human eye. The f/1.7 offers extremely good cost performance and is ideal to keep in the bag as a cheap fast aperture lens for low lighting conditions.

Both lenses feature a built-in lens hood.

The f/1.7 lens is of Dynax/Maxxum specification.

Telephoto lenses

85mm f/1.4 G

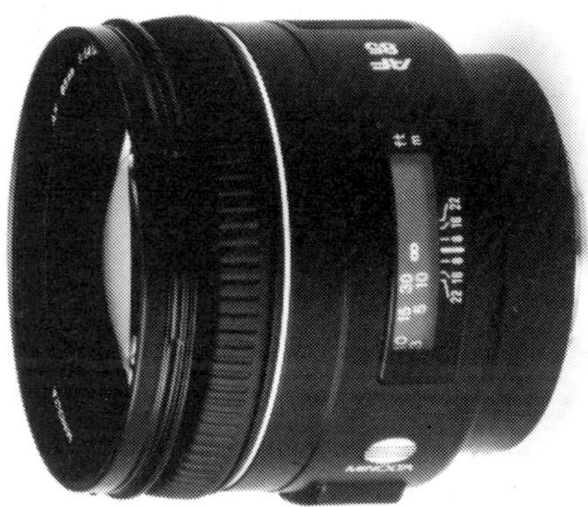

Words cannot express the optical performance of this lens. It is an excellent choice for anyone specialising in portraiture. Its very fast maximum aperture allows precise control of depth of field. In addition, the use of a circular diaphragm produces natural background highlights.

Recently updated to Dynax/Maxxum specification and given a large manual focusing ring and focus lock button.

100mm f/2

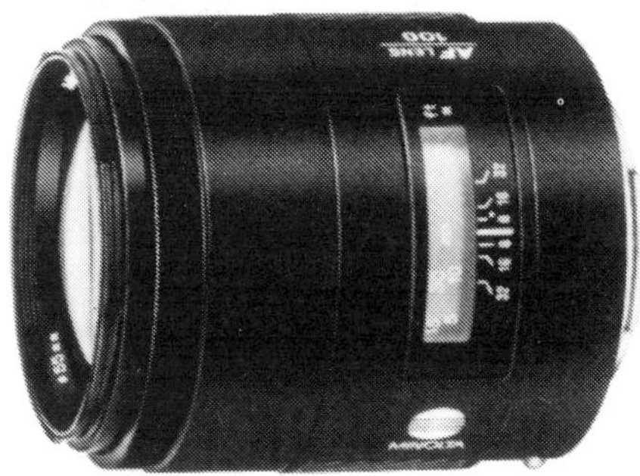

The 100mm focal length has always been regarded as the perfect focal length for portraiture due to its natural perspective and depth of field control. The large aperture also makes it suitable for indoor sports photography.

Heat Expansion

Ever wondered why the APO lenses are painted white rather than the usual black? Due to the size of the lens barrel, when used in high temperatures the lens barrel expands affecting the focus. The white paint is used to help reflect the heat and therefore minimize expansion. If you look at the infinity setting on the distance scale you will notice that it is represented as a line rather than a specific point. This is because at varying temperatures the infinity focus point will change slightly. Depending on the lens in use this can be as much as a 7° rotational shift.

Reflex 500mm f/8

Another unique lens to Minolta. This is the world's first and **ONLY** autofocus mirror lens.

Originally when autofocus was introduced, other manufacturers said that this type of lens was impossible to produce due to 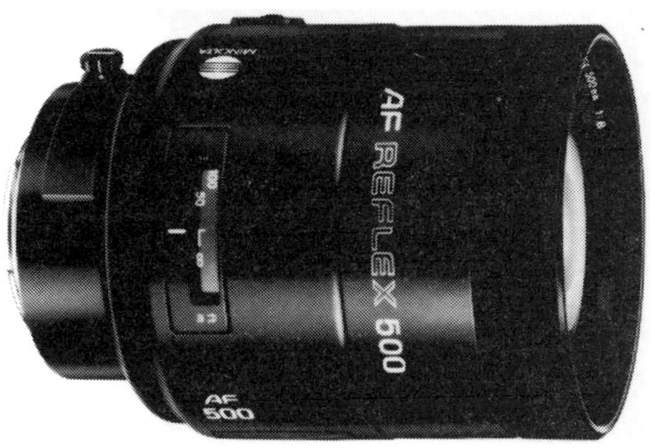 the very small working aperture. F/5.6-6.7 is normally the smallest aperture that autofocus will still function. Minolta found a way though!

By utilising two mirrors, one at each end of the lens, the light is folded so that the lens is one third of the length of a conventional lens of this focal length. Because of this the weight is considerably less as well.

The short, "chubby" design improves handling considerably and allows it to be used hand held at much slower shutter speeds than with a conventional 500mm lens.

Autofocusing is amazingly fast for a lens of this type. A focus hold button is provided on the lens barrel.

The large rubber covered lens hood also acts as an extension of the manual focusing ring. The front filter thread is 82mm. Drop in filters can be used. The lens is supplied with a normal and a ND4x neutral density filter.

Due to the reflex optical design, there is no aperture control, it is effectively fixed. Due to this, in aperture priority and manual exposure modes the aperture is fixed at f/8 and therefore cannot be changed. The use of a neutral density filter can be used to reduce the amount of light entering the camera and therefore reduce the shutter speed in bright conditions.

Note: Due to the optical design of this lens only the centre AF sensor can be used. It is not possible to select any other sensor. Because of this, metering will be from the central seven honeycomb segments only.

Multi-dimensional Predictive focus will not function. However, the 700si will use conventional predictive focus control.

200mm f/2.8 G; 300mm f/2.8 G; 600mm f/4 G

These three lenses offer the highest possible optical performance available for applications requiring telephoto lenses. In addition their large apertures make them particularly suitable for sports and wildlife photography.

The 200mm f/2.8 is my personal favourite. This is due to its outstanding optical performance, compact dimensions and light weight, which make it ideal for panning and hand holding for long periods. I tend to make extensive use of the 1.4 and 2x converters to give 280mm and 400mm focal

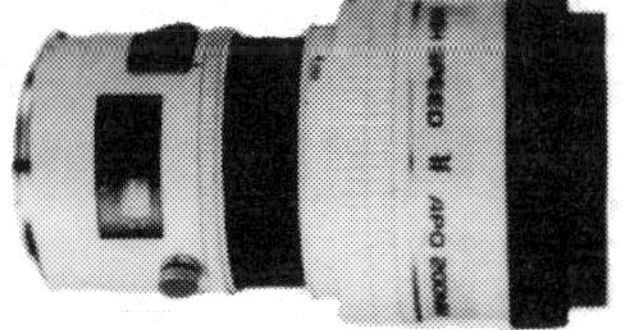

200mm f/2.8 G

lengths respectively. I do not enjoy using the 300mm or the 600mm due to their size and weight; you really do need a tripod for these lenses. Having said that, they are approximately 2/3 to 1/2 the size and weight of their counterparts from other manufacturers!

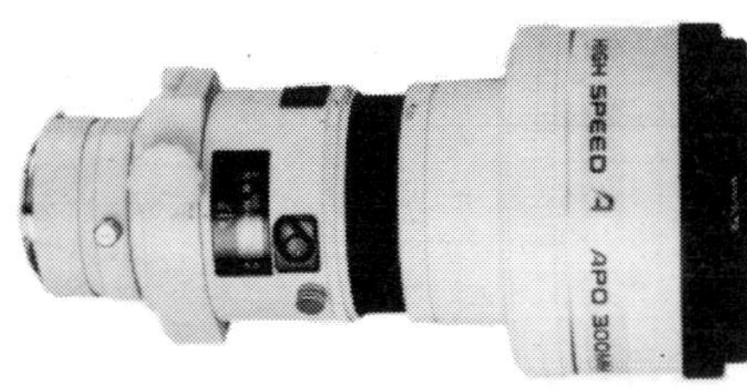

300mm f/2.8 G

Due to the size and weight of the 300mm and 600mm lenses, a tripod mount is provided on the lens barrel. Ensure that you use this when using these lenses on a tripod or monopod, unless you want to see what the camera looks like without a lens mount!

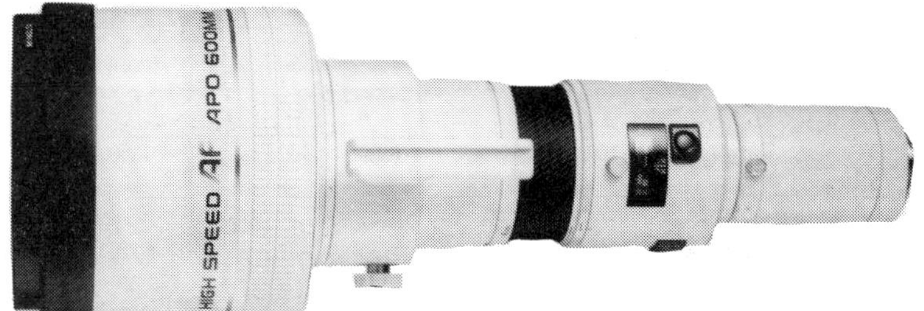

600mm f/4 G

All three lenses feature built-in lens hoods. The front of which is rubber armoured to protect the front of the lens so that it can be stood upright on the ground when the hood is extended and locked in to position. They also feature focus lock buttons (2 on the 300mm and 600mm for vertical or horizontal framing).

The filter thread on the front of the 200mm is 72mm, the 300mm is 114mm and the 600mm is 154.5mm. They are supplied with a clear filter to protect the large and very costly-to-replace front element. However, to replace the filter on the 600mm is certainly not cheap!

Because of the extremely large diameter filter threads on the 300mm and 600mm lenses, 42mm diameter filters may be dropped in at the rear of the lens.

Slow autofocus performance is normally associated with lenses of this type, but not these. Due to an internal rear focusing optical design, only the rear lighter lens elements are moved for focusing therefore allowing very fast autofocus to be maintained without the need for lens integral autofocus motors.

To further reduce focusing times, the focusing range can be limited from either the closest distance to a preset distance, or from infinity to a preset distance.

When in autofocus, a metal sheath is slid over the large focusing ring to prevent this from being obstructed during focusing as the lens is normally held in this region.

Teleconverters

Minolta produce two converters exclusively for the 200mm f/2.8, 300mm f/2.8 and 600mm f/4 lenses. They **CANNOT** be used on any other lens as they will not physically fit.

It is normally accepted that teleconverters significantly reduce the optical performance. Although there is inevitably a slight performance loss when using these converters, the quality is still extremely high: many users may never notice the optical fall-off with these lenses. The use of Minolta's achromatic lens coating and AD glass helps maintain optimum image quality even at maximum aperture.

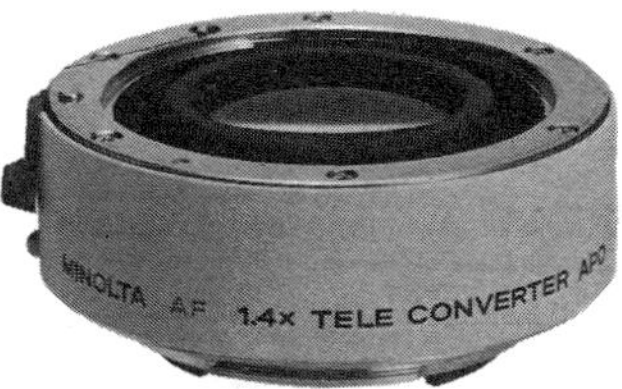

1.4x Teleconverter

The 1.4x converter extends the focal length by 1.4 times. There is a loss of one f-stop in light transmission, therefore the 200mm f/2.8 becomes 280mm f/4, the 300 f/2.8 becomes 420mm f/4 and the 600mm f/4 becomes 840mm f/5.6.

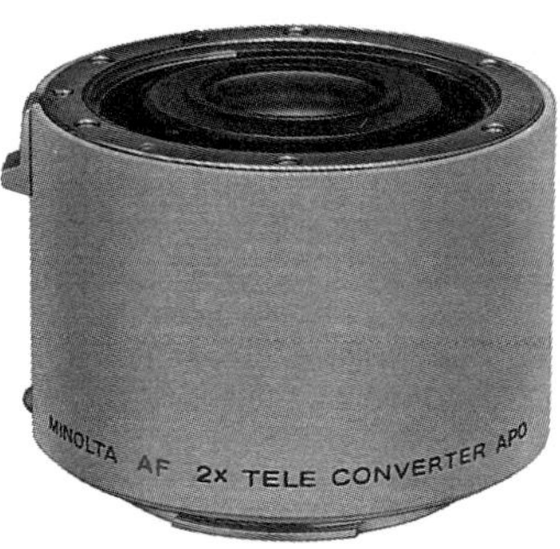

2x Teleconverter

The 2x converter extends the focal length by 2 times. There is a reduction in light transmission of two f-stops. Therefore the 200mm f/2.8 becomes 400mm f/5.6, the 300mm f/2.8 becomes 600mm f/5.6 and the 600mm f/4 becomes 1200mm f/8.

Both converters feature a built-in ROM IC to provide the 700si with the necessary compensation data so that the effective aperture is displayed at all times.

Autofocus cannot be used with the 600mm lens when the 2x converter is used.

Macro lenses

Another strong point in the Minolta lens range, are the macro lenses. There are four macro lenses available.

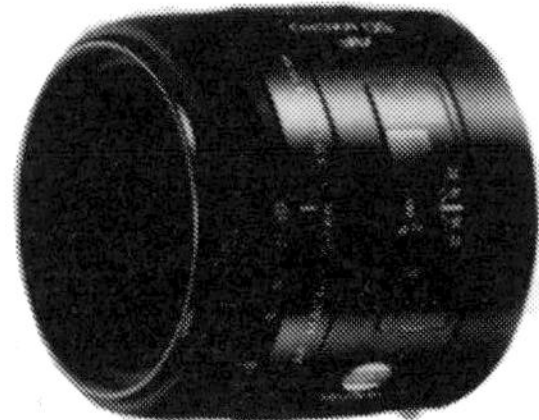

The 50mm f/3.5 Macro is the newest addition to the macro range. It offers 1:2 (1/2 lifesize) reproduction. A "floating element" optical lens design is used to virtually eliminate close focus aberrations.

50mm f/3.5 Macro

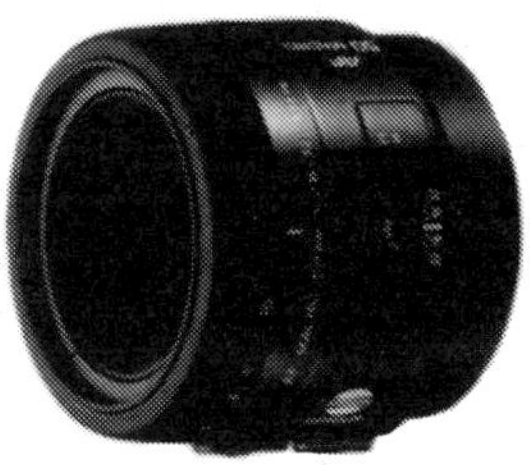

The 50mm f/2.8 and 100mm f/2.8 lenses allow 1:1(lifesize) reproduction. Both of these lenses employ a "double-floating element" optical design to virtually eliminate close-focus aberrations and to allow for faster autofocusing. Both lenses also feature a circular diaphragm to produce a softer more natural background.

50mm f/2.8 Macro

Each lens features a wide rubberised manual focusing ring to aid manual control.

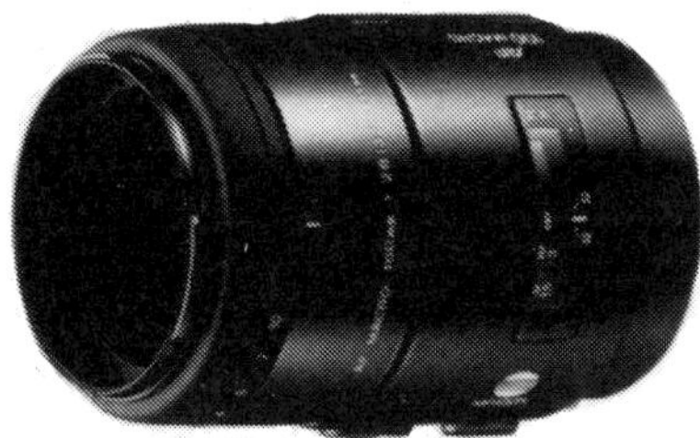

The 50mm f/2.8 and 100mm f/2.8 feature a focus limiter to reduce focusing times when working at one end of the focusing range. In addition they also feature a focus lock button on the lens barrel.

100mm f/2.8 Macro

When using the 50mm f/2.8 macro lens at close to 1:1 magnification it is recommended that you use the 1200AF macro flash. This is because, shooting at this magnification results in you becoming so close to the subject that you end up blocking most of the available light, which then leads to slow shutter speeds. When using the 100mm f/2.8 macro lens, because the shooting distance is very much greater, the above problem is not normally encountered.

The 100mm f/2.8 macro can also be used very successively as a portraiture lens.

Macro Zoom 3x-1x f/1.7-2.8

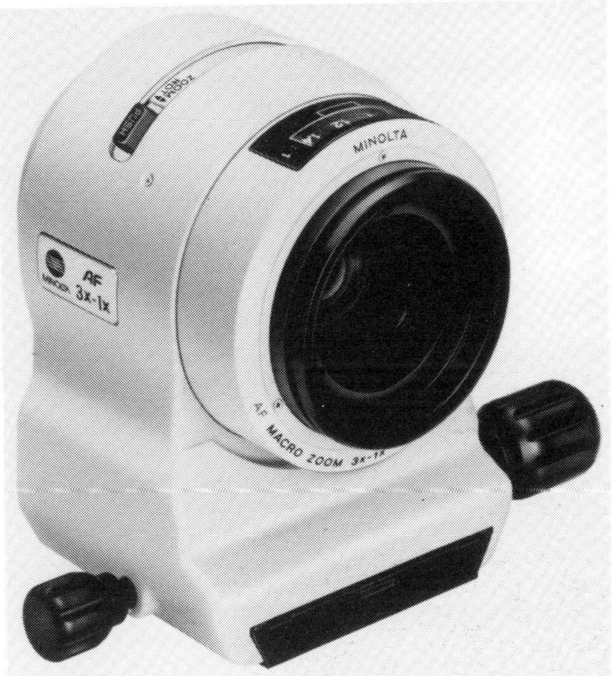

This is the world's first and only AF lens to operate in the 3x-1x magnification range.

It is exclusively for macro photography as its operating range is limited to 25.1 - 40.1mm from the subject to the front of the lens. The zoom is motorized as well as the lens barrel, which can be rotated through 90° when fitted to its supplied table top stand. Full autofocus and autoexposure are maintained.

It is almost essential that the 1200AF macro flash be used to allow autofocusing to take place. There is no manual focusing option.

As with the other macro lenses this lens features a floating element optical design to reduce both spherical and chromatic aberrations.

Zoom lenses

xi Zoom lenses:

xi 28-80mm f/4-5.6, xi 28-105mm f/3.5-4.5, xi 35-200mm f/4.5-5.6, xi 80-200mm f/4.5-5.6, and xi 100-300mm f/4.5-5.6

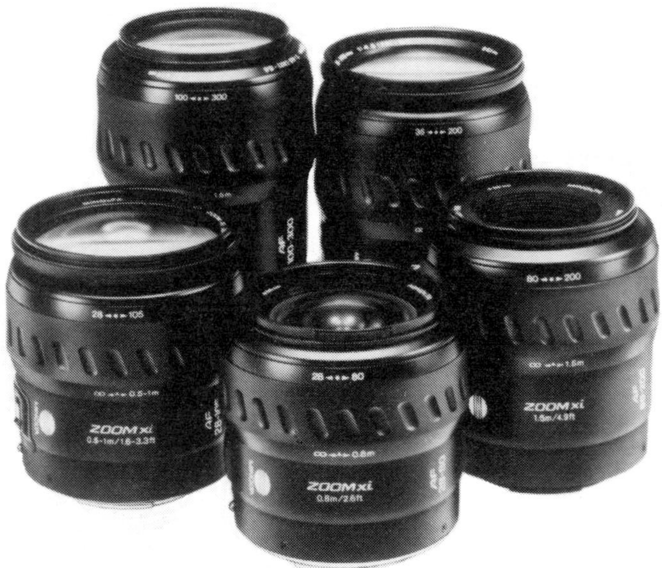

There are five xi zoom lenses. They allow powered zoom operation as well as powered manual focus. Turning the lens control ring to the left zooms the lens to wide focal lengths, turning the ring to the right selects telephoto settings. The further the ring is turned the faster the zooming speed. There are five speeds. Once you have acclimatised to the degree of rotation required to select the various zooming speeds you soon appreciate the control available. The main benefit is stable comfortable zoom control, especially when operating the camera in low lighting conditions whilst still trying to maintain a sturdy support for the camera. Many people are not open to the benefits of the power zoom lenses. I must admit that I did not like the operation initially, but given the choice now, I would have no hesitation in choosing either the xi 28-105mm or the excellent xi 35-200mm, which are the smoothest of all the xi zoom's.

Incidentally, using the fastest zoom speed causes the lens to change from one end of the range to the other in only 7/10 of a second (35-200mm - 1.0 second).

Pulling the ring back and turning in either direction selects powered manual focus. Once again the further the ring is turned the faster the speed. There are three focusing speeds. This I do find a little too fiddly, fortunately the AF system is so good now that we do not have to rely too heavily on this operation.

All of the xi lenses feature a switch on the lens barrel, (except the 28-80mm, due to its "U-turn" optical zoom design) labelled **AZ/MZ**. In the **AZ** position zooming is powered. In the **MZ** position zooming is performed as on conventional zoom lenses, either by twisting the ring at the end of the lens or pushing and pulling, depending on the lens in use.

Image Size Lock

Also on the lens barrel is a button (28-80mm included) to select the Image Size Lock facility.

Once the subject has been framed, press and hold the function button on the lens barrel. **ISL ON** should appear in the viewfinder in place of the aperture/shutter speed

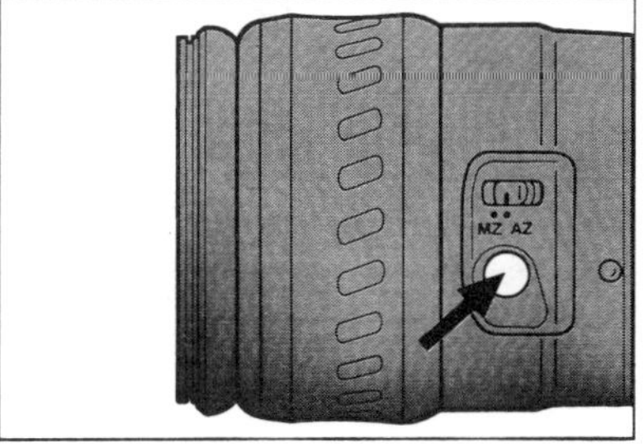

display. If the display indicates **ISL --**, move closer or zoom in more on the subject. Press the function button again. **ISL ON** should now appear in the display.

As the subject moves towards or away from the camera the focal length will be controlled automatically to maintain approximately the same image size in the frame.

Focal length display

If you pull the zoom ring back, the focal length set will appear in both the viewfinder and body LCD panels for a few seconds. As you zoom the lens, the focal length display will also change.

Note: When these lenses are used with the Child or Sports Action 2 card, zooming is controlled continuously as the subject moves without having to keep the function button pressed.

Electronic Compensation

In all zoom lenses, one or more elements move together to keep the image in focus as the focal length changes. Most lenses accomplish this by moving several elements either together or the same amount individually with the use of a special cam. The first method results in a large and bulky lens design, whilst the second, although more compact, requires extremely precise design and manufacture.

The 28-105 f/3.5-4.5 and 35-200mm f/4.5-5.6 feature a very compact vari-focal design and a method called electronic compensation, which requires no cam or any other mechanical method to keep the image in focus as the lens is zoomed. Basically the shape of the cam is programmed into the lens' CPU. As the focal length changes the lens microprocessor passes the focus compensation information to the 700si's autofocus system which then automatically adjusts focus as the lens is zoomed.

The 28-80mm, 28-105mm and the 35-200mm all feature an aspheric lens element which contributes to the compact dimensions whilst still maintaining optimum lens performance.

Manual Zoom Lenses

Over the last year or so Minolta have added a number of new zoom lenses and upgraded some of the original lenses.

All Minolta zoom lenses are extremely compact and therefore lightweight in comparison with their rivals.

The current range is as follows:

      24-50mm f/4
      24-85mm f/3.5-4.5
      28-70mm f/2.8 G
      28-80mm f/4-5.6
      28-85mm f/3.5-4.5
      28-105mm f/3.5-4.5 (new)
      35-70mm f/3.5-4.5
      70-210mm f/4.5-5.6
      80-200mm f/4.5-5.6
      80-200mm f/2.8 APO G
      100-300mm f/4.5-5.6
      100-300mm f/4.5-5.6 APO

I am frequently asked which lenses in the range I would buy. Below I have listed three suitable combinations. These lenses complement each other in optical performance.

1. 28-70mm f/2.8 G and 80-200mm f/2.8 APO G

2. 24-85mm f/3.5-4.5, 28-85mm f/3.5-4.5 or 28-105mm f/3.5-4.5 and 100-300mm f/4.5-5.6 APO

3. 28-80mm f/4-5.6 and 70-210mm f/4.5-5.6 or 100-300mm f/4.5-5.6

The first combination I would describe as superb, the second excellent and the third very good.

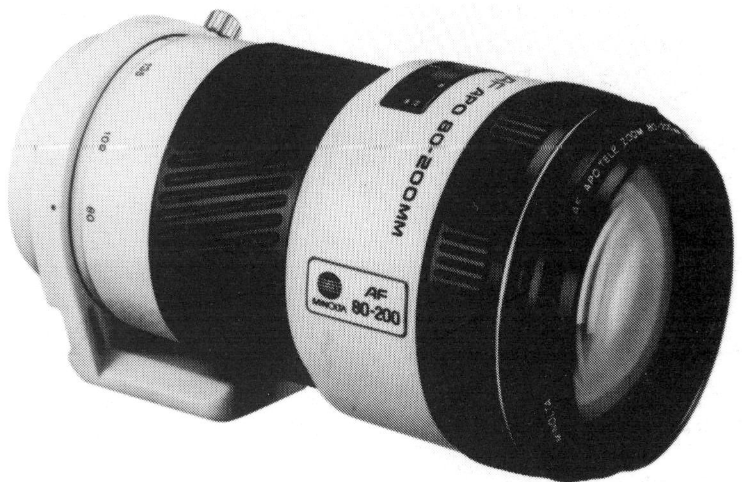

The 80-200mm f/2.8 APO G is one of the best zoom lenses available. Many users of this lens state that they find it difficult, if not impossible to differentiate this lens from the fixed focal length 200mm f/2.8 APO.

The 28-70mm f/2.8 G was developed to be used with this lens as it offers very similar optical performance. The designers have gone to great lengths to produce the highest possible performance from these lenses. Firstly, they have incorporated a more circular aperture diaphragm in both lenses, and in the 28-70mm they have built-in an internal lens flare reduction mask. This moves up and down the lens axis as well as increasing and

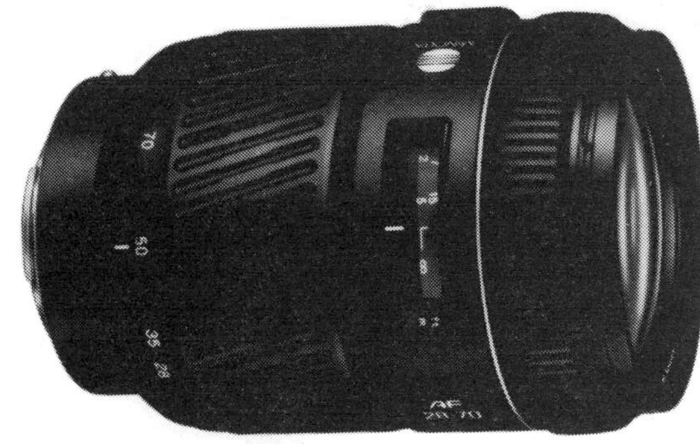

decreasing in diameter to reduce lens flare to an absolute minimum.

28-70mm f/2.8 APO G

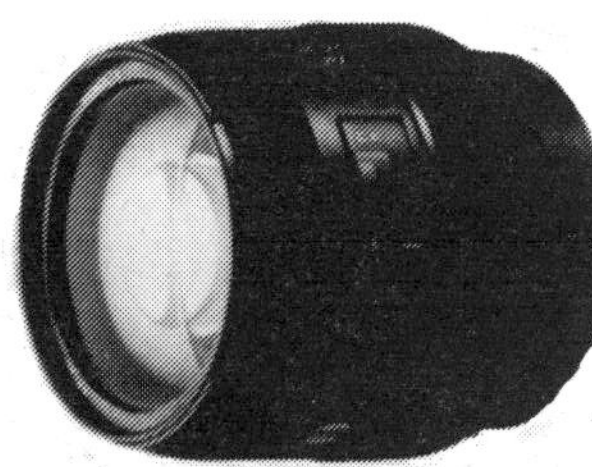

24-85mm f/3.5-4.5

The 24-85mm and the 100-300mm APO lenses were recently introduced to be used together as their optical performance complement each other. The 24-85mm is the world's first lens to feature this zoom range. It uses two aspherical lenses primarily to reduce distortion at the wide focal length settings. The use of an internal focusing mechanism ensures fast and quiet autofocusing as well as providing a minimum focusing distance of 0.5m at all focal lengths, which enables a maximum magnification ratio of 1:5.9. The internal focusing mechanism also results in the front of the lens remaining fixed during focusing and zooming, therefore making it far more convenient when using filters such as the polarizing and graduated filters.

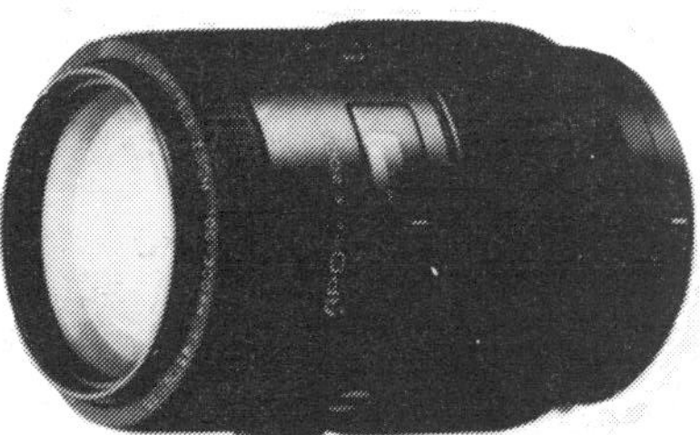

100-300mm f/4.5-5.6 APO

The 100-300mm APO employs a similar optical design to that of the normal 100-300mm. However, the front two elements are made from AD glass which gives improved resolution and colour rendition as well as higher contrast. It should be noted that this lens is extremely compact and lightweight for the zoom range and quality that it delivers. This is due to Minolta's unique "double-telephoto" optical design.

It also offers a maximum magnification of almost 1/4 lifesize.

Extra Information:

Ever wondered why Minolta rear lens caps open the aperture when fitted to the lens?

This is to protect the lens diaphragm when in transit. By opening the diaphragm the aperture blades cannot be damaged due to any extreme vibrations. Therefore if you lose one of these caps, be sure to replace it with the real thing, as independent caps tend not to do this.

What to do when using non-Minolta lenses

If a lens or accessory with no electrical contacts in the mount, such as some independent lenses, microscope adaptors, bellows, extension tubes or slide copiers, is fitted to the 700sl the shutter will not fire with a film loaded in the camera.

This is a safety feature designed to reduce the chance of wasting film due to the camera not being able to communicate with the lens. Reasons for this occurring other than when using a non compatible lens are, grease or dirt on the camera/lens contacts, the lens not fitted correctly or the contacts being damaged. Should the camera not be able to communicate with the lens, — will be displayed where the aperture is normally shown.

To override this feature, perform the following operation:

Press and hold both **CARD** and **SPOT** buttons whilst switching the camera from **LOCK** to **ON**. The body LCD panel will display **OFF** for a few seconds to confirm the setting.

To reactivate the safety feature, perform the same operation. The display will indicate **On** to confirm the new setting.

Note: Switching the camera off and back on again or removing the battery will not reset the feature.

Close-Up lenses

Minolta produce three close-up lenses. Unlike many close-up lenses which are a single element, they are two elements cemented together. They are colour corrected and designed to be attached to regular Minolta lenses to allow them to focus closer for close-ups and copying.

The No.0 is used with focal lengths of 100 to 135mm

The No.1 and No.2 are intended for use with standard lenses. However, focal lengths down to 35mm and up to 135mm can also be used.

They can also be used in any combination. E.g. No.0 + No.1, No.0 + No.2 or No.1 + No.2. for greater magnification.

When using two lenses together attach the one with the smaller number first.

It is recommended to use apertures of f/5.6 and smaller.

When the No.1 lens is used with a 50mm f/1.7 lens, the close focusing distance is reduced by approximately 30%, with the No.2 the distance is reduced by approximately 45% and with both the No.1 and No.2 the distance is reduced by approximately 50%, giving almost half lifesize magnification.

FILTERS

Until very recently I was never aware of the effect that a filter could have on the image sharpness.

I was using for the first time a polarizing filter on the end of my 200mm f/2.8 lens. Normally when shooting sports photography I only keep a clear or skylight filter attached to the lens, purely to protect it. However, on this occasion I was unable to get hold of a Minolta polarizer, but was able to get my hands on an independent's filter. I was looking through the viewfinder down the straight towards the start line, before the race, deciding on where I was going to start shooting etc. when it dawned on me that the image did not look as sharp as I am used to. I initially thought that it could possibly be a problem with the AF system, so I switched to manual focus, no difference. I removed the filter, **and my word!** You would not believe the difference.

Whilst I would of course not reveal the name of the manufacturer, apart from to say that they are well respected, I have learnt my lesson and since then, I only ever use Minolta filters.

Minolta use the same optical glass for producing their filters as they do for their lenses, they are also ground absolutely flat to ensure that they give maximum image quality. They are then mounted in satin finish metal rings.

In addition (with the exception of the 46mm diameter filters and the 49mm and 55mm polarizing filters) all Minolta filters are coated using Minolta's exclusive achromatic lens coating.

Filters for Black and White Photography

L37 (UV)

This filter is used to absorb excessive ultraviolet rays for when shooting mountain, snow and other distant scenes. A good filter to leave on permanently as a protector.

Why use coloured filters for black and white photography?

Normal black and white film (panchromatic) dyes are not capable of giving the film the same sensitivity as the eye. Compared to the eye, black and white film is too sensitive to blue, violet and ultraviolet. It is fairly insensitive to greens and too responsive to red. If filters are not used, blues will appear too light, greens a little dark and reds pale. Therefore, the use of filters is obviously recommended.

GO (Green/Orange)

For correct monochromatic rendition of coloured subjects as they appear to the eye when using panchromatic film use this filter.

Y52 (Yellow)

When this filter is used, red and yellow subjects are rendered lighter than the eye sees them. In addition the overall contrast is increased and therefore makes this filter a good choice to darken the sky and emphasize the clouds.

O56 (Orange)

Similar effect to that of the yellow filter but the effect is more pronounced.

R60 (Red)

This greatly lightens red, produces strong contrast and can be used once again to further emphasize the clouds. If used in conjunction with infra-red film, it eliminates atmospheric haze and produces extremely high contrast effects.

Filters for Colour Photography

1B (Skylight)

Used mainly as a means of protecting the front lens element, it also improves bluish rendition of subjects in shade illuminated by blue sky, on overcast or rainy days, or obscured by atmospheric haze.

A12 (85)

This filter is used when using tungsten film (balanced to 3400° Kelvin colour temperature) in daylight conditions.

B12 (80B)

Used to balance daylight type films for use under tungsten lighting (balanced to 3400° Kelvin), such as photofloods.

For use with either Black and White or Colour

ND4X (Neutral Density)

Used to reduce the light entering the camera by 2 f-stops, when shooting in very bright conditions with slow speed film. The 700si's TTL metering system will take into account the reduction in light transmission automatically.

Circular Polarizer

Ideal for darkening blue skies and improving colour saturation. Best effects can be obtained by shooting at 90° to the sun's position.

This filter can also be used to reduce reflections.

Rotating the filter increases/decreases the polarizing effect, therefore after focusing and/or zooming, if the front element of the lens rotates, rotate the filter in its mount until the desired effect is obtained.

Because the filter reduces light transmission by 1 1/2 stops, it can also be used to act as a neutral density filter. No adjustment is necessary as the TTL metering system will effectively take the effect of the filter into account.

Important: Linear polarizing filters must not be used, as they affect the performance of the metering and autofocusing systems.

Portrayer Filters

These filters are available in two sets, the S series, comprising of two filters, S1 and S2, and the P series, comprising of three filters, P1, P2 and P3. Each set is available in either 55mm or 72mm filter thread sizes.

The S series soften the image, with the S2 offering greater diffusion than the S1. The effect is more pronounced as the focal length is increased.

The P series are like no other filters available. Rather than softening the image they reduce blemishes in the skin, such as freckles and veins. This is achieved by filtering the green wavelengths which causes red wavelengths to blend smoothly with other colours and yet greens and blues retain their original definition.

The effect is more noticeable with the P3 than it is with the P1. Best results are experienced when using them with focal lengths between 85 and 135mm. As with the S series, increasing the focal length strengthens the effect.

ACCESSORIES

Vertical Control Grip VC-700

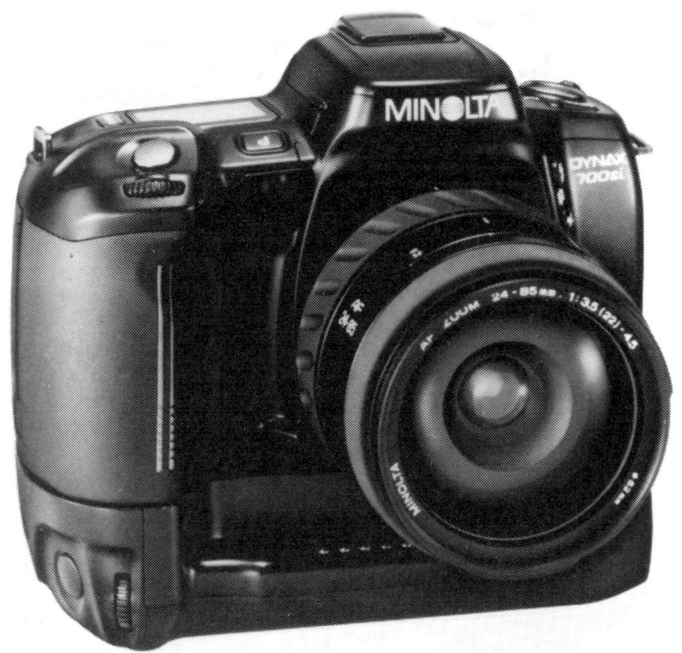

700si with Vertical Control Grip VC-700

The most useful accessory for the 700si is the Vertical Control Grip VC-700. It includes all of the necessary camera controls to enable vertical operation to be the same as that of horizontal operation. It also allows three different power sources to be used, the normal lithium 2CR5, four alkaline or rechargeable AA size batteries. In addition a threaded PC flash terminal is provided to allow studio and non-dedicated flash units to be used with the 700si.

700si controls that are carried over to the grip include the shutter release, front and rear control dials, spot/slow sync flash button, AF button, grip sensor and a tripod socket. In addition there is a switch to deactivate the grip controls to prevent accidental operation.

Not only does the VC-700 provide comfortable vertical operation but it even improves horizontal operation by extending the normal grip down, therefore increasing the 700si's surface area, to enable a more secure grip for those of us with large hands.

What does appear surprising is that, when not using the built-in flash, alkaline batteries will provide more rolls of film than the lithium battery in normal operating temperatures.

The grip also features two extra strap lugs to allow the strap to be attached in three different ways.

To attach the grip to the 700si, the camera's battery cover is removed. To prevent it from being lost there is a storage area on the grip where it can be attached. The grip is then attached to the 700si by aligning all of the electrical contacts carefully and then tightening the attaching screw which threads into the 700si's tripod socket.

Note: When using the PC connection, ensure that the shutter speed set does not exceed 1/200 second.

Holding Strap HS-700

This is for exclusive use with the 700si and the VC-700 vertical control grip. It attaches to one of the strap fixing lugs on the VC-700 and one on the 700si's body. The padded strap then runs over the back of the right hand to help provide extra support and grip on the 700si.

Remote Control Accessories

IR-1(n) Set

The IR-I(n) infra-red remote controller allows the shutter to be fired from up to 60m away from the camera. There are two modes of operation, single and continuous. In single mode, the shutter will fire once with every press of the button on the

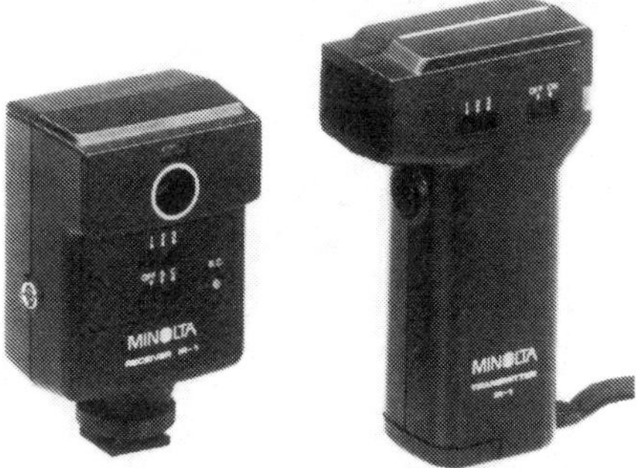

transmitter. In continuous mode the shutter continues to fire until the button is pressed a second time.

The receiver can either be mounted on the 700si's accessory shoe using the FS-1100 shoe adaptor, or on a bracket which can be fitted between the camera body and the tripod.

Note: Autofocus cannot be used with this accessory.

RC-1000L/RC-1000S Remote Releases

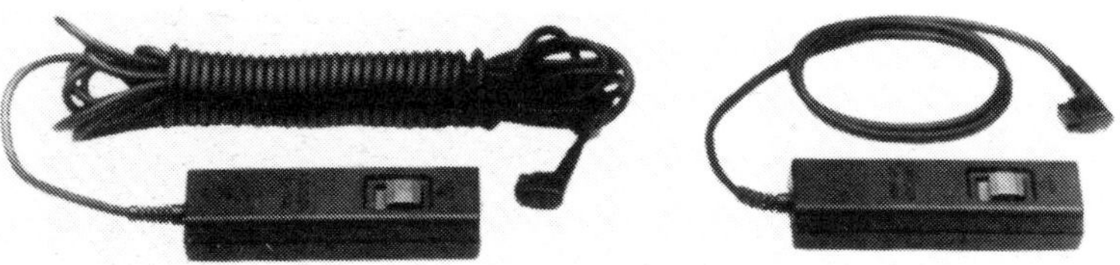

The RC-1000S measures 50cm and is suitable for when using the camera on a tripod. The RC-1000L measures 5m and is ideal for when you wish to operate the camera remotely from some distance.

Both remote releases activate autofocus and autoexposure systems, as well releasing the shutter. A lock setting allows the shutter to be locked open for when using BULB exposure.

Panorama Head II

This unique accessory is used to shift the camera a set angle for each picture to form a 360° panoramic picture once all of the images have been spliced together.

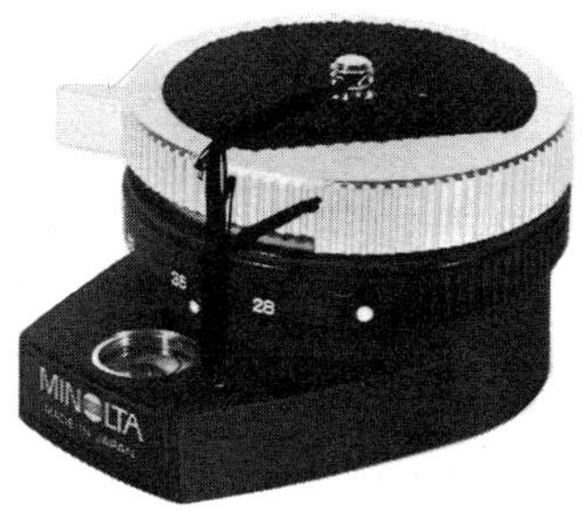

The head is mounted between the tripod and camera. It features a very accurate spirit level to allow for easier setting up.

The focal length of the lens in use is first set from a choice of 28, 35, 50, 85 and 100mm focal lengths. Once this has been set the camera is then rotated until a positive click-stop is felt, which denotes the picture taking position.

Panorama Adaptor

The Panorama adaptor is fitted over the shutter in the film plane and is used to mask the normal film area of 24x36 mm, so that it becomes 13x36 mm. When the film is processed the negative is effectively "enlarged" to the equivalent of a 10x8" print. However, the top and bottom areas of the print which are not printed because they were masked by the adaptor are not used, therefore, the end print measures approximately 10x3.5".

Although best results are obtained when using wideangle lenses it can be used with all lenses.

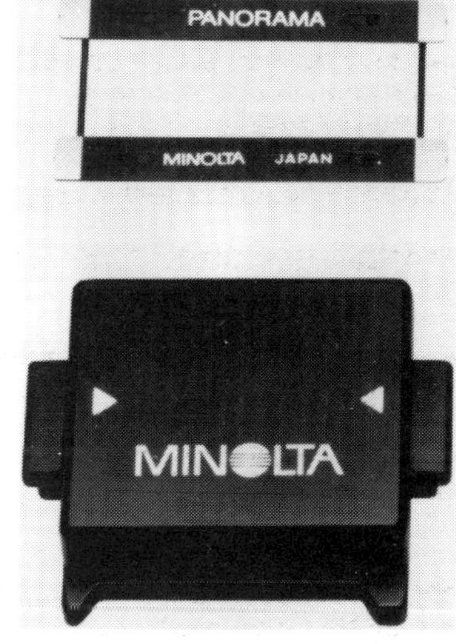

The adaptor is installed prior to the film being loaded with the use of a special holder, to prevent any damage to the shutter. Once this has been done, pressing and holding the **CARD** and **AF** buttons whilst switching the camera on will display the Panorama indicator on the viewfinder screen. This is used to indicate the new picture area for composition.

Extra Information:

When in program the Expert Program area is shifted slightly to bias smaller apertures. In addition, the AF area is automatically changed to the area normally used when shooting vertically. However, the top centre sensor can still be selected manually.

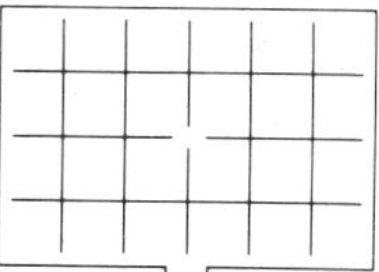

Type L Focusing Screen

Focusing Screens

There are two optional focusing screens to choose from, Type S and Type L. Type S features vertical and horizontal scales, which makes it ideal for macro photography and copying. Type L has vertical and horizontal

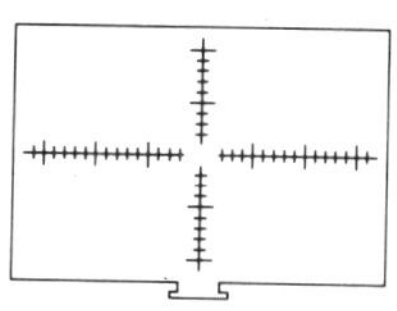

Type S Focusing Screen

lines forming a grid which is suitable for architecture and landscape photography for checking verticals and horizontals.

Due to the close proximity of the transparent LCD panel to the focusing screen, the screen must be fitted by a Minolta Service Facility. In addition, if the screen were not to be fitted correctly, the image in the viewfinder may appear to be out of focus, although the camera has focused correctly.

Insulation Case

In addition to the normal ever-ready cases Minolta produce for the 700si, there is an Insulation Case to reduce camera operating noise and to insulate the camera from the extreme cold. The camera is completely encapsulated, with the exception of the lens which protrudes outside of the case. The hand is positioned inside the case in a similar way to using a film changing bag.

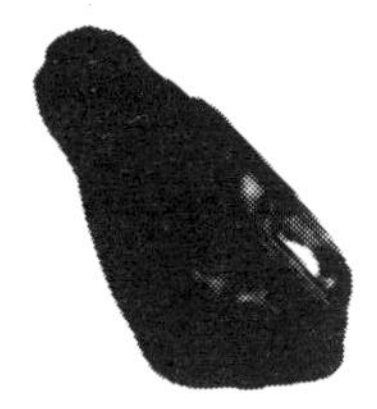

The 700si can still be used with the VC-700 and can still be attached to a tripod, but a flashgun cannot be fitted.

Accessories for close-up photography and copying

Minolta produce a number of accessories to aid macro photography and copying.

Macro Stand 1000

This is designed to be used with the 50mm f/2.8 macro and 100mm f/2.8 macro lenses and the Slide Copy Unit 1000.

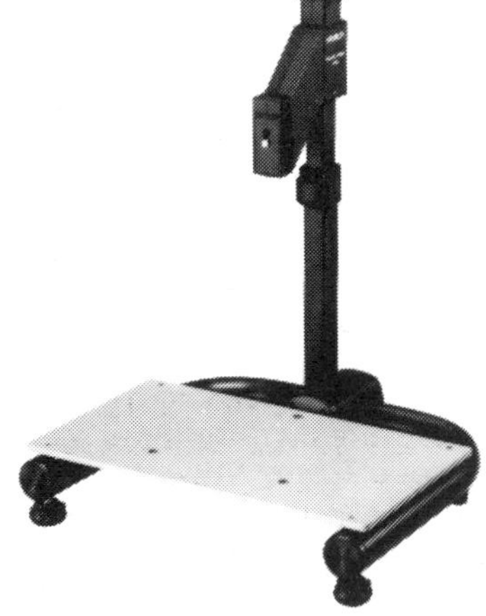

Slide Copy Unit 1000

This accessory allows copying mounted or unmounted slides using the 100mm f/2.8 macro, 50mm f/2.8 macro or 3x-1x macro zoom lenses. The macro flash 1200AF must be used to provide the illumination.

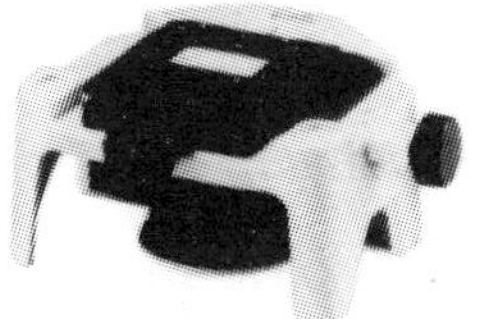

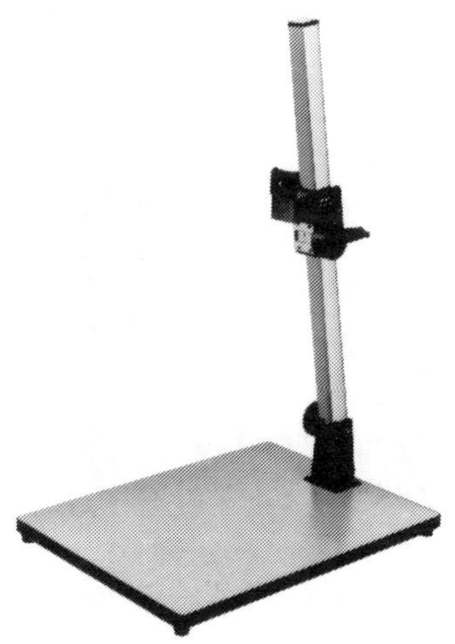

Copy Stand III

In addition, Minolta also produce a conventional copy stand with a large base board and sturdy support arm which can be slid up and down vertically to adjust the copy ratio.

Anglefinder V$_N$

The anglefinder is particularly useful for copying, macro photography and low level photography.

The image is corrected so that it appears right side up and unreversed.

It attaches to the 700si's eyepiece frame. You can choose to view the entire viewfinder area or select a 2 times magnification setting which enlarges the centre of the viewfinder to allow for precise manual focusing.

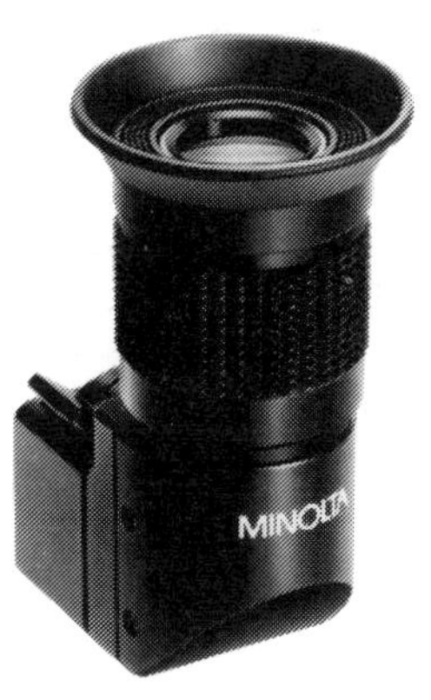

In addition the barrel can be rotated to provide eyesight correction between -9 and +3 dioptres. The rubber eyecup can also be folded back to provide more comfortable viewing when wearing spectacles.

The eyepiece can be rotated freely through 360°. It can be turned to any position or to one of four click stops at 90° increments.

Magnifier Vn

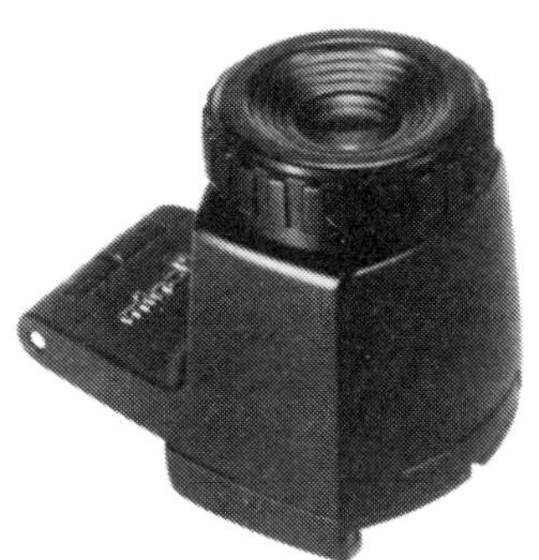

Ideal for macro photography and copying where focusing is critical. It enlarges the centre of the viewfinder image by a factor of 2.3x. It can also be folded out of the way to allow for normal viewing.

As with the Anglefinder, eyesight correction is available by rotating the eyepiece.

Eyepiece Corrector 1000

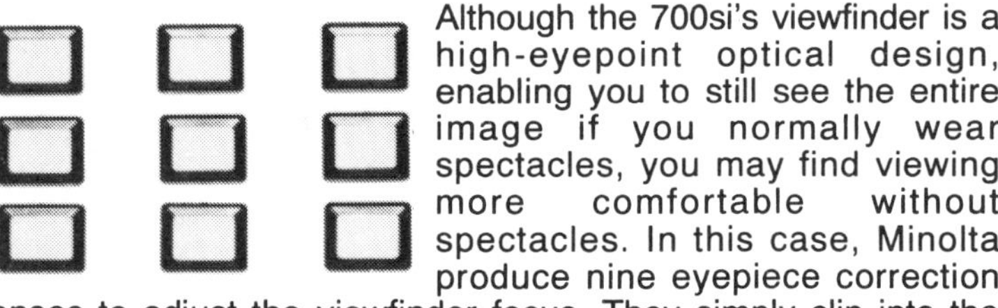

Although the 700si's viewfinder is a high-eyepoint optical design, enabling you to still see the entire image if you normally wear spectacles, you may find viewing more comfortable without spectacles. In this case, Minolta produce nine eyepiece correction lenses to adjust the viewfinder focus. They simply clip into the viewfinder frame, thus allowing the standard eye-cup to still be used.

Strengths available are as follows:

-4, -3, -2, -1, +0.5, +1, +1.5, +2, +3.

Remember the eyepiece is set to -1 as standard. Therefore if your prescription is for -3, you will need a -2 correction lens.

HELP Message

Should the 700si ever indicate **HELP** in the body LCD data panel remove the battery and then re-insert it after 10 seconds. This should clear the problem. If the **HELP** message is displayed again within a small period of time or cannot be cleared by removing the battery, return the camera to a Minolta service facility.

THE END

And to think in 1981 they said it couldn't be done!

ACCESSORIES WELL WORTH LOOKING AT!

OP/TECH

The world's most comfortable cameras, bag and tripod straps (binoculars too). Op/tech has a built-in weight reduction system that makes equipment feel 50% lighter and 100% more comfortable. From the famous 'Pro-Camera Strap' to the 'Bag Strap' and the 'Tripod Strap', the style, colours and comfort which along with the non-slip grip, ensure that you have a wonderful combination of comfort and safety.

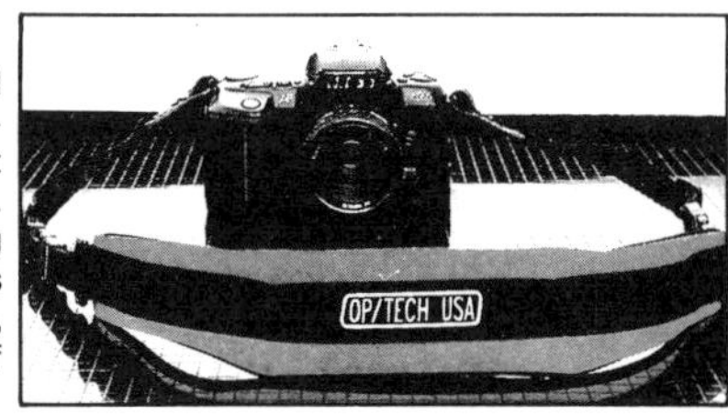

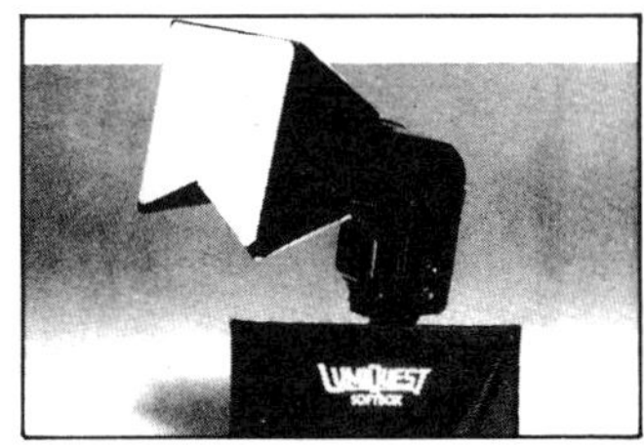

BAG STRAP

The **OP/TECH USA Bag Strap** is the answer to the problem of carrying a heavy bag for extended periods of time. By combining the patented weight reduction system with the Non Slip Grip™, you have the perfect strap for camera/video bags and cases as well as garment bags. Adjustable from 29" to 52", this strap is one of a kind. You will feel the difference!

LUMIQUEST

For any portable flashgun that has a bounce head. Lumiquest is an accessory system that has a place in everybody's camera bag. Not just to reduce 'red-eye', but from the simple 'Pocket Bounce' through to the 'Softbox', added diffusion for flash portrait or close-up's of still life can be achieved while at the same time Metallic Inserts in silver will give spectacular highlights and in gold, a warm sunset tone. Snoots and Barndoors are part of the system for the creative flash photographer.

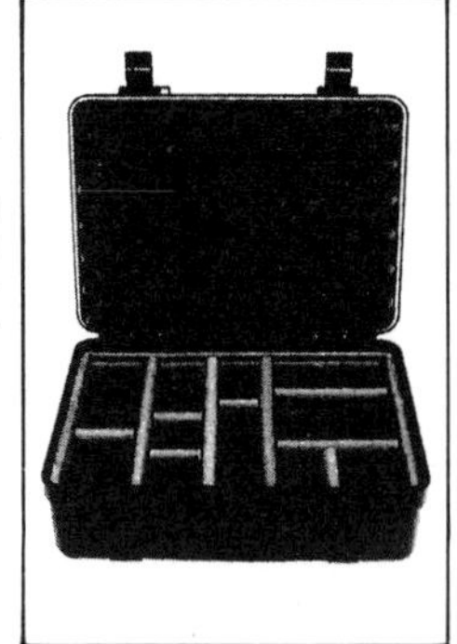

PELI-PELICAN CASES

Watertight and airtight to 30 feet for the ultimate in protection. Constructed of light weight space age structural resin with a neoprene "O" ring seal and exclusive purge valve. Supplied complete with pre-scored pick n'pluck foam or padded dividers. Also includes locking flanges, massive multiple latches for absolute security and best of all, a comfortable molded grip handle.